The MAYA

MICHAEL D. COE

The MAYA

Sixth edition, fully revised and expanded

With 172 illustrations, 17 in color

 Thames & Hudson

Ancient Peoples and Places
FOUNDING EDITOR: GLYN DANIEL

Frontispiece: Wood carving of a Maya lord from Tabasco, Mexico. See ill. 50 for whole figure.

Second edition published in the United States of America in 1980 by Thames & Hudson Inc., 500 Fifth Avenue, New York, New York 10110

thamesandhudsonusa.com

Third edition 1984
Fourth edition 1987
Fifth edition 1993
Sixth edition 1999
Reprinted 2002

Library of Congress Catalog Card Number 98-60191
ISBN 0-500-28066-5

Printed and bound in Singapore by C.S. Graphics

Contents

Preface

It has been over three decades since the first edition of *The Maya* appeared. A reader would only have to compare that book with this, the Sixth Edition, to appreciate how profoundly our knowledge of the ancient Maya has changed and grown over the intervening years. To take just one example, in 1966 the sympathetic position that I took regarding Yuri Knorosov's claim to have "cracked" the Maya script was held by only a few other scholars, and scorned by the majority. We then knew very little of any dynastic history, hardly anything of Maya warfare, and virtually nothing of the Maya Creation. Nobody would have dreamed of finding the Hero Twins and their sinister adversary, the arrogant bird-monster 7 Macaw (Wuqub' Kaqix), in Classic Maya art. Of the tangled relationship between the highland Mexican city of Teotihuacan and the Maya area, we could speak of little but "influences."

I first wrote The Maya in the belief that the time was ripe for a concise, accurate, yet reasonably complete account of these people that would be of interest to students, travelers, and the general public – one, preferably, that could be carried in the pocket while visiting the stupendous ruins of this great civilization. In all subsequent editions, I have tried to keep to these goals. As the decipherment of the hieroglyphs proceeded, it became possible to let the Maya speak in their own voice, as the previously mute inscriptions began to speak.

Since the previous edition, there have been some notable advances in Maya research; perhaps the most striking, based upon new glyphic and iconographic information, concerns probable military incursions by Teotihuacan forces in the northern Peten and at Copan in the southeast, with the establishment of new dynasties and new ideologies of foreign origin. Yet some puzzles still remain to be solved, above all what really happened at the transition between the Classic and Post-Classic periods, and whether there was or was not a "Toltec-Maya" occupation of the huge site of Chich'en Itza. Unfortunately, until the day that Chich'en becomes treated more as a major site crying for broad-scale excavation, and less as a venue for mass tourism, those questions will not be answered. As for the modern Maya, the terrible events which took place in the 1970s and 1980s in Guatemala apparently have been superseded by an era of peace and hope for the future; sadly, over the border in Mexico, the reverse seems to be the case. These developments will be described in the final chapter.

In making this revision, I have enormously benefited from advice and help generously given me by many leaders in the field of Maya research – none of them, of course, are responsible for any errors I might commit with their information. In particular, I wish to thank Dr Nikolai Grube of the University of Bonn, who completely annotated a copy of the Fifth Edition; I have incorporated most (but not all!) of his suggestions. Ever since meeting her at the First Palenque Mesa Redonda, my late friend Dr Linda Schele was a constant source of new ideas and insights, and I want to pay tribute to her. While making this revision, I had the good fortune to have had at my fingertips the proof pages of her new book, co-authored by Peter Mathews, *The Code of Kings*. Simon Martin generously provided the dynastic lists of Maya rulers at the end of this book – the result of many years of research by him and his colleagues. Others to whom I owe profound gratitude are James Brady, Clifford Brown, Richard Hansen, Peter Harrison, Stephen Houston, Justin Kerr, Mary Miller, and David Stuart.

Heretofore, I have used a traditional orthography for Maya words and names; this system came to us from the early Spanish missionaries who were attempting to record in Latin letters the native language of Yucatan. Some of the consonantal sounds were unknown in Spanish and even other Romance languages, so the friars had to devise new ways of writing them (such as the use of *u* followed by a vowel to write an initial sound like English *w*). Particularly troubling to these Franciscans – all good linguists – was an important distinction that the Mayan languages make between consonants that are glottalized (pronounced with constricted glottis) and those that are non-glottalized. For the various highland Maya languages, other orthographies came into use during the Colonial period.

In 1989, the Guatemalan Ministry of Culture, advised by linguists who were themselves Maya, adopted a standardized orthography for all Mayan languages that has now come into general use, not only among anthropologists and archaeologists, but among the Maya themselves. This is the orthography that will be found in this book. Here, glottalized consonants are indicated by a following apostrophe (as in *Tik'al*). An important change to be noted by readers of this edition is that unglottalized *c* (as in *Coba*) is now *k* (as in *Koba*). Throughout, vowels have about the same pronunciation that they have in Spanish; and unglottalized consonants approximately as in English, with these exceptions:

‘   the glottal stop (in initial position, or between two vowels). It most closely resembles the *tt* in the Cockney English pronunciation of *bottle*.

q   a postvelar stop, like a guttural *k*, restricted to highland Mayan languages

tz   a voiceless sibilant consonant, with the tip of the tongue held against the back of the teeth

x   like English *sh*

This is the orthography to be found here, with some important exceptions that are already well established in the world literature and would be confusing to change. Some of these are well known geographical and other place names, such as "Yucatan"; and words and names that either are clearly of Spanish origin (e.g. "Caracol") or else hispanicized (like "Seibal").

Certain of the words that the reader will encounter here are in Nahuatl, the national tongue of the Aztec state, which was used as a great trading *lingua franca* at the time of the Conquest. Nahuatl names were transcribed in Roman letters in terms of the language spoken by the *conquistadores* of the sixteenth century. Neither they nor Maya names have been accented here, since both are regularly stressed: Maya ones almost always on the final syllable, and Nahuatl ones on the penultimate.

Readers may well wonder about the sources of the exotic-sounding names for ancient cities and archaeological sites that appear in these pages. Some of these are in bona fide Yucatec Maya, and were in use in early Colonial-period Yucatan, such as Uxmal, Chich'en Itza, Koba (Coba), and Tulum; but these may or may not have been the *original* names of these places. Mayapan in Yucatan definitely was so. Others are patently Hispanic, for example Piedras Negras ("black rocks"), Seibal ("place of ceiba trees"), Palenque ("fortified place"), Naranjo ("orange"), and El Mirador ("the overlook"). Not a few have been bestowed by the archaeologists themselves, drawing upon one or another Mayan language; among these are Bonampak', Waxaktun (formerly Uaxactún), Xunantunich, Kaminaljuyu, and Abaj Tak'alik'. Recent epigraphic work has shown that the Peten site of Yaxha was really called exactly that in Classic times; but also that the true Classic name for Tik'al was "Mutul", and that for Palenque, "Lakamha." Other ancient city names are sure to emerge as hieroglyphic research progresses.

There have been important advances in the accurate correlation of dates derived from radiocarbon determinations with those of the Christian calendar. Dendrochronological studies of the bristlecone pine now show that before about 700–800 BC there is an increasing deviation from "true" dates back to a maximum of some 800 years at radiocarbon 4500 BC. In this edition, all radiocarbon dates have been calibrated to take this into account. Radiocarbon dating has no real bearing on the chronology of the Classic Maya period (*c.* AD 250–900), which depends upon the accuracy of the correlation between the Long Count calendar and the European Christian calendar. My late colleague Dr Floyd Lounsbury has provided incontrovertible proof that the calendar correlation first advanced by the late Sir Eric Thompson (the 584285 constant, for specialists) is correct, and that is the one used here. All Christian equivalents are given in terms of the Gregorian Calendar.

DATES	PERIODS	SOUTHERN AREA		CENTRAL AREA	NORTHERN AREA	SIGNIFICANT DEVELOPMENTS
Calibrated		Pacific Coast	Highlands			
1530	**Late Post–Classic**	Aztec Xoconocho	Mixco Viejo	Tayasal ↑	Independent states	*Spanish Conquest* *Highland city-states*
1200	**Early Post–Classic**	Tohil Plumbate	Ayampuk		Mayapan	*League of Mayapan*
					Toltec Chich'en	*Toltec hegemony in Yucatan*
925	**Terminal Classic**	Cotzumalhuapa	Quen Santo	Bayal/ Tepeu 3	Puuk, Maya Chich'en	*Toltec arrive in Yucatan* *Classic Maya collapse, Putun ascendancy*
800	**Late Classic**		Amatle– Pamplona	Tepeu 2 1	Early Koba	*Bonampak' murals* *Height of Maya civilization* *Reign of Hanab Pakal at Palenque*
600	**Early Classic**	Tiquisate	Esperanza	· 3 Tzak'ol 2 1	Regional styles, Acanceh	*Teotihuacan interference and influence*
250	**Late Preclassic**	Izapan styles ↑ Crucero	Aurora Santa Clara Miraflores	Matzanel Holmul I Chikanel	Late Preclassic	*First lowland Maya dated stela at Tik'al* *Massive pyramid-building in lowlands* *Spread of Izapan civilization, calendar, writing*
AD/BC						
300	**Middle Preclassic**	Conchas Jocotal	Las Charcas Arévalo	Mamom Xe, Swasey	Middle Preclassic	*Earliest lowland Maya villages*
1000	**Early Preclassic**	Cuadros Cherla Ocós Locona Barra				*Early Olmec influence on Pacific Coast* *Beginnings of social stratification* *Origins of village life, pottery, figurines*
1800	**Archaic**	Chantuto		Belize Archaic		*Hunting, fishing, gathering*
3000						

Chronological Table

1 · Introduction

The Maya are hardly a vanished people, for they number at least seven-and-a-half million souls, the largest single block of American Indians north of Peru. Most of them have resisted with remarkable tenacity the encroachments of Spanish American civilization, although in the past few decades these have taken an increasingly violent and repressive form. Besides their numbers and cultural integrity, the Maya are remarkable for an extraordinary cohesion. Unlike other more scattered indigenous peoples within Mexico and Central America, at the time of the Conquest the Maya were confined with one exception (the Huaxtec) to a single, unbroken area that includes all of the Yucatan Peninsula, Guatemala, Belize, parts of the Mexican states of Tabasco and Chiapas, and the western portion of Honduras and El Salvador. Such homogeneity in the midst of such a miscellany of tongues and peoples testifies to their relative security from invasions by other native groups – the Aztecs, for instance, never extended their empire to include any part of Maya territory, although they had important trading relationships with them.

There are few parts of the world where there is such a good "fit" between language and culture: a line drawn around the Mayan-speaking peoples would contain all those remains, and hieroglyphic texts, assigned to the ancient Maya civilization. It would be an error, though, to think of these peoples as existing in some kind of vacuum. An earlier generation of archaeologists, which included the late Sylvanus G. Morley of the Carnegie Institution of Washington, thought of the Maya as the great innovators and culture-givers to the rest of the peoples of Mexico and Central America. A later generation, which included myself, came to view this fundamentally "Mayacentric" outlook as wrong: the ancient Maya had received much more from the non-Maya Mexican civilizations than they had given. I must now admit that Morley may have been more right than wrong, for reasons that will be made clear in this book. The point to remember is that the Maya were probably always in contact with their sister civilizations in this part of the New World, and that all these peoples profoundly influenced each other throughout their development; this will become abundantly clear when we examine the relations between the Early Classic Maya and the great city of Teotihuacan in the Valley of Mexico.

In pre-Spanish times the Maya belonged to the larger grouping christened "Mesoamerica" by Paul Kirchhoff. The northern frontier coincided approximately with the limits of aboriginal farming in Mexico, the desiccated plateau beyond holding out only the possibility of humble collecting and hunting. To the southeast, the Mesoamerican border ran from the Caribbean

1 Major topographical features and culture areas.

to the Pacific across what is now Honduras and El Salvador, although in late pre-Conquest times it is apparent that northwesternmost Costa Rica was thoroughly Mesoamerican in culture; the southeastern frontier generally divided the civilized Maya from simpler peoples of foreign tongue. All the Mesoamerican Indians shared a number of traits which were more or less peculiar to them and absent or rare elsewhere in the New World: hieroglyphic writing, books of fig-bark paper or deerskin which were folded like screens, a complex permutation calendar, knowledge of the movements of the planets (especially Venus) against the background of the stars, a game played with a rubber ball in a special court, highly specialized markets, human sacrifice by head or heart removal, an emphasis upon self-sacrifice by blood drawn from the ears, tongue, or penis, and a highly complex, pantheistic religion which included nature divinities as well as deities emblematic of royal descent. Also in all Mesoamerican religions was the idea of a cosmic cycle of creation and destruction, and of a universe oriented to the four directions with specific colors and gods assigned to the cardinal points and to the center.

138

While there are profound differences between the subsistence base of the lowlands and that of the highlands, the ancient foursome of maize, beans, chile peppers, and squash formed then, as it still does, the basis of the Mesoamerican diet but of course these foods were widely spread elsewhere – from the southwestern United States to Peru and Argentina in pre-Conquest times – wherever native cultures had advanced beyond a level of semi-nomadic simplicity. In Mesoamerica, none the less, the preparation of maize is highly distinctive: the hard, ripe kernels are boiled in a mixture of water and white lime, producing a kind of hominy (*nixtamal*) which is then ground into unleavened dough on a quern (*metate*) with a handstone (*mano*, from the Spanish *mano de piedra*), later to be fashioned into steamed *tamales* or into the flat cakes called by the Spanish term *tortillas*. The latter, perhaps introduced into the Maya area in late pre-Conquest times from Mexico, are characteristically toasted on a clay griddle which rests upon a three-stone hearth.

131

The importance of the *nixtamal* process cannot be overstressed. Maize is naturally deficient in essential amino acids and in niacin (a member of the vitamin B complex): a population whose diet consisted solely of untreated maize would develop pellagra, and would be malnourished. Cooking with lime (in Mesoamerica and the American Southwest) or with ashes (in North America) enhances the balance of essential amino acids and frees the otherwise unavailable niacin. Without the invention of this technique, no settled life in Mesoamerica would have been possible.

Given the similarities among the diverse cultures of Mesoamerica, one can only conclude that its peoples must have shared a common origin, so far back in time that it may never be brought to light by archaeology. Yet there is some consensus among archaeologists that the Olmecs of southern Mexico had elaborated many of these traits beginning about 3,000 years ago, and that much of complex culture in Mesoamerica has an Olmec origin. It is also reasonable to assume that there must have been an active interchange of ideas and things among the Mesoamerican elite over many centuries, a state of affairs which can be documented in the Terminal Classic epoch thanks to recent research; this in itself would tend to bring about cultural homogeneity – for example, it might explain why both the Classic Maya and the very late Aztec held a snake-footed god to be the supernatural ruling their respective royal houses. It was out of such a matrix of cultural evolution and diffusion that Maya civilization was born.

The setting

There can be few parts of the globe as geographically diverse as Meso-america, which includes almost every ecological extreme from the snow-swept wastes of the high volcanoes to parched deserts and to rain-drenched jungle. The Maya area is situated in the southeastern corner of this topsy-turvy land, but actually is somewhat less varied than the larger unit of which it is a part. For instance, high-altitude tundra is not found, and deserts are confined to narrow stretches along the upper Río Negro and middle Río Motagua. It is also true that tropical forest is more extensive here than in Mexico outside the Maya area.

There are really two natural settings in the land of the Maya: highlands and lowlands. In geology, in animal and plant life, and in the form that human cultures took, these are well set off from each other. The Maya highlands by definition lie above 1,000 ft (305 m) and are dominated by a great backbone of volcanoes both extinct and active, some over 13,000 ft (3,960 m) in altitude, which curves down from southeastern Chiapas toward lower Central

2 Lake Atitlan in the Maya highlands, Guatemala. This view, taken by Eadward Muybridge in the 1880s, shows native traders carrying loads of pottery to market.

3   Lakandon Maya in the Chiapas rain forest.

America. This mighty cordillera has been formed principally by massive explosions of pumice and ash of Tertiary and Pleistocene age which have built up a mantle many hundreds of feet thick, overlain by a thin cover of rich soil. Millennia of rain and erosion have produced a highly dissected landscape, with deep ravines between hog-back ridges, but there are a few relatively broader valleys, such as those of Guatemala City, Quetzaltenango, and Comitán, which have long been important centers of Maya life. Not all of the highlands are so recent in origin, however, for to the north of the volcanic cordillera is a band of more ancient igneous and metamorphic rocks, and beyond this a zone of Tertiary and Cretaceous limestones which in the more humid country bordering the lowlands take the fantastically eroded appearance of a Chinese landscape. Isolated to the northeast are the Maya Mountains, a formation of similar antiquity.

Highland rainfall is dependent, as in the rest of the New World tropics to the north of the Equator, upon a well-defined rainy season which lasts from May through early November. In effect, this follows a double-peaked distribution in both highlands and lowlands, with heaviest falls in June and in October. For the highlands, the highest figures are registered along the Pacific slopes of Chiapas and Guatemala, a zone noted in pre-Conquest days for its cacao production, but in general total precipitation for the Maya highlands is no greater than for the temperate countries of northern Europe.

The highland flora is closely related to soils and topography; on the tops of slopes and ridges, pines and grasses dominate, while further down in ravines where there is moisture, oaks flourish. Compared with that of the lowlands, the wild fauna is not especially abundant, but this may be due to a far denser human occupation.

Native farming practices in the highlands are quite different from those of the lowlands, although inhabitants of both regions depend upon the burning of unwanted vegetation and upon rest periods for farm plots. The moderate fallowing practiced in the highlands depends upon the position of the field on the slope, with only about 10 years of continuous cultivation possible in higher fields, after which the plot must be abandoned for as much as 15 years, while further down up to 15 years continuous use with only a 5-year rest is practicable. In densely populated areas of highland Guatemala, almost all the available land may be cleared or in second-growth. Several kinds of maize are planted over the year; tilling is by furrowing and, after the sprouts have appeared, by making hillocks. In these maize fields, or *milpas*, secondary crops like beans and squashes, or sweet manioc, are interplanted, as well as chile peppers of many sizes, colors, and degrees of "hotness." In summary, while it utilizes the same kinds of plants as in the lowlands, the highland system of agriculture seems to be well-adapted to an area of high population with good, deep soils where the competition posed by heavy forests and weeds is not a major problem.

But it is the lowlands lying to the north which are of most concern to the story of Maya civilization. A greater contrast with the highland environment can hardly be imagined, as every tourist flying to the ruins of Tik'al from Guatemala City must have realized. The Peten-Yucatan peninsula is a single, great limestone shelf jutting up into the blue waters of the Gulf of Mexico which borders it on the west and north; its reef-girt eastern shores face the Caribbean. These limestones have risen from the sea over an immense period of time. In the older Peten and Belize region of the south, the uplift has been greatest, and the topography is more rugged with broken karst hills rising above the plain. As one moves north to Yucatan itself, the country becomes flatter – it looks like a featureless, green carpet from the air – but this is deceptive, for on foot the pitting of the porous limestone is all too apparent. In the northern reaches of our peninsula, about the only topographical variation of any note is the Puuk range, a chain of low hills no more than a few hundred feet high strung out like an inverted "V" across northern Campeche and southwestern Yucatan.

Unlike the sierra to the south, there are few permanently flowing rivers in the lowlands, except in the west and in the southeast, where extensive alluvial bottom-lands have been formed. The great Usumacinta with its tributaries is the most important system, draining the northern highlands of Guatemala and the Lakandon country of Chiapas, twisting to the northwest past many a ruined Maya "city" before depositing its yellow silts in the Gulf of Mexico.

3

Opposite

I Portion of a building in the Nunnery complex at Uxmal, as seen in a lithograph of 1844 by Catherwood.

II View of the cracked and fallen Stela C at Copan in a storm, from a lithograph published in 1844 by the English topographical artist Frederick Catherwood. Dedicated on 5 December AD 730, the monument depicts the 13th Copan ruler Waxaklahun Ubah K'awil.

I

II

III Reconstruction view of the site of El Mirador, in the northern Peten, Guatemala. This Late Preclassic city was one of the greatest ever built in the Pre-Columbian Americas, and is testimony that Maya civilization flourished here centuries before the opening of the Classic.

IV

V

VI

IV View of the upper part of the west side of the Rosalila Structure, as reconstructed in the Copan Museum. Dating to the Early Classic, the painted stucco surface of Rosalila was perfectly preserved by being encased within later building phases.

V Detail of the facade of the Rosalila Structure, Copan, depicting Wukub' Kaqix, the monstrous bird deity that claimed to be the Sun of the last creation in the Popol Vuh legend.

VI Palenque's Temple of the Inscriptions, seen from the Palace. This temple-pyramid is the funerary monument of the great 7th-century king Hanab Pakal, who was laid to rest in a massive sarcophagus deep within its base. The temple superstructure contains a very long hieroglyphic record of Hanab Pakal's reign.

VII View of the Caracol, Chich'en Itza, Mexico. This unique circular building of the Terminal Classic period functioned as an observatory.

VIII General view of Uxmal, looking north from the Great Pyramid. In the middle distance is the House of the Turtles, and beyond it the Nunnery Quadrangle (*left*) and the House of the Magician (*right*). These structures belong to the Terminal Classic period.

IX The great four-sided Castillo at Chich'en Itza, a Toltec-Maya temple dedicated to the god K'uk'ulkan; the view is from the Temple of the Warriors. In the foreground is a so-called "chacmool," a reclining figure which may have been used for heart sacrifice. Early Post-Classic period.

VII

IX

VIII

X

Sizeable rivers flowing into the Caribbean are the Motagua, which on its path to the sea cuts successively through pine and oak-clad hills, cactus-strewn desert, and tropical forest; the Belize River; the New River; and the Río Hondo which separates Belize from Mexico.

The lowland climate is hot, uncomfortably so toward the close of the dry season. In May come the rains, which last until December, but compared with other tropical regions of the world these are not especially abundant. In much of the Peten, for instance, only about 70–90 inches (178–229 cm) fall each year, and as one moves north to Yucatan there is a steady decrease from even this level. Nor is there total reliability in these rains, for in bad years there may be severe droughts. Really heavy precipitation is found in the far south of the Peten and Belize; in the Lakandon country of Chiapas; and in the Tabasco plains which are covered with great sheets of water during much of the summer and for that reason were largely shunned by the pre-Conquest Maya.

Lakes are rare in the lowlands, especially in the Yucatan Peninsula. The absence of ground water in many regions makes thirst a serious problem. In the Peten of northern Guatemala, there are broad, swampy depressions or *bajos* which fill during the summer but are often dry in the rainless winter season. Smaller and similarly seasonal water-holes called *aguadas* are found in some places in Yucatan, but there the major source of drinking (and bathing) water for the inhabitants is the *cenote,* a word corrupted by the Spaniards from the Maya *tz'onot.* These are circular sinkholes, some of great size, formed by the collapse of underground caves. Because the deeper parts of *cenotes* are perennially filled with water percolating through the limestone, these have necessarily served as focal points for native settlement since the first occupation of the land.

The relative dryness of the northern half of the peninsula presented especially grave problems to the inhabitants of the Puuk area, where *cenotes* are largely nonexistent. According to geographer Nicholas Dunning and art historian Jeff Kowalski, the water table is at least 210 ft (65 m) below the surface, and while deep caves may be a source of drip water, they could never have supplied the needs of the dense populations of the Puuk. As a response, the Maya excavated and constructed thousands of underground, bottle-shaped cisterns called *chultunob* (sing. *chultun*), the entrances of which were surrounded by broad, plastered aprons to catch the water which fell during the rainy season.

Opposite

X Putun Maya influence is powerfully present on this representation of a young Eagle Warrior from Cacaxtla, a hilltop acropolis in Tlaxcala, Mexico. His eagle feet rest on the back of a Feathered Serpent, and he carries in his arms a Maya "ceremonial bar," emblematic of rulership. AD 700–900, Terminal Classic period.

A high monsoon forest (now badly destroyed by unrestrained lumbering, farming, and cattle-ranching) covers the southern lowlands, dominated by mahogany trees towering up to 150 ft (45 m) above the jungle floor, by sapodillas, which gave wood to the ancients and chewing-gum to ourselves, and by the breadnut tree. In the middle and lower layers of this formation grow many fruit trees important to the Maya, such as the avocado. The forest is only partly evergreen, however, for in the dry season many species drop their leaves; but in a few places favored by higher rainfall, there is real, non-deciduous rain forest.

Interspersed in the monsoon forest, particularly in the Peten and southern Campeche, are open savannahs covered with coarse grasses and dotted with stunted, flat-topped trees. There is no real agreement on the origin of the savannahs, but modern opinion is against the idea that they were created by the ancient Maya through over-cultivation of the land. On the other hand, they are certainly maintained by the hand of man, for while they are avoided by farmers, they are periodically burned off by hunters so as to attract game to new grasses which sprout in the ashes. When Cortés and his army crossed these grasslands on their way to the Itza capital of Tayasal, they came upon a herd of sacred deer that had no fear of man, and thus allowed themselves to be easily slaughtered by the *conquistadores*.

To the north and west, where there is a profound drop in the annual rainfall, the forest turns into a low, thorny jungle, finally reaching the state of xerophytic scrub along the northern shore of the Yucatan Peninsula.

There is a rich fauna in the lowlands. Deer and peccary abound, especially in Yucatan, which the Maya called "The Land of the Turkey and Deer." Spider monkeys and the diminutive but noisy howler monkeys are easy to hunt and well-favored in the native cuisine. Among the larger birds are the ocellated turkey, with its beautiful golden-green plumage, the currasow, and the guan. More dangerous beasts are the jaguar, largest of the world's spotted cats, which was pursued for its resplendent pelt as well as for sacrificial offerings, and the water-loving tapir, killed both for its meat and for an incredibly tough hide employed in making shields and armor for Maya warriors.

Of more importance to the development of Maya civilization is the agricultural potential of the lowlands, which is by no means uniform. Apart from the clay-filled *bajos*, some of the soils of the Peten, for instance, are relatively deep and fertile, while those of Yucatan (except for the Puuk area) are the reverse. The sixteenth-century Franciscan bishop, Diego de Landa, our great authority on all aspects of Maya life, tells us that "Yucatan is the country with least earth that I have seen, since all of it is one living rock and has wonderfully little earth." It is little wonder that the early Colonial chronicles speak much of famines in Yucatan before the arrival of the Spaniards, and it might be that the province relied less upon plant husbandry than upon its famed production of honey, salt, and slaves.

It is now almost universally recognized, albeit unwillingly, that many tropical soils which are permanently deprived of their forest cover quickly decline in fertility and become quite unworkable as a layer of brick-like laterite develops on the surface. Tropical rainfall and a fierce sun, along with

4 Burning a lowland *milpa* or maize field at Waxaktun, Peten, Guatemala.

erosion, do their destructive work in a surprisingly brief span, and agricultural disaster results. On such soils about the only kind of farming possible is that practiced by the present-day lowland Maya – a shifting, slash and-burn system under which the forest is permitted to regenerate at intervals. While seemingly simple, it requires great experience on the farmer's part. A patch of forest on well-drained land is chosen, and cut down in late fall or early winter; the larger trees are usually left for shade and to prevent erosion. The felled wood and brush are fired at the end of the dry season, and all over the Maya lowlands the sun becomes obscured by the smoke and haze which cover the sky at that time. The maize seed is planted in holes poked through the ash with a dibble stick. Then the farmer must pray to the gods to bring the rain.

4

A cleared plot or *milpa* usually has a life of only 2 years, by which time decreasing yields no longer make it worthwhile to plant a third year. The Maya farmer must then shift to a new section of forest and begin again, leaving his old *milpa* fallow for periods which may be from 4 to 7 years in the Peten, and from 15 to 20 years in Yucatan. In inhabited regions, the forest seen from the air looks like some great patchwork quilt of varying shades of green, a veritable mosaic of regenerating plots and new clearings.

The long-held notion that shifting cultivation was the *only* system of food production practiced by the ancient Maya has now been discarded. In 1972, the geographer Alfred Siemens and the late Dennis Puleston reported their discovery from the air of extensive areas of raised fields in southern Campeche; these are narrow, rectangular plots elevated above the low-lying, seasonally inundated land bordering rivers or in *bajos*, and are remarkably similar to the *chinampas* on which Aztec agriculture was based in central Mexico. Ancient raised fields have since been found over a wide area in northern Belize and in adjacent Quintana Roo, where water levels vary little through the annual cycle of dry and wet seasons.

Recent research suggests that at least some of the raised field systems of the southern lowlands may have been initiated in swampy areas as far back as the Late Preclassic (prior to AD 250), thus providing the subsistence base for the remarkably precocious increase in population which we know for that period.

Stone-walled terraces which probably acted as silt traps are common in various localities in the lowlands, especially in western and northern Belize and in the Río Bec region of southern Campeche. Both these and the raised fields show that in favorable areas, perhaps in response to population pressure, the Maya turned to intensive, highly productive, fixed-field systems. At the same time, it should be remembered that the artificial aquatic environment created by raised field agriculture would have harbored abundant edible fish, crocodilians, turtles, and snails.

And yet the claims that the Classic Maya were almost totally dependent upon the techniques of intensive maize agriculture are probably exaggerated through the understandable enthusiasm created by new finds. Much of the Maya lowland area is and was unsuitable for raised fields or for terracing, and it remains a certainty that most of the maize eaten by the pre-Conquest lowland Maya was grown in *milpa* plots by the still-used methods of shifting cultivation.

Puleston, tragically struck down in 1978 by a bolt of lightning on the Castillo of Chich'en Itza, was a provocative champion not only of the raised-field theory, but also of the idea that the lowland Classic Maya may well have relied as much upon the cultivation of the breadnut or *ramón* tree (*Brosimum alicastrum*) as upon maize, since the breadnut fruit stores well and the tree itself is remarkably common around old Maya ruins. Stimulating though the idea was, recent research suggests that the breadnut was never much more than a famine food for the Maya, and that the frequency of its distribution near Maya sites is largely due to edaphic, or soil, factors and has little to do with human intervention.

Nevertheless, plants other than maize, particularly root crops, may have played an important role in the Maya diet, as was first suggested by Bennett Bronson. Sweet manioc, for instance, does very well in the lowlands, is easy to propagate, and requires very little attention. Also to be mentioned are the house gardens, still ubiquitous in Maya villages and hamlets; in these would have been planted avocados, papayas, sweetsops, guavas, and a host of other native fruits.

5 Prehistoric Maya raised fields in the Río Hondo area, northern Belize. Rectangular plots can be seen extending out from the *terra firma* side of the floodplain.

What all this means is that the lowlands could have been far more densely occupied by the Classic Maya than we would have estimated under the old *milpa* hypothesis. This conclusion is reinforced by a recent aerial survey and mapping of ancient ruins in northern Yucatan, which revealed virtually continuous occupation from one end of the survey area to the other, implying a pre-Conquest population far higher than today's. Perhaps we should be talking of eight to ten million people in the lowlands at about AD 750. These new facts and hypotheses also bear upon the question of what proportion of this population would have been released from their agricultural pursuits to engage as full-time participants in the making of Maya civilization; they may also bear upon the question of why it collapsed (Chapter 6).

Natural resources

From the time of their initial contact with the Maya, the Spaniards learned to their bitter disappointment that there were no sources of gold and silver in the Maya lowlands, and the foreign colonizers soon came to look upon the region as a hardship post. Yet the native inhabitants, to whom the yellow metal was of little value and in fact unknown until about AD 800, had abundant resources which were of far greater importance to them in their daily life, in their rituals, and in their trade.

Construction materials in the form of easily quarried limestone occurred almost everywhere; since it only hardens after prolonged exposure to the air, it was easily worked with their stone-age technology. In some of the limestone beds of the southern lowlands, the Maya found deposits of flint and chert, from which they chipped the axes that were absolutely essential for slash-and-burn farming. Even in very early times, flint-working communities sprang up to exploit this resource, the great workshop at Kolha in northern Belize, for example, having been founded far back in the Preclassic period.

But rock harder than limestone was necessary for the production of the *manos* and *metates* used in grinding maize dough; trading networks brought vast quantities of these objects down from the volcanic regions of Guatemala, and from the granitic outcrops of the Maya Mountains in Belize.

As archaeologist Robert Cobean has noted, obsidian – a natural volcanic glass – was to ancient Mesoamerica what steel is to modern civilization. It was turned into knives, lance and dart points, prismatic blades for woodworking and shaving, and a host of other tools. For the Maya, the sources necessarily lay in the volcanic highlands, above all the great pumice and obsidian exposures at El Chayal, northeast of Guatemala City, and at San Luis Jilotepeque, about 42 miles (70 km) east of El Chayal.

It is a human universal that the body demands a constant concentration of sodium in the blood, as this element is lost by excretion. Meats are rich in sodium, so that a primarily hunting people such as the Inuit (Eskimo) do not need to take in salt, but tropical farmers like the Maya require about 8 grams of salt a day to maintain their sodium balance. Anthony Andrews calculates that a great Classic city like Tik'al, with a population conservatively estimated at 45,000, would have had to import over 131 tons of salt each year.

Happily, the greatest salt sources in all Mesoamerica lie within the Maya area. The major one consisted of the salt beds along the lagoons of Yucatan's north coast. There, grids of shallow, rectilinear pans (still in use) allowed the lagoon water to evaporate during the dry season. Once a thick layer of salt had hardened, it was raked up and transported in baskets. On the eve of the Conquest, these beds were controlled by Yucatan's most powerful kingdoms, and their product was traded to places as distant as the Río Pánuco in northern Veracruz. Similar conditions existed along the Pacific Coast, but there and at important, inland, mineral-spring sources such as Bolontewitz on the Río Chixoy, the brine was cooked down rather than sun-evaporated. Regardless of method, access to salt sources or to salt trade networks was critical to the growth and security of Maya states.

The Maya elite had their special needs, above all jade, quetzal feathers, and marine shells. Green jade was obtained along the middle reaches of the Río Motagua, where it occurs as pebbles and boulders in the river deposits. The highly prized tail feathers of the quetzal, which flash blue, green, and gold in dazzling iridescence, were obtained from the bird's natural habitat, the cloud forests of Alta Verapaz and the Sierra de las Minas in Guatemala, Chiapas in southeastern Mexico, and Honduras. Many thousands of such feathers saw their way into the gorgeous costumes of Maya rulers and their retinues, so that the quetzal may well have been near extinction by the time Maya civilization collapsed in the ninth century AD. The most prized shell was the beautiful, red-and-white, thorny oyster (*Spondylus* sp.), obtained by divers from deep waters off the Caribbean and Pacific coasts; also imported by the inland Maya were large numbers of conch shells (*Strombus* sp.), to be used as trumpets in ceremonies, in warfare, and in the chase.

Areas

The Maya occupied three separate areas, which is hardly surprising considering the great environmental contrasts within the Maya realm: Southern, Central, and Northern, the latter two entirely within the lowlands.

The Southern Area includes the highlands of Guatemala and adjacent Chiapas, together with the torrid coastal plain along the Pacific and the western half of El Salvador. In general, the Southern Area is somewhat aberrant (many books on the Maya ignore it altogether), almost surely because of the Mexican influence which has been powerful here over a very long time. Some of the most characteristically "Maya" traits are missing: the corbel vault in architecture and, except in Late Preclassic times, the Maya Long Count and the stela-altar complex. We must admit that in many ways the Southern Area hardly seems Maya at all from a purely archaeological standpoint, while some of it, such as the central and eastern Chiapas highlands, was only occupied by Maya-speakers at a relatively late date.

In the Central Area, on the other hand, Maya civilization soared to its greatest heights. Focused upon what is now the Department of Peten in northern Guatemala, it reaches from Tabasco, southern Campeche and Quintana Roo across the densely forested southern lowlands to include Belize, the Río Motagua of Guatemala, and a narrow portion of westernmost Honduras. All the most typically "Maya" traits are present – architectural features such as the corbel vault and roof comb, the fully developed Long Count with all its complexities, hieroglyphic writing, the stela-altar complex, and many others. These triumphs, however, were registered during the Classic period. Since the opening decades of the tenth century AD, much of the area has been a green wilderness.

As one would expect, the Northern and Central Areas have much in common, since there are virtually no natural barriers to cultural exchange or to movements of peoples between the two. There is, none the less, a good deal of individuality to the Northern Area. In part this may be due to the fact that agricultural potentialities in much of Yucatan are poorer, and that places where people may live in large concentrations (cities and towns) are often dictated by the distribution of *cenotes* and waterholes; but it may also partly be the result of Mexican influences which are almost as strong here as in the Southern Area. In contrast with the situation in the southern lowlands, there was no mass abandonment of the Northern Area (although many of the cities were depopulated), and overall native population figures remain high even today.

Periods

The discovery of the ancient Maya civilization was a piecemeal process. Following the imposition of Spanish power in the Yucatan Peninsula, various persons such as the formidable Bishop Landa, or Fray Antonio de Ciudad Real who visited the famous site of Uxmal in 1588, wondered at the age of the mighty ruins which lay scattered across the land, but they could discover little from the natives. Real interest in Maya remains only began after the publication, in a London edition of 1822, of the pioneering explorations and excavations which Antonio del Río, a Spanish captain of dragoons, had made at the site of Palenque in the late eighteenth century. Modern Maya archaeology, however, stems from the epic journeys undertaken between 1839 and 1842 by the American diplomat and lawyer, John Lloyd Stephens, and his companion, the English topographical artist Frederick Catherwood, which revealed the full splendor of a vanished tropical civilization to the world.

Stephens and Catherwood were the first since Bishop Landa to assign the ruined "cities" which they encountered to the actual inhabitants of the country – to the Maya Indians rather than to the peripatetic Israelites, Welshmen, Tartars, and so forth favored by other "authorities"- but they had no way of even roughly guessing at their age. It was not until the Maya calendrical script had been studied by Ernst Förstemann, the State Librarian of Saxony, and others, and the Maya inscriptions magnificently published by the Englishman Alfred P. Maudslay at the close of the nineteenth century, that a real breakthrough was achieved in Maya chronology. In addition, large-scale excavations in Maya sites were begun at this time by the Peabody Museum of Harvard, to be followed by the Carnegie Institution of Washington, Tulane University, the University of Pennsylvania, and the Institute of Anthropology and History in Mexico.

The dating of the ancient Maya civilization now rests on four lines of evidence: "dirt" archaeology itself, particularly the stratification of cultural materials like pottery; radiocarbon dating, in use since 1950; native historical traditions passed on to us by post-Conquest writers but bearing on the late pre-Conquest period; and the correct correlation of the Maya and Christian calendars.

The correlation problem is an unbelievably complex and still controversial topic which demands a few words of explanation. The Maya Long Count, which will be explained in greater detail in Chapters 3 and 9, is an absolute, day-to-day calendar which has run like some great clock from a point in the mythical past. Long Count dates began to be inscribed in 36 BC on present evidence and subsequently, during the Classic period, all over the ancient cities of the Central and Northern Areas. By the time of the Conquest, however, they were expressed in a very abbreviated and somewhat equivocal form. Now, it is explicitly stated in the native chronicles (the so-called Books of Chilam Balam) that the Spanish foundation of Mérida, capital city of

Yucatan, which in our calendar took place in January 1542, also fell shortly after the close of a specified period of the truncated Long Count. Bishop Landa, an impeccable source, tells us that a certain date in a more primitive Maya system, the 52-year Calendar Round, fell on 16 July 1553 in the Julian calendar. All attempts to fit the Maya calendar to the Christian must take these two statements into account.

It so happens that there are only two correlations which meet these requirements as well as those of "dirt" archaeology. These are the 11.16 or Thompson correlation, and the 12.9 or Spinden correlation, which would make all Maya dates 260 years earlier than does the former. Which of these is correct? The ancient Maya spanned the doorways of their temples with sapodilla wood beams, and these have not only survived but can be dated by the radiocarbon process. A very long series of such samples from Tik'al was run by the University of Pennsylvania, giving overwhelming support to the Thompson correlation. Most Mayanists gave sighs of relief, for any other chronology would have played havoc with what we now think we know about the development of Maya culture over two millennia. Even further, any displacement in the dating of the Maya Classic period would have disrupted the entire field of Mesoamerican research, for ultimately all archaeological chronologies in this part of the world are cross-tied with the Maya Long Count. Further details on the Maya-Christian correlation will be given in Chapter 9, for it bears directly on what we now know about ancient Maya astronomy.

As it now stands, the cultural sequence in the Maya area runs something like this. The earliest occupation of both highlands and lowlands was during the Early Hunters period, beginning by at least 13,000 years ago, and ending with the close of the Pleistocene, or Ice Age, about 7500 BC. Before 2000 BC there were simple horticulturalists, hunters, and farmers following a way of life called "Archaic," far better known for the upland peoples of Mexico. During the Preclassic (or Formative) period, between 2000 BC and AD 250, village-farming became firmly established in all three areas, marking the first really intensive settlement of the Maya land. More advanced cultural traits like pyramid-building, the construction of cities, and the inscribing of stone monuments are found by the terminal centuries of the Preclassic, and some have even wondered why this early florescence should not be included in the Classic which it presages. The spectacular Classic period, lasting from AD 250 to 900, is defined as that interval during which the lowland Maya were erecting stone monuments dated in the Long Count. A great and as yet unexplained cataclysm shook the lowlands from the late eighth through the ninth century, by the end of which the Classic cities had been largely abandoned, while the Northern and Southern Areas seem to have received the impact of invasions either by Mexicans, or more likely, by Mexicanized Maya. Thus was inaugurated the Post-Classic, which endured until the arrival of the bearded adventurers from across the seas.

66

Peoples and languages

While the cohesion of the Maya-speaking peoples is quite extraordinary for any time or place, the linguistic family called "Mayan" contains a number of closely related but mutually unintelligible languages, the result of a long period of internal divergence. A Maya from Yucatan would have the same trouble understanding an Indian from highland Chiapas as an Englishman would a Dutchman. There have been several attempts to correlate the various Mayan tongues in larger groups; the most recent one by the linguists Terrence Kaufman and Lyle Campbell is the one we adopt here. An ingenious method of vocabulary comparison developed by the late Maurice Swadesh has enabled linguists to suggest approximate dates for the splitting-off of these from the ancestral Mayan language and from each other. It should be stressed, however, that there are many uncertainties built into this methodology, above all the assumption that the rate of change or divergence in "basic" vocabularies is constant throughout time and space. Nevertheless, even if these dates prove to be wrong in absolute terms, they would still be valid for the relative sequence of events.

Prior to 2000 BC, near the end of the Archaic period, there was a single Mayan language, Proto-Mayan, perhaps located in the western Guatemalan highlands. About this time, according to the linguistic scenario, Huaxtecan and Yucatecan split off from the parent body, with Huaxtec migrating up the Gulf Coast to northern Veracruz and Tamaulipas in Mexico, and Yucatecan occupying the Yucatan Peninsula. Of the Yucatecan languages, Yucatec today is the dominant tongue, spoken by townspeople and rural farmers alike, while Lakandon is represented by only a few hundred remaining natives – isolated Maya who wear their hair long and still make bows and arrows (now entirely directed at the tourist trade) – inhabiting the Chiapas rain forest, or what is left of it, southwest of the Usumacinta. The Lakandon appear to be pathetic survivors of a larger group which began diverging from Yucatec after the Classic Maya collapse, but which was probably always marginal to the more major tribes; they may have been driven out of the Peten by the Itza during the Late Post-Classic.

The parent body then split into two groups, a Western and an Eastern Division. In the Western group, the ancestral Cholan-Tzeltalan moved down into the Central Area, where they split into Cholan and Tzeltalan about AD 1. The subsequent history of the Tzeltalans is fairly well known from linguistics and archaeology, for they seem to have left the Central Area by AD 400 and returned to the highlands, pioneering the settlement of the mountain valleys around San Cristobal de las Casas, Chiapas. There many thousands of their descendants, the Tzotzil and Tzeltal, maintain unchanged the old Maya patterns of life. Of the Cholans, who played a major role in the Maya story, we will see more later. Other Western language groups include the little known Kanjobal, Tojolabal, Motozintlec, and Chuj, which stayed close to the parental homeland and which seem to have had little to do with the main developmental line of Preclassic and Classic Maya civilization.

The Eastern Division includes the Mamean group of languages; Mam

6　Colonial and present-day distribution of languages in the Maya area.

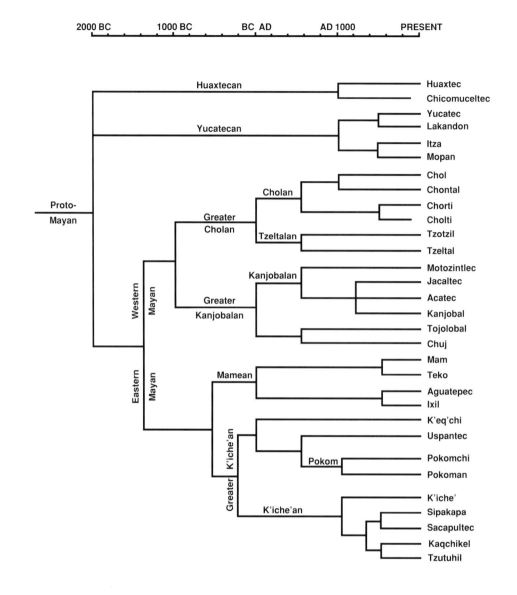

7   Classification and time depth of the Mayan languages.

itself is a rather archaic tongue which has spilled down to the Pacific coastal plain in relatively late times. Another Mamean language is spoken by the Ixil, a very conservative Maya group centered on the ancient town of Nebaj; they have been the principal target of a particularly bloody repression in recent times. Much of the late pre-Conquest history of the Southern Area concerns the powerful K'iche' and Kaqchikel of the Eastern Division. They and their relatives, the Tzutuhil, who live in villages along the shores of the volcano-girt Lake Atitlan, speak languages which only 1,000 years ago were one, K'ich'ean. Since the Spanish Conquest, a more dominant role has been taken by the K'eq'chi, who have expanded from a center in the Alta Verapaz of Guatemala to colonize southern Belize and the once Cholan-speaking lowlands around Lake Izabal, Guatemala, and who are now the predominant linguistic group in the Peten.

What, then, was the language recorded by the ancient Maya inscriptions and books? A glance at the linguistic map will show that the Yucatan Peninsula is occupied by Yucatec to the exclusion of all others, and there can be no quibbling that this was the daily speech of the Maya scribes of the Northern Area, including those who produced three of the four surviving codices – but it was not necessarily the language written down in these books, as we shall see.

Yucatecan was probably spoken over much of Belize during the Classic, for Mopan in the southern part of the country belongs to this group, and some phonetically-written words on the walls of Naj Tunich cave, not far from the Belize border in Guatemala, indicate that Yucatecan was in use there during the Late Classic.

But much of the Central Area appears as a blank on the map, with the exception of those lands occupied by the Lakandon, by the surely recent K'eq'chi, and by the Yucatecan Itza, who are known to have moved into the Peten from the north no earlier than the thirteenth century AD and probably a good deal later. The idea that the language of most of the inscriptions of the Central Area was Yucatecan has little to recommend it.

Some years ago the late Sir Eric Thompson proposed that the Central Area was inhabited by Cholan-speakers during the Classic period. From its present distribution alone – with Chontal and Chol in the low hills and plains in the northwest, and Chorti in the southeast – it seems certain that Cholan once predominated across a great arc extending right through the Central Area, at least to the Belize border, and we have some Spanish documents which confirm this point.

Recent linguistic and epigraphic research has thrown new light on this puzzle: the language of the inscriptions is neither Yucatecan nor even Western Cholan (Chontal and Chol proper), but rather an ancestral form of Eastern Cholan now called "Southern Classic Mayan". Its direct descendants are Cholti, once spoken in the Motagua Valley, but which eventually became extinct when these people were relocated by the Spaniards to the highlands in the seventeenth century; and Chorti, still spoken by about 52,000 Maya living in the Department of Chiquimula, eastern Guatemala – directly west of the great Classic city of Copan. Tourists who travel overland from Guatemala to that beautiful site pass through villages where the inhabitants speak in a tongue that was once spoken at Copan, Tik'al, and Palenque over one thousand years ago!

Early on, Southern Classic Mayan became a literary language with high prestige value among scribes throughout the Maya lowlands, even among the Yucatec-speakers of the northern peninsula (it is recorded at the site of Oxk'intok' as early as AD 475): there is ample evidence that even the inscriptions and Late Post-Classic screenfold codices of the Northern Area basically record this same language, rather than Yucatec, although a certain amount of bilingualism is evident in these writings. In this, it played a role for the Maya similar to that of prestige languages in other civilizations. One thinks of Sumerian in Mesopotamia, Middle Egyptian along the Nile, Sanskrit in India and in the Hinduized cultures of Southeast Asia, and Literary Chinese: these, like Southern Classic Mayan, continued to be the preferred written languages long after the spoken ones had died out, or been transformed into something else.

Languages other than Mayan were found in isolated pockets, indicating either intrusions of peoples from foreign lands or remnant populations engulfed by the expansion of the Mayan tongues. The somewhat shadowy Pipil, whose speech was very close to Nahuatl, the official language of the Aztec Empire, were concentrated in western El Salvador, but there were other Pipil communities on the Pacific Coast and in the Motagua and Salamá valleys of Guatemala. Some authorities think that they invaded the Maya country from Mexico during the Toltec disruptions of the Early Post-Classic, an idea which is not out of line with the lexicostatistic evidence on them, but they could have come earlier. Tiny populations of Zoquean speakers near the Pacific Coast in the Chiapas-Guatemala border region were probably vestiges of a once more-widespread distribution of the Mixe-Zoquean language family. Xincan, with no known affiliations, seems to have extended over all the eastern part of the Pacific coastal plain before the arrival of Mayan and Pipil, but the Xincan territory is an archaeological and ethnological blank. Nahuatl itself, as a great trading *lingua franca*, was spoken at the time of the Conquest at the port of Xicallanco on the Laguna de los Términos in southern Campeche.

Loan words from other languages do appear in Mayan, testifying to early contacts and cultural contributions. Those from the Mixe-Zoquean family of the Isthmus of Tehuantepec (locus of the very early Olmec civilization) include high-culture words such as *may, 'to count or divine', and *pom, "copal incense," and it has been suggested that Mixe-Zoquean was the tongue of the Olmecs, of whom we shall speak more in the next chapter. The Zapotecs of Oaxaca, who probably invented the essentials of the Mesoamerican calendar and who might have been the first to use hieroglyphic writing, contributed several names for the days in the 260-day count so fundamental to Maya thought. And in late times, during the Post-Classic epoch, many words, names, and titles were introduced into the Maya area from Nahua speech by Mexican or Mexicanized warlords.

Climate change and its cultural impact

We have usually assumed that the climatic conditions which now prevail in the Maya area have always been the same, all through Maya prehistory and history. That assumption now seems wrong, as proved by recent paleoclimatic research undertaken by three University of Florida scientists – Jason Curtis, David Hobell, and Mark Brenner – based on sediment cores which they took in Lake Punta Laguna, not far from the Classic site of Koba in the eastern Yucatan Peninsula. What they did was to test the remains of ostracods (tiny freshwater crustaceans) contained in these sediments for oxygen-18; in water of enclosed tropical lakes of this sort, the abundance of this isotope is controlled by the ratio of evaporation and precipitation. Low oxygen-18 means low rainfall conditions, while relatively high oxygen-18 spells drought. Because they were able to date their samples with some degree of precision, there is now a continuous record of climate changes for the Maya lowlands extending over a period of 3,500 years.

Their results are striking, with profound implications for the study of the pre-Conquest Maya (and, obviously, for the ancient Maya themselves). During much of the Preclassic period, the climate was wet (low oxygen-18 values), but by the beginning of the Classic at about AD 250, there was a shift to somewhat drier conditions. As we shall see, this transition corresponds to the demise of the extraordinarily large Late Preclassic cities of the northeastern Peten. Then, with a dated peak at about AD 585, there is a major "dry event," which they reasonably suggest might correspond to the "Great Hiatus" marking the boundary between the Early and Late Classic – a time when no new stelae were erected in the northern Peten, and in which earlier ones were defaced, with clearcut abandonment of some areas.

Their most dramatic finding was that there had been an unusually severe drought that lasted from AD 800 to 1050, peaking at 862. In fact, this was one of the driest intervals to be recorded within the past three millennia and a half. As we shall see in Chapter 6, this was the period that saw the collapse of Maya civilization in the southern Maya lowlands, to be followed somewhat later by the abandonment of the Puuk cities in the north. Now, we have solid evidence from a number of sources that by the ninth century the Classic lowland Maya had severely degraded their environment to the point that extremely high populations could no longer be sustained; there were lesser factors which probably played a part in the Collapse. But conditions of extreme drought, and year after year of crop loss, must have been the "nail in the coffin" that ended this brilliant cultural florescence.

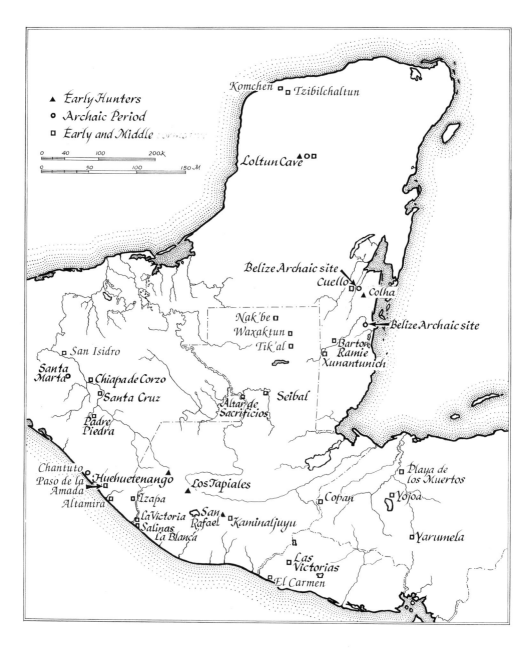

Early Hunters
Archaic Period
Early and Middle (Preclassic)

Komchen □ ▪ Tzibilchaltun

0   40   100   200 K
0   50   100   150 M

Loltun Cave ▲ o □

Belize Archaic site
Cuello o ▪ Colha
□

Nak'be □
Waxaktun □
Tik'al □

Belize Archaic site

San Isidro
Santa o
Marta □ Chiapa de Corzo
□ Santa Cruz
Padre
Piedra

Barton
Ramie
Xunantunich

Altar de
Sacrificios
Seibal

Chantuto
Paso de la ▲ Huehuetenango
Amada □
Altamira □ Izapa
La Victoria □ San
Salinas Rafael ▲ Kaminaljuyu
La Blanca

Los Tapiales ▲

Copan

Playa de
los Muertos
□ Yojoa

□ Yarumela

Las
Victorias
El Carmen

8   Sites of the Early Hunters, Archaic, and Early and Middle Preclassic periods.

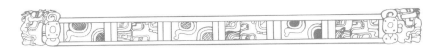

2· The Earliest Maya

The Popol Vuh, the great epic of the K'iche' Maya, recounts that the forefather gods, Tepew and Q'ukumatz, brought forth the earth from a watery void, and endowed it with animals and plants. Anxious for praise and veneration after the creation, the divine progenitors fashioned man-like creatures from mud, but to mud they returned. Next a race of wooden figures appeared, but the mindless manikins were destroyed by the gods, to be replaced by men made from flesh. These, however, turned to wickedness and were annihilated as black rains fell and a great flood swept the earth. Finally true men, the ancestors of the K'iche', were created from maize dough.

Neither tradition nor archaeology have thrown much light on Maya origins. Tribal memories are weak, and a combination of luxuriant vegetation and unfavorable geological conditions has made the search for really early remains difficult. There are few caves and rock-shelters suitable for habitation by primitive hunters and gatherers, and open sites are virtually impossible to detect, especially in the monsoon forests.

8

Early hunters

In spite of over six decades of research, there is little agreement among archaeologists as to when the first settlement of the New World took place. Some geologists have held that the initial colonization of this hemisphere must have been made by Siberian peoples crossing over the Bering Strait land bridge at about 14,000 years ago, during the last maximum of the Pleistocene when sea level was far lower than it is today. Yet long before this, boats must have been available to the peoples of Eurasia, for recent evidence shows that Australia, which was never connected to Asia by a land bridge, was settled as far back as 50,000 years ago. The presence or absence of a land bridge from Siberia to Alaska is thus not necessarily relevant to the problem, for the first Americans may well have taken a maritime route.

While radiocarbon dates from human occupations in Pennsylvania, the Valley of Mexico, the Andean highlands of Peru, and more recently Brazil suggest to some scholars that American Indians had colonized both North and South America by at least 20,000 years ago, many authorities still do not accept these dates as valid, preferring a post-14,000 year arrival. Nonetheless, the recently discovered site of Monte Verde in Chile has revealed a very early occupation of southern South America by hunter-gatherers, with radiocarbon dates clustering around 11,000 BC. There, excavations by Thomas Dillehay have uncovered a small village with houses built of logs;

wooden stakes had been driven into the ground to hold down structures. While the toolkit of these people lacks chipped projectile points, unifacial stone tools and pointed weapons of wood and bone were part of the artifact assemblage. By the ninth millennium BC, the first Indians were already camped on the wind-swept Straits of Magellan, at the southern tip of South America, and so we may assume that primitive hunters had by then occupied all that part of the Americas that was worth inhabiting. Large areas of both continents were grassland over which roamed great herds of herbivores – mammoths, horses, camels, and giant bison.

In the western United States, Canada, and Alaska, where a number of camps belonging to this ancient epoch have been located, the earliest culture which has stood up to archaeological scrutiny is called Clovis, well dated to about 11,500–11,000 years ago. If we can rely upon the remains in several slaughtering sites in the American Southwest, the Clovis people lived mainly off mammoth-hunting, although in lean times they must have been content with more humble foods. These great elephants were killed with darts hurled from spear-throwers, fitted with finely chipped and "fluted" points from the bases of which long channel flakes had been removed on one or both faces. Clovis points are widely distributed, from Alaska to Nova Scotia, down through Mexico and into Central America. They have even been found in Costa Rica and Panama.

One of the earliest known artifacts from Maya country is a small projectile
9   point of obsidian, found by a picnicking schoolboy at San Rafael, in the pine-clad hills just west of Guatemala City. Even a neophyte would recognize this as a Clovis: fluting has been carried out on one side, and the edges are ground down where the object was to be lashed to a dart or spear shaft. It is remarkably similar in outline to several such points which have been collected in Mexico, and to the smaller Clovis points of the United States.

In 1969 the archaeologists Ruth Gruhn and Alan Bryan discovered the highland Guatemalan site of Los Tapiales, which they excavated in 1973; it lies in an open meadow on the Continental Divide, in a cold, rainy, foggy environment, and probably represents a small, temporary camp of hunters located on an important pass. The stone tool industry is mainly basalt, and includes the base of a fluted point, bifaces, burins (for slotting bone), gravers, scrapers, and blades. Unfortunately no bone material has survived, but the site did produce radiocarbon dates extending back to 8760 BC.

The kind of game that these ancient people may have hunted may be revealed by a butchering site on the outskirts of the highland town of Huehuetenango, first investigated in 1977 by Herbert Alexander. This was located on or near the edge of a large, Pleistocene lake. Limited excavations have turned up the bones of at least three mastodons and one or more horses. Butchering marks are frequent on the bones, and four stone tools used in the process were found in situ, comprising a granite chopper and three unifacially worked tools.

The difficulties of prospecting for stone tools of the Early Hunters period in the Maya lowlands have already been mentioned. One of the few areas favorable for this kind of search is northern Belize, where there are extensive

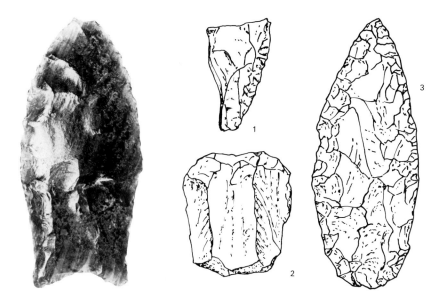

9,10 (*Left*) A fluted point of the Early Hunters period from San Rafael. L. 2 ¼ in. (5.7 cm). (*Right*) Early Hunters period stone tools from Los Tapiales, Totonicapan, Guatemala. *1*, burin; *2*, scraper; *3*, obsidian uniface.

inland areas of low, eroded, sandy ridges with widely scattered pine cover. There, the Belize Archaic Archaeological Project directed by Richard S. MacNeish found four different sites of what he calls the Lowe-Ha Phase, perhaps to be dated on typological grounds to 9000–7500 BC. These were the campsites of nomadic microbands; although little bone has survived in this acid environment, projectile points similar to fluted examples from Panama and Ecuador show that they hunted, and snub-nosed scrapers and side-scrapers testify to skin-working. Bifacial stone choppers found at Lowe-Ha sites may have been used in butchering and general food preparation.

Further north, in Yucatan, a Mexican project has discovered an Early Hunters period occupation with bones from extinct animals including wild horses in a corner of Loltun Cave, an enormous cavern complex utilized by the Maya for millennia.

Archaic collectors and cultivators

By about 7000 BC, the ice sheets which had covered much of North America in the higher latitudes were in full retreat, and during the next 5,500 years the climate of the world was everywhere warmer than it is today. In Europe, this interval has been called the "Climatic Optimum," but in many parts of the New World conditions were by no means so favorable, least of all for hunters. A fatal combination of hot, dry weather, which turned grasslands into desert, and over-hunting by humans had finished off the big game. In upland Mexico, the Indians were diverted to another way of life, based on an intensified collection of the seeds and roots of wild plants, and upon the killing of smaller, more solitary animals. In their economy, in their semi-nomadic pattern of settlement, and even in the details of their tool-kits, the Mexican Indians of the Archaic period were only part of the "Desert Culture," extending at that time all the way from southern Oregon, through the Great Basin of the United States (where it survived into the nineteenth century), and down into southeastern Mexico.

It was in Mexico, however, and in this "Desert Culture" context, that all the important plant foods of Mesoamerica – maize, beans, squashes, chile peppers, and many others – were first domesticated. It seems likely that the practice of plant cultivation must have reached the Maya area at some time during the Archaic period.

An earlier generation of scholars, particularly Sylvanus G. Morley, firmly believed that the Maya themselves had been the first to domesticate Indian corn *(Zea mays)*. This idea was rooted on the often-revived premise that the wild progenitor of maize was *teosinte*, a common weed in cornfields of the western Guatemalan highlands. Whether this premise is correct is still a subject of acrimonious dispute among botanists. One school of thought, led by the late Paul C. Mangelsdorf, contended that *teosinte* was not the ancestor of maize but its offspring through hybridization with another grass, *Tripsacum*, and that the real progenitor was a tiny-cobbed wild species of corn with small, hard kernels that could be popped. Cobs of this sort have been found by MacNeish and his colleagues in dry caves in the Tehuacan Valley of Puebla, Mexico, in levels dating to about 3000 BC. According to Mangelsdorf, they represent ancestral maize; according to his opponents, they are probably *teosinte*. This complex problem has not yet been resolved.

Even if *teosinte*, which admittedly is extremely close botanically to maize, should prove to be the antecedent of domestic maize, this does not necessarily mean the domestication process took place in Guatemala, for it is widespread in southern and western Mexico as well. Nevertheless, Guatemala (which is no larger than the state of Ohio) has more distinct varieties of maize than can be found in all the United States put together, which suggests that this must have been a very old center for the evolution of this plant under the tutelage of man. Quite probably all the uplands, from southern Mexico through Chiapas and highland Guatemala, were involved in the processes leading to the modern races of this most productive of all food plants.

It will be recalled that, according to a linguistic method of dating called lexicostatistics, the Proto-Mayan language was already present in the high-lands of western Guatemala, and probably Chiapas too, before 2000 BC, well within the Archaic span and before the most ancient pottery-using cultures, and it may have been they who brought maize and other cultigens to our area.

8   Beyond the western border of the Maya area, the rock-shelter of Santa Marta in Chiapas may record traces of this *ur*-Maya group. Unfortunately, somewhat wetter conditions than those in the Tehuacan Valley have destroyed any perishables which may have been left by the ancient inhabitants of the shelter, but nut-cracking stones with pecked depressions, and

11 Milling stones from Archaic sites in northern Belize.

pebble *manos* and *metates* tell us that seeds and other plant foods were well
exploited. Other artifacts of the Santa Marta Complex, including chipped
projectile points, choppers, and scrapers, strongly resemble those of the
Tehuacan and Tamaulipas caves, and the whole assemblage, which is
estimated to last from 7000 to 3500 BC, obviously belongs with the Mexican
Archaic and more generally with the "Desert Culture." 11

Evidence for the Archaic period is generally poor in the highlands, but it is
improving in the Maya lowlands. We have some idea of what the Peten
looked like then, based on analysis of windblown pollen recovered from a
long core drilled into the bottom of Lake Petenxil, in the heart of the Central
Area. It used to be thought that the savannahs which punctuate the tropical
forest had resulted from an over-use of their fields by the Classic Maya, with
a consequent invasion of unwanted grasses. This notion has now been turned
upside-down. At 2000 BC, the Peten was like a parkland, with broad
savannahs surrounded by copses of oak, the tropical forest being considerably more restricted than at present. The strong dominance of forest over
grasslands has been shown to have begun only with the opening of the
Classic period at about AD 250, reaching peak intensity after the Maya had
fairly deserted the Peten.

The same pollen core has also provided an unexpected bit of information,
namely that by 2000 BC a little maize was being grown near the margins of the

lake, a good 1,000 years before the first pottery-using farmers are known for the region. Who were these people? If we accept the word of the linguists, they could have been the Yucatec on their trek north to Yucatan from the Maya homeland, but since their sites have not been located this is mere speculation. While some African peoples raise their crops in tropical grass-lands, it is unlikely that the pioneer Maya, lacking metal tools, could have tilled the savannahs. More plausibly, they would have colonized patches of tropical forest which offered good soils and the possibility of clearing by the slash-and-burn method, avoiding the open country as assiduously as did the early Neolithic farmers of Europe.

In 1980, Richard S. MacNeish of the R. S. Peabody Foundation began a three-year investigation of the Archaic or Preceramic occupation of Belize. With his long experience in uncovering the early, incipient agricultural pre-history of highland and northeast Mexico, MacNeish was in a good position to recognize similar sequences in the Maya lowlands, unlike the usual Maya archaeologist more familiar with Classic pyramids than with humble, chipped-stone artifacts. The result has been the establishment of a tentative Archaic sequence running from about 7500 BC until after 2000 BC, with a slowly increasing number of grinding tools related to the processing of seeds and other vegetal materials, and gradually expanding and perhaps seasonal dependence upon marine resources. Unfortunately, preservation of plant materials and faunal remains is poor in his Belize sites, so that the data on the introduction and use of domesticated plants are virtually non-existent. Nevertheless, the question of whether native populations, ancestral Maya or not, had occupied the lowlands prior to the beginning of the Preclassic has now been answered in the affirmative.

Early Preclassic villages

Really effective farming, in the sense that densely inhabited villages were to be found throughout the Maya area, was an innovation of the Preclassic period, which lasted from about 1800 BC to about AD 250. What brought it about? Although some scholars favor the theory that it was a major improve-ment in the productivity of the maize plant, the adoption of the *nixtamal* process, which enormously increased the nutritional value of corn, may have been of more significance. Whatever the underlying cause, villages made up of thatched-roof houses, in no way very different from those in use among the modern Maya peasantry, now dotted the land.

Still, the evidence shows that the advance to Preclassic life did not take place everywhere at the same time. As will be seen, the Maya lowlands were remarkably backward in this respect, for reasons that are as yet unclear. The crucial area for an understanding of the Early Preclassic in southeastern Mesoamerica is not the Peten or the Yucatan Peninsula, or even the Maya highlands, but the hot, humid Pacific littoral of Chiapas, Guatemala, and westernmost El Salvador, a region of winding rivers, fertile soils, and an extensive lagoon-estuary system just in back of the barrier beaches.

Research in this zone has focussed on the old Aztec province of

Xoconochco (modern Soconusco), covering part of the coastal plain of Chiapas and adjacent Guatemala. There, sedentary villages were fore-shadowed by the Late Archaic Chantuto phase, radiocarbon-dated to 3000–2000 BC. Numerous shell middens located in the mangrove-lined estu-aries seem to represent seasonal occupation by somewhat mobile, non-farming groups that largely subsisted upon hunting and fishing.

The Early Preclassic begins in Soconusco about 1800 BC, and is marked by profound changes in settlement pattern, subsistence, technology, and even society. During this period, which lasted until about 1000 BC, settlements were located further inland, and consisted of real villages, occupied through-out the year. Significantly, they were placed next to a series of *bajos* – old stream channels or oxbow lakes – which flooded during the rainy season. As they dried up, fish became concentrated in these and could be easily taken; at the height of the dry season, as archaeologists John Clark and Michael Blake have noted, the *bajos* could have served as sunken fields for agriculture, as they retained enough moisture for a third corn crop to be raised in addition to the two that are normal for the Soconusco plain.

What crop or crops were being grown to support these developments? Maize cobs are found in Soconusco sites beginning about 1700 BC, but these are from small and not very productive ears; further, carbon pathway analysis of human skeletal material has shown that maize was not very important in the diet of these Early Preclassic villagers. Gareth Lowe, of the New World Archaeological Foundation, and myself once speculated that they might have been relying on manioc or cassava, an ancient root crop of the New World tropics, rather than maize, but the evidence for this remains elusive, and the case is unproven.

From a technological point of view, the most significant innovation was the invention or introduction of pottery, which appears at the beginning of the Barra phase at about 1800 BC. Although Barra ceramics may well be the oldest in Mesoamerica, they are of remarkable sophistication and beauty. They largely consist of thin-walled, neckless jars (called *tecomates* by archae-ologists), the remainder comprising deep bowls. Vessel surfaces include monochromes, bichromes, and trichromes, and have been manipulated by the potter by grooving, incising, and modeling. 12

As Clark and Blake make clear, these were not mere cooking vessels; based on forms and decoration of gourd prototypes, they were more likely containers for liquids and foods used during rituals. Then how did they cook? Quantities of fire-cracked rock indicate that the technique was stone-boiling: rocks were heated, then dropped into water contained in water-proofed baskets.

Barra also marks the beginning of fired clay figurines in Mesoamerica, a tradition that was to continue throughout the Preclassic. These objects, generally female, were made by the thousands in many later Preclassic villages of both Mexico and the Maya area, and while nobody is exactly sure of their meaning, it is generally thought that they had something to do with the fertility of crops, in much the same way as did the Mother Goddess figurines of Neolithic and Bronze Age Europe. 13

10 cm

Pottery becomes even more complex in the succeeding Locona phase (1700–1500 BC), with the addition of rocker-stamping (carried out with the edge of a shell, by "walking" the edge of the shell in zigzags across the wet clay), and of striping with a pinkish-iridescent slip; and true cooking vessels make their first appearance. But more significant than these is the evidence for the first ranked societies in this part of the New World. Clusters of villages and communities were organized under a single polity, dominated by a large "capital" village, which could have contained over 1,000 people. At one such "capital," excavators found the clay foundations of a very large, long house with apsidal ends; the floor area covered by its once thatched roof would have been 1313 square ft (122 square m). This surely was a chiefly residence where public rituals were carried out, and perhaps occupied over several generations.

Social differentiation in Locona is also suggested by the burial of a child who had been covered with red pigment and who had a mica mirror on his forehead, and by figurines depicting enormously fat men, perhaps shaman chiefs, seated on stools and wearing chest mirrors and sometimes animal masks.

The subsequent Ocós phase (1500–1400 BC), discovered by my wife and me in 1958, is in most respects a continuation of Locona, with the addition of a pottery decoration known as cord-marking, made by impressing the wet surface of the clay with a paddle wrapped in fine cotton twine – a technique unique in Mesoamerica, but common on the most ancient ceramics of east Asia and North America. Ocós figurines are highly sophisticated, many appearing to be almost human caricatures out of the imagination of Da Vinci, but some being anatomically perfect (but armless) representations of beautiful young women. After Ocós, the Soconusco region was strongly

12 (*Left*) Reconstructed Barra phase pottery, Pacific Coast of Chiapas, Mexico.

13 (*Right*) Early Locona phase hollow figurine head, from San Carlos, coastal Chiapas. Ht 3 ½ in. (9 cm).

influenced by the Early Preclassic Olmec civilization of the Mexican Gulf Coast, but that is another story.

Now, Early Preclassic sites with materials and settlement pattern very similar to the Soconusco cultures have been located all along the Pacific littoral of Guatemala as far as El Carmen in El Salvador. In stark contrast, in spite of decades of intensive search and excavation, no pottery-using village culture on this time level has yet been uncovered anywhere in the Central and Northern Maya Areas, or, for that matter, on the level of the earliest known Olmec civilization of the Gulf Coast. This is one of the unexplained mysteries of Mesoamerican archaeology.

The Middle Preclassic expansion

If conditions before 1000 BC were less than optimum for the spread of effective village farming except for the Pacific littoral, in the following centuries the reverse must have been true. Heavy populations, all with pottery and most of them probably Mayan-speaking, began to establish themselves in both highlands and lowlands during the Middle Preclassic period, which lasted until about 300 BC. In only one instance (Nak'be) do we have remains suggesting that these were anything more than simple peasants: there was no writing, little that could be called architecture, and hardly any development of art. In fact, nothing but a rapidly mounting population would make us think that the Maya in this period were much different from their immediate ancestors.

There was, however, something very different that had been taking place in Mexico, in the hot coastal plain of southern Veracruz and adjacent Tabasco. This was the developing Olmec civilization, which began in the Early Preclassic, reached its peak toward the end of the Middle Preclassic, and then collapsed as suddenly as did the Maya at a much later time. So far, the oldest known Olmec site is San Lorenzo, lying near a branch of the Coatzacoalcos River in Veracruz. Excavated by a Yale expedition between 1966 and 1969, fully developed Olmec culture, represented typically by gigantic basalt sculptures fashioned in a distinctive style, proved to date back to 1400 BC. By 1000 BC, San Lorenzo had been destroyed by an unknown hand, but during the four centuries of its *floruit*, Olmec influence emanating from this area was to be found throughout Mesoamerica, with the curious exception of the Maya domain – perhaps because there were few Maya populations at that time sufficiently large to have interested the expanding Olmecs.

During the Middle Preclassic, following the demise of San Lorenzo, the great Olmec center was La Venta, situated on an island in the midst of the swampy wastes of the lower Tonalá River, and dominated by a 100-ft-high (30 m) mound of clay. Elaborate tombs and spectacular offerings of jade and serpentine figurines were concealed by various constructions, both there and at other Olmec sites. The Olmec art style was centered upon the representations of creatures which combined the features of a snarling jaguar with those of a weeping human infant; among these were-jaguars almost surely was a rain god, one of the first recognizable deities of the Mesoamerican pantheon. From the unity of the art style, from the size and beauty of the sculptured monuments, and from the massive scale of the public architecture, there can be no doubt that there was a powerful Olmec state on the Gulf Coast which even at this early time was able to command enormous resources both in manpower and in materials.

More important to the study of the Maya, there are also good reasons to believe that it was the late Olmecs who devised the elaborate Long Count calendar. Whether or not one thinks of the Olmecs as the "mother culture" of Mesoamerica, the fact is that many other civilizations, including the Maya, were ultimately dependent on the Olmec achievement. This is especially true during the Middle Preclassic, when lesser peasant cultures away from the Gulf Coast were acquiring traits which had filtered to them from their more advanced neighbors, just as in ancient Europe barbarian peoples in the west and north eventually had the benefits of the achievements of the contemporaneous Bronze Age civilizations of the Near East.

One of the greatest of all archaeological sites in the New World is Kaminaljuyu, on the western margins of Guatemala City in a broad, fertile valley lying athwart the Continental Divide. Although it consisted of several hundred great temple mounds in Maudslay's day, all but a handful have been swallowed up by the rapidly expanding slums and real estate developments of the capital. Rescue operations by the Carnegie Institution of Washington and Pennsylvania State University have shown that whereas part of the site was constructed during the Early Classic, the great majority of the mounds

14 (*Right*) Monument 52 at San Lorenzo, Veracruz, a representation of the Olmec rain god as an infant. San Lorenzo phase (1400–1000 BC). Early Preclassic period.

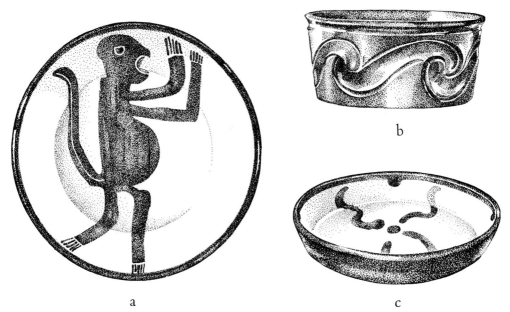

15 Pottery vessels of the Las Charcas culture (Middle Preclassic period). *a, c*, interiors of red-on-white bowls; *b*, grey-brown bowl with modeled decoration. *a*, 12 in. (30.5 cm) diam.; *b, c*, to scale.

were definitely Preclassic. The loss to science through the depredations of brickyards and bulldozers has been incalculable.

It has been no easy task, under these circumstances, to work out an archaeological succession for Kaminaljuyu, but the oldest culture is probably Arévalo, for which we have little more than some sherds from *tecomates* and red-slipped bowls. This is followed by Las Charcas, which marks a major occupation of the Valley of Guatemala, for Las Charcas remains are scattered widely. Its stratigraphic position underneath deposits of the Late Preclassic, backed up by a number of slightly contradictory radiocarbon dates, suggests that this village culture falls toward the end of the Middle Preclassic, around the fifth or fourth century BC.

The best-preserved Las Charcas remains come from a series of bottle-shaped pits which had been cut in ancient times down through the topsoil into the underlying volcanic ash. No one has a firm idea of the purpose of these excavations. Perhaps some may have been cooking pits, and it is entirely possible that, as among the historic Hidatsa Indians of the Great Plains, others may have been for the storage of maize and beans, but surely their final use was as refuse containers. In them have been found carbonized avocado seeds, maize cobs, and remnants of textiles, basketry and probably mats, and rope fragments. The magnificent Las Charcas white ware, manufactured from a kaolin-like clay, is extremely sophisticated, with designs in red showing spider monkeys with upraised arms, grotesque dragon masks, and other more abstract motifs. Las Charcas figurines are predominantly female, with a liveliness of concept seldom found elsewhere.

16 (*Right*) A Middle Preclassic pottery figurine of a seated woman, from the Las Charcas culture site of Copolchi. Ht *c*. 4 in. (10 cm).

In the Maya lowlands, both in the Central and in the Northern Areas, we now have for the first time substantial evidence for a Maya population. Presumably, prior to that time, the lowland forests and savannahs contained only small groups of preceramic hunters and gatherers of unknown tongue, but in lieu of solid archaeological evidence, that is pure speculation.

One of the oldest Middle Preclassic cultures in the lowlands is the little-known Xe phase of the western Peten, which appears in deep levels at the site of Altar de Sacrificios and at Seibal, and may represent some kind of intrusion from the highlands via the Lakantun drainage system. While on the one hand Xe ceramics are related to coeval hard, white pottery of Chiapas, there are ties with the Olmecs of the Gulf Coast, for at Seibal Gordon Willey and his Harvard group found a cache of jade celts and a jade perforating instrument of probable La Venta manufacture.

The spread of Mayan-speakers in the Peten, Belize, and the Northern Maya Area is almost surely to be associated with the adoption of red and mottled orange ceramics, the earliest manifestation of which seems to be in the Swasey/Bladen phase, at the site of Cuello in northern Belize; its excavator, Norman Hammond, once assigned it to the Early Preclassic, but radiocarbon evidence places it at about 1000–700 BC. In Swasey deposits there have been preserved tiny cobs of pop corn, and root crops such as native yam *(Dioscorea)*, cocoyam *(Xanthosoma)*, and possibly manioc. There is also some evidence of architectural beginnings, with plastered platforms that once supported perishable superstructures.

Swasey/Bladen leads directly into the Mamom culture, dated from 700 to about 400 BC. Mamom is spread over almost all of the Maya lowlands, and looks like a simple village culture, since until recently there were no real examples of public architecture on the scale of La Venta, for instance. However, the special conditions of excavation in the Peten must be considered. The lowland Maya almost always built their temples over older ones, so that in the course of centuries the earliest constructions would eventually come to be deeply buried within the towering accretions of Classic period rubble and plaster. Consequently, to prospect for Mamom temples in one of the larger sites would be extremely costly in time and labor.

The recent discoveries by Richard Hansen of the University of California, Los Angeles, at the northern Peten site of Nak'be (to be further considered in the next chapter) have drastically changed our minds about Mamom temple architecture. At first no more than a large Middle Preclassic village, by 750 BC, Nak'be had begun to look like a city, with buildings and platforms as high as 59 ft (18 m) covering up the old village structures. While these lack the spectacular mask-panels that were to be a hallmark of this and other cities in the Late Preclassic, the Nak'be temples testify that the lowland Maya had begun to emerge at even this early date from simple peasant life to a more complex society.

Mamom pottery appears quite simple when compared with Las Charcas to which it seems related. The commonest wares are red and orange-red monochromes, with polychrome decoration absent. Usually the only embellishment is simple incising on the inside of bowls, or daubing of necked jars with red blobs. Nonetheless, new information from Nak'be suggests that this simplicity has been overstated: there, according to Dr Hansen, up to 17 percent of Mamom ceramics recovered from well-preserved contexts were waxy monochromes that had been covered with an extremely fine and delicate, brilliantly polychromed stucco. Such polychroming may have been present in other Peten sites, but inadvertently washed off in the laboratory.

The figurine cult, if such it may be called, is present in Mamom, with a wide range of stylistic treatment carried out by punching and with applied strips of clay. At Tik'al, a cache of Mamom ceramics was discovered in a sealed *chultun*. This is a bottle-shaped chamber below the plaza floor, quite comparable in shape and perhaps in use to those of Las Charcas. *Chultunob* are ubiquitous in sites of the Central and Northern Areas, cut down into the limestone marl from the surface. We know that by the Classic, they were used as cisterns in the Puuk region, and in the Central Area for burials and perhaps sweat baths. Initially, they could have been utilized as sources of the fine lime employed in construction by Maya architects, but their use as storage pits (perhaps for the fruit of the breadnut tree, as suggested by Dennis Puleston) should not be overlooked. However, they are often so damp that stored food may have rotted. Whatever the answer to the "*chultun* mystery,*" they are as old as the Mamom phase.

In the southeastern corner of the Central Area, the pioneers who first settled in the rich valley surrounding the ancient city of Copan had other roots. Towards the end of the Early Preclassic, village cultures all along the Pacific littoral as far as El Salvador had become "Olmec-ized," a tradition that was to continue into the Middle Preclassic, and that was to be manifested in carved ceramics of Olmec type and even in Olmec stone monuments. This Olmec-like wave even penetrated the Copan Valley, during the Middle Preclassic Uir phase (900–400 BC), with the sudden appearance of pottery bowls incised and carved with such Olmec motifs as the paw-wing and the so-called "flame eyebrows." In a deep layer of an outlying suburb of the Classic city, William Fash discovered a Uir phase burial accompanied by Olmecoid ceramics, 9 polished stone cells, and over 300 drilled jade objects. Although the rest of the Maya lowlands seems to have been of little interest to the Olmec peoples, the Copan area definitely was.

There is still a great deal to understand about the Middle Preclassic, the base on which the flowering of Maya culture took place. Certainly it was during this period when the Maya area became truly "Maya." But Maya civilization as we know it – the vaulted masonry architecture, the naturalistic painting and relief style, the Long Count calendar and writing – had not even begun to germinate during this epoch.

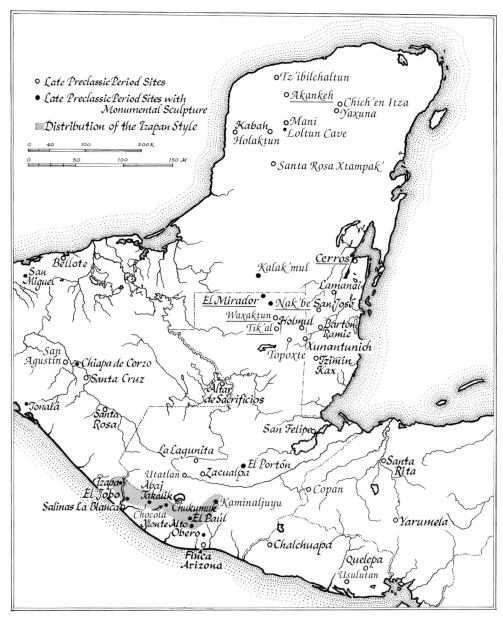

Late Preclassic Period Sites

○ Late Preclassic Period Sites

● Late Preclassic Period Sites with Monumental Sculpture

▨ Distribution of the Izapan Style

```
0   40    100      200K
0    50    100     150 M
```

Tz'ibilchaltun

Akankeh
Chich'en Itza
Yaxuna

Kabah
Holaktun

Mani
Loltun Cave

Santa Rosa Xtampak'

Bellote
San Miguel

Cerros

Kalak'mul

Lamanai

El Mirador
Nak'be
San José

Waxaktun
Holmul
Barton Ramie
Tik'al

Xunantunich

San Agustin
Chiapa de Corzo

Topoxte
Tzimin Kax

Santa Cruz

Tonalá

Altar de Sacrificios

Santa Rosa

San Felipe

La Lagunita

El Portón

Santa Rita

Utatlan
Zacualpa

Izapa
El Jobo
Abaj Takalik

Chukumuk
Kaminaljuyu

Copan

Salinas La Blanca

Chocola
Monte Alto
El Baúl

Obero

Yarumela

Finca Arizona

Chalchuapá

Quelepa

Usulutan

17 Sites of the Late Preclassic period. Underlined sites have giant architectural masks.

3· The Rise of Maya Civilization

It is a long step from the village cultures that we have thus far been considering to the awe-inspiring achievements of the Classic Maya, but by no means an impossible one. The all-important questions are, what happened during the intervening time covered by the Late Preclassic period, 17 and how did those traits that are considered as typical of the Classic Maya actually develop?

There have been a number of contradictory theories to account for the rise of Maya civilization. One of the most persistent holds that the previously undistinguished Maya came under the influence of travelers from shores as distant as the China coast; as a matter of interest to the lay public, it should be categorically emphasized that *no* objects manufactured in any part of the Old World have been identified in any Maya site, and that ever since the days of Stephens and Catherwood few theories involving trans-Pacific or trans-Atlantic contact have survived scientific scrutiny.

The possibility of some trans-Pacific influence on Mesoamerican cultures cannot, however, be so easily dismissed. Its most consistent proponent has been David Kelley of the University of Calgary, who has long pointed out that within the twenty named days of the 260-day calendar so fundamental to Mesoamericans (see below) is a sequence of animals that can be matched in similar sequence within the lunar zodiacs of many East and Southeast-Asian civilizations. To Kelley, this resemblance is far too close to be merely coincidental. Furthermore, Asian and Mesoamerican cosmological systems, which emphasize a quadripartite universe of four cardinal points associated with specific colors, plants, animals, and even gods, are amazingly similar. Both Asian and Mesoamerican religions see a rabbit on the face of the full moon (whereas we see a "Man in the Moon"), and they also associate this luminary with a woman weaving at a loom.

Even more extraordinary, as the historian of science the late Joseph Needham reminded us, Chinese astronomers of the Han Dynasty as well as the ancient Maya used exactly the same complex calculations to give warning about the likelihood of lunar and solar eclipses. These data would suggest (but by no means prove) that there was direct contact across the Pacific. As oriental seafaring was always on a far higher technological plane than anything ever known in the prehispanic New World, it is possible that Asian intellectuals may have established some sort of contact with their Mesoamerican counterparts by the end of the Preclassic.

Lest this be thought to be idle speculation along the lines of the lunatic fringe books so common in this field, let me point out one further piece of evidence. Paul Tolstoy of the University of Montreal has made a meticulous study of the occurrence of the techniques and tools utilized in the manufacture of bark paper around the Pacific basin. It is his well-founded conclusion that this technology, known in ancient China, Southeast Asia and Indonesia, as well as in Mesoamerica, was diffused from eastern Indonesia to Mesoamerica at a very early date. The main use of such paper in Mesoamerica was in the production of screenfold books to record ritual, calendrical, and astronomical information. It is not unreasonable to suppose that it was through the medium of such books, which are still in use by Indonesian people like the Batak, that an intellectual exchange took place.

This does *not* mean that the Maya – or any other Mesoamerican civilization – were merely derivative from Old World prototypes. What it does suggest is that at a few times in their early history, the Maya may have been receptive to some important ideas originating in the Eastern Hemisphere.

Another school of thought holds that, because of the supposedly low agricultural potential of the Peten and Yucatan, civilization was introduced to the lowlands from an outside area with a more favorable ecology. There are still others who claim that this potential has been gravely underrated, and that Maya culture as it is known for the Classic period is completely *sui generis*, with no trace of outside influence. Needless to say, both of these points of view are overstated, and both are at least partly wrong. The fact is that the Maya of both highlands and lowlands have never been isolated from the rest of Mesoamerica, and that Mexican influences have sporadically guided the course of Maya cultural history since very early times, as we shall see in this and subsequent chapters. It is also increasingly apparent that the reverse was also the case: strong Maya influence can be detected in central Mexico and the Gulf Coast of Veracruz, particularly during the last phase of the Classic.

How are we to define the word "civilization"? How do the civilized differ from the barbaric? Archaeologists have usually dodged this question by offering lists of traits which they think to be important. Cities are one criterion. The late V. G. Childe thought that writing should be another, but the obviously advanced Inca of Peru were completely illiterate. Civilization, in fact, is different in degree rather than in kind from what precedes it, but has certainly been achieved by the time that state institutions, large-scale public works, temple buildings, and widespread, unified art styles have appeared. With few exceptions, the complex state apparatus demands some form of records, and writing has usually been the answer: so has the invention of a more-or-less accurate means of keeping time.

Yet all civilizations are in themselves unique. The Classic Maya of the lowlands had a very elaborate calendar; writing; temple-pyramids and palaces of limestone masonry with vaulted rooms; architectural layouts emphasizing buildings arranged around plazas with rows of stone stelae lined up before some; polychrome pottery; and a very sophisticated art style expressed in bas-reliefs and in wall paintings. These traits are now known to have been developed in the Late Preclassic (300 BC–AD 250) period.

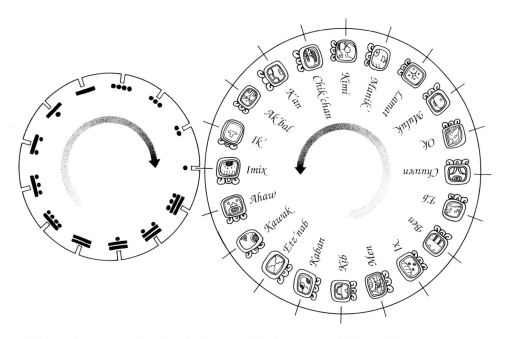

18 Schematic representation of the 260-day count. The day-names are in Yucatec Maya.

The birth of the calendar

Some system of recording time is essential to all higher cultures – to fix critical events in the lives of the persons ruling the state, to guide the agricultural and ceremonial year, and to record celestial motions. The Calendar Round of 52 years was present among all the Mesoamericans, including the Maya, and is presumably of very great age. It consists of two permutating cycles. One is of 260 days, representing the intermeshing of a sequence of the numbers 1 through 13 with 20 named days. Among the Maya, the 260-day count (sometimes called by the *ersatz* term *tzolk'in*) began with 1 Imix, followed by 2 Ik', 3 Ak'bal, 4 K'an, until 13 Ben had been reached; the day following was Ix, with the coefficient 1 again, leading to 2 Men, and so on. The last day of the 260-day cycle would be 13 Ahaw, and it would repeat once again commencing with 1 Imix. How such a period of time even came into being remains an enigma, but the use to which it was put is clear. Every single day had its own omens and associations, and the inexorable march of the 20 days acted as a kind of perpetual fortune-telling machine guiding the destinies of the Maya and of all the peoples of Mexico. It still survives in unchanged form among some indigenous peoples in southern Mexico and the Maya highlands, under the care of calendar priests.

Meshing with the 260-day count is a "Vague Year" or *Haab* of 365 days, so called because the *actual* length of the solar year is about a quarter-day more, a circumstance that leads us to intercalate one day every four years to keep our calendar in march with the sun. Although the Maya were perfectly aware

18

19

19 Signs for the months in the *Haab* or 365-day count. The names of the months are in Yucatec Maya.

that the *Haab* was shorter than the tropical year, they did not change the calendar accordingly. Within the *Haab*, there were 18 named "months" of 20 days each, with a much-dreaded interval of 5 unlucky days added at the end. The Maya New Year started with 1 Pop, the next day being 2 Pop, etc. The final day of the month, however, carried not the coefficient 20, but a sign indicating the "seating" of the month to follow, in line with the Maya

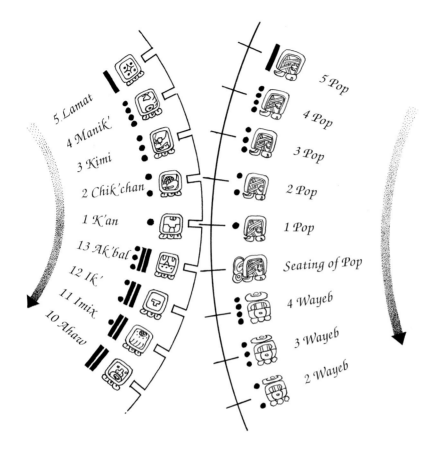

5 Lamat
4 Manik'
3 Kimi
2 Chik'chan
1 K'an
13 Ak'bal
12 Ik'
11 Imix
10 Ahaw

5 Pop
4 Pop
3 Pop
2 Pop
1 Pop
Seating of Pop
4 Wayeb
3 Wayeb
2 Wayeb

20 Schematic representation of part of the 52-year Calendar Round.

philosophy that the influence of any particular span of time is felt *before* it actually begins and persists somewhat beyond its apparent termination.

From this it follows that a particular day in the 260-day count, such as 1 K'an, also had a position in the *Haab*, for instance 2 Pop. A day designated as I K'an 2 Pop could not return until 52 *Haabs* (18,980 days) had passed. This is the Calendar Round, and it is the only annual time count possessed by the highland peoples of Mexico, one that obviously has its disadvantages where events taking place over a span of more than 52 years are concerned.

Although it is usually assumed to be "Maya," the Long Count was widely distributed in Classic and earlier times in the lowland country of Meso-america; but it was carried to its highest degree of refinement by the Maya of the Central Area. This is really another kind of permutation count, except that the cycles used are so large that, unlike the Calendar Round, any event within the span of historical time could be fixed without fear of ambiguity. Instead of taking the Vague Year as the basis for the Long Count, the Maya and other peoples employed the tun, a period of 360 days. The Long Count cycles are:

145

20 k'ins	1 winal or 20 days
18 winals	1 tun or 360 days
20 tuns	1 k'atun or 7,200 days
20 k'atuns	1 bak'tun or 144,000 days.

Long Count dates inscribed by the Maya on their monuments consist of the above cycles listed from top to bottom in descending order of magnitude, each with its numerical coefficient, and all to be added up so as to express the number of days elapsed since the end of the last Great Cycle, a period of 13 bak'tuns whose ending fell on the date 4 Ahaw 8 Kumk'u. The starting point of the present Great Cycle corresponds, in the Thompson correlation, to 13 August 3114 BC (Gregorian calendar). Thus, a Long Count date convention- ally written as 9.10.19.5.11 10 Chuwen 4 Kumk'u would be:

9 bak'tuns	1,296,000 days
10 k'atuns	72.000 days
19 tuns	6,840 days
5 winals	100 days
11 k'ins	11 days

or 1,374,951 days since the close of the last Great Cycle, reaching the Calen- dar Round position 10 Chuwen 4 Kumk'u.

Something should also be said about the coefficients themselves. The Maya, along with a few other groups of the lowlands and the Zapotecs and Mixtecs of Oaxaca, had a number system of great simplicity, employing only 144 two symbols: a dot with the value of "one" and a horizontal bar for "five." Numerals up to four were expressed by dots only, six was a bar with a dot above, and ten two bars. Nineteen, the highest coefficient in calendrical use, took the form of four dots above three bars. The treatment of higher numbers, for which the "nought" symbol (a stylized shell) was essential, will be discussed in Chapter 9.

It is generally agreed that the Long Count must have been set in motion long after the inception of the Calendar Round, but by just how many centuries or millennia is uncertain. Be that as it may, the oldest recorded 17 Long Count dates fall within Bak'tun 7, and appear on monuments which lie *outside* the Maya area. At present, the most ancient seems to be Stela 2 at Chiapa de Corzo, a major ceremonial center which had been in existence since Early Preclassic times in the dry Grijalva Valley of central Chiapas: in a vertical column are carved the numerical coefficients [7.16.]3.2.13, followed by the day 6 Ben, the "month" of the Vague Year being suppressed as in all these early inscriptions. This would correspond to 7 December 36 BC. Five years later, the famous Stela C at the Olmec site of Tres Zapotes in Veracruz was inscribed with the date 7.16.6.16.18 6 Etz'nab. On the Chiapa de Corzo monument, the initial coefficients are missing but reconstructable.

Now, the sixteenth k'atun of Bak'tun 7 would fall within the Late Preclassic, and we can be sure that unless these dates are to be counted forward from some base *other* than 13.0.0.0.0 4 Ahaw 8 Kumk'u (as the end of the last Great Cycle is recorded), which seems improbable, then the "Maya" calendar had reached what was pretty much its final form by the first century BC among peoples who were under powerful Olmec influence and who may not even have been Maya.

Who might they have been? It will be remembered from Chapter 1 that the most likely candidate for the language of the Olmecs was an early form of Mixe-Zoquean; languages belonging to this group are still spoken on the Isthmus of Tehuantapec and in western Chiapas. Many scholars are now willing to ascribe the earliest Long Count monuments outside the Maya area proper to Mixe-Zoquean as well, and a recent discovery in southern Veracruz may provide confirmation. This is Stela 1 from La Mojarra, a magnificent monument inscribed with two Bak'tun 8 dates corresponding respectively to AD 143 and 156. These are accompanied by a text of about 400 signs, in a script which is now called "Isthmian" (the famous "Tuxtla Statuette," also found in southern Veracruz, is in the same system, and dates to AD 162). In 1993, Terrence Kaufman and John Justeson announced their decipherment of the Isthmian script and the text on Stela 1, which they assert is in Mixe-Zoquean, but this decipherment has not yet been fully accepted by other glyph specialists.

From the Mixe-Zoqueans, then, it appears that writing and the calendar were spread along the Pacific Coast of Guatemala and into the Maya highlands, eventually reaching the developing states of the Peten forests and Yucatan.

Izapa and the Pacific Coast

Crucial to the problem of how higher culture came about among the Maya is the Izapan civilization, for it occupies a middle ground in time and in space between the Middle Preclassic Olmecs and the Early Classic Maya. Its hallmark is an elaborate art style, found on monuments scattered over a wide zone from Tres Zapotes on the Veracruz coast, to the Pacific plain of Chiapas and Guatemala, and up into the Guatemala City area.

17

Izapa itself is a very large site made up of over eighty temple mounds of earthen construction faced with river cobbles, just east of Tapachula, Chiapas, in the moist, slightly hilly country about 20 miles (32 km) inland from the Pacific shore. Whether it belongs with Mexico, culturally speaking, or with the Maya area is debatable, but the tongue anciently spoken here was not Maya but Tapachulteco, a vestigial member of the once more widespread Mixe-Zoquean group. While Izapa was founded as a ceremonial center as far back as Early Preclassic times and continued in use until the Early Classic, the bulk of the constructions and probably all of the many carved monuments belong to the Late Preclassic era. The Izapan art style consists in the main of large, ambitiously conceived but somewhat cluttered scenes carried out in bas-relief. Many of the activities shown are profane, such as a richly attired person decapitating a vanquished foe, but there are deities as well. One of these is a "Long-lipped God," part human and part fish (most likely shark), who apparently is an ancestral form of Chak, the ubiquitous Maya

7

patron of lightning and rain. Another supernatural being present at Izapa has one leg ending in a serpent's body and head, and is thus the earliest known representation of the god K'awil, in Classic times the presiding deity of Maya ruling houses. But by far the leading figure in the crystallizing Maya pantheon as seen in Izapan monumental art, extending to the giant stucco masks of Late Preclassic temples in the Peten and Belize, is the monstrous form of Wuqub' Kaqix, an anthropomorphic bird who shows up in the Popol Vuh as the arrogant "sun" of the creation preceding this one.

146d   Certain recurrent elements must represent well-understood iconographic motifs, such as a U-shaped form between diagonal bars above the principal scene, perhaps an early occurrence of the sky-band so ubiquitous in Classic Maya art; the "U" itself is most likely the prototype of the Maya glyph for the moon, and is found repeated many times on the same relief.

Izapa, then, is a major center with some of the features which we consider more typical of the lowland Maya already in full flower – the stela-altar complex, the Long-lipped God who becomes transformed into the Maya rain god Chak, and a highly painterly, two-dimensional art style which emphasizes historical and mythic scenography with great attention to plumage and other costume details. Writing and the calendar are absent, but as one moves along the Pacific slopes east into Guatemala, one finds sites with inscriptions and Bak'tun 7 dates.

One of these Guatemalan stations is Abaj Tak'alik', situated in a lush, well-watered Piedmont zone that in the days of the Conquest was a great producer of chocolate, and is now devoted to coffee. Like Izapa, it is made up of earthern mounds scattered about the site with little attention to formal arrangement. That the Olmecs had once intruded here is apparent from a large boulder located less than a mile from the main group of mounds, carved in relief with a bearded were-jaguar in the purest Olmec style. Stela 1 from the site is purely Izapan but dateless. On the other hand, Stela 2, now somewhat damaged, bore on its carved face two richly attired Izapan figures with tall, plumed headdresses, facing each other across a vertical row of glyphs, below a cloud-like mass of volutes from which peers the face of a sky god. The topmost sign in the column is beyond doubt a very early form of the Introductory Glyph which in later Classic inscriptions stands at the head of a Long Count date. Just beneath is the bak'tun coefficient, which is pretty clearly the number 7. In recent decades, a University of California expedition has found a number of significant new monuments at Abaj Tak'alik', including a stela with two Bak'tun 8 dates, so that this site may have equaled Izapa in importance.

21   A more complete Bak'tun 7 inscription appears on Stela 1, the "Herrera Stela," from El Baúl, a coffee plantation considerably to the southeast of Abaj Tak'alik' in a region studded with Early Classic centers of the Cotzumalhuapa culture. This object has attracted fairly hot debate ever since it was found in 1923, some refusing to believe that it is even as old as the Classic period, and its very discoverer claiming it as Aztec! On the right, a profile figure is stiffly posed with spear in hand below a cloud-scroll; over the lower part of his face is some sort of covering, while to his headdress is attached a

21 Stela 1 from El Baúl, the earliest dated monument from the Maya area proper. On the right a figure in profile stands stiffly posed below a face looking down from a cloud-scroll.

22 Monument 1 at Monte Alto, a site of the Late Preclassic period. Ht 4 ft 8 in. (1.42 m).

chin strap, a feature known to be extremely early in the Maya lowlands. In front of him are two vertical columns of glyphs, the right-hand of which consists of little more than empty cartouches which were probably meant to be painted. Let us, however, consider the row on the extreme left, for this is almost surely the earliest dated monument in the Maya area proper. At the top is the coefficient 12 above a fleshless jaw, a Mexican form of the day sign Eb. Then there are four indecipherable signs, followed by a series of Long Count numbers which can be reconstructed as 7.19.15.7.12, reaching the Calendar Round position 12 Eb; in terms of our own calendar, this would be in the year AD 36, some 256 years prior to the first such date in the Maya lowlands, but significantly later than the precocious inscriptions of Chiapas and the Veracruz coast.

We cannot leave the Pacific coastal zone without mentioning a second sculptural tradition which reaches some degree of popularity both there and at Kaminaljuyu. This is expressed in large, crude, pot-bellied statues with puffy faces and lower jaws so inflated that they have been compared with Italy's one-time Fascist leader, Mussolini. At Monte Alto, not far from El Baúl, a group of these monstrous forms is placed in a row along with a colossal head carried out in the same style, and some believe that the entire

22

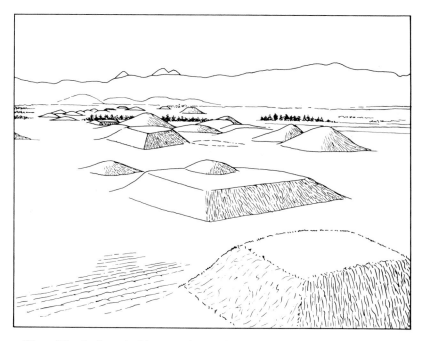

23 View of Kaminaljuyu, looking west, from a photograph taken by A. P. Maudslay. Most of the earthen mounds – now largely disappeared – were temple substructures of the Miraflores culture.

pot-bellied complex is connected with the Olmec culture and precedes the Izapan. However, since Monte Alto is strewn with Late Preclassic pottery sherds, it is most likely that this was a subsidiary cult that coexisted with the Izapan Rain God, just as Egyptian and Graeco-Roman religious art flourished side-by-side in ancient Alexandria. But a cult to what deity? A fairly good case can be made out for this being none other than the Fat God, without known functions but ubiquitous among the peoples of Mexico and the Northern Maya Area in Classic times.

Kaminaljuyu and the Maya highlands

A Late Preclassic rival to Izapa in size and number of temple mounds and in the splendor of its carved monuments was Kaminaljuyu during the Miraflores phase. This, it will be recalled, was once a major ceremonial site on the western outskirts of Guatemala City. The majority of the approximately 200 mounds once to be found there were probably constructed by the Miraflores people, whose rulers must have possessed a formidable economic and political power over much of the Maya highlands at this time.

The excavation of two Miraflores tombs has thrown much light on the luxury to which these rulers were accustomed. Mound E-III-3 at Kaminaljuyu consists of several superimposed temple platforms, each a flat-topped, stepped pyramid fronted by a broad stairway; in its final form it reaches a height of more than 60 ft (18 m). In lieu of easily worked building

23

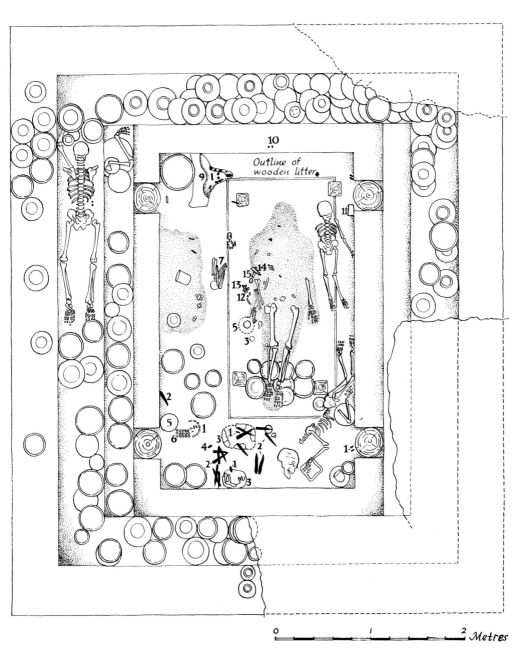

24 Plan of Tomb II, Mound E-III-3, a burial of the Miraflores culture at Kaminaljuyu.
1, jade beads; *2*, obsidian flake-blades; *3*, mica sheets; *4*, jade mosaic element; *5*, stuccoed gourds; *6*, pebbles; *7*, basalt implements; *8*, human teeth; *9*, jade mosaic mask or headdress; *10*, obsidian stones; *11*, pyrite-incrusted sherd; *12*, soapstone implement; *13*, bone objects, fish teeth, and quartz crystals; *14*, sting-ray spines; *15*, spatulate bone object. All other circular objects are pottery vessels.

Kaminaljuyu

25 (*Above*) A Late Preclassic effigy of grey–green chlorite schist from Tomb I, Mound E-III-3 (Miraflores culture) at Kaminaljuyu. Overall length 8 ¼ in. (21 cm).

26 (*Right*) A grey soapstone jar from Tomb I, Mound E-III-3 at Kaminaljuyu. Ht 3 ½ in. (9.2 cm).

27 (*Below*) A fine-line incised bowl from Tomb I, Mound E-III-3 at Kaminaljuyu. W. 12 in. (30.5 cm).

28 A ruler wearing a mask of the Principal Bird Deity (Wuqub' Kaqix) is carved on this granite stela from Kaminaljuyu. Ht 6 ft (1.8 m).

stone, which was unavailable in the vicinity, these platforms were built from ordinary clay and basketloads of earth and household rubbish. Almost certainly the temples themselves were thatched-roof affairs supported by upright timbers. Apparently each successive building operation took place to house the remains of an exalted person, whose tomb was cut down from the top in a series of stepped rectangles of decreasing size into the earlier temple platform, and then covered over with a new floor of clay. The function of Maya pyramids as funerary monuments thus harks back to Preclassic times.

The corpse was wrapped in finery and covered from head to toe with cinnabar pigment, then laid on a wooden litter and lowered into the tomb. Both sacrificed adults and children accompanied the illustrious dead, together with offerings of an astonishing richness and profusion. In one tomb, over 300 objects of the most beautiful workmanship were placed with the body or above the timber roof, but ancient grave-robbers, probably acting after noticing the slump in the temple floor caused by the collapse of the underlying tomb, had filched from the corpse the jades which once covered the chest and head. Among the finery recovered were the remains of a mask or headdress of jade plaques perhaps once fixed to a background of wood, jade flares which once adorned the ear lobes of the honored dead, bowls carved from chlorite-schist engraved with Miraflores scroll designs, and little carved bottles of soapstone and fuchsite.

Miraflores pottery vessels from E-III-3 and elsewhere belong to a ceramic tradition prevalent throughout southeastern Mesoamerica during the Late Preclassic horizon, from Izapa to El Salvador, and up into the Central and Northern Maya Areas, but are set off from this tradition in their refinement and sophistication. Shapes have now become exuberant, with re-curved outlines, elaborate flanges on rims and bodies, and the appearance of vessel feet. Some of the most amusing examples of the potter's art are effigy vessels, a few of which show smiling old men. Painted stucco is often used to achieve effects in colors such as pink and green, unobtainable in fired slips. Most bowls and jars are embellished with engraved and carved scroll designs. A more peculiar kind of decoration which is virtually a marker for the Late Preclassic period in the Maya area is found on Usulutan ware, believed to originate in El Salvador where it attained great popularity. On this widely traded ware, a resistant substance such as wax or thin clay was applied to bowls with a multiple-brush applicator; after smudging or darkening in a reducing fire, the material was removed to leave a design of yellowish wavy parallel lines on a darker orange or brown background.

As for stone carving on a large scale, it was once believed that the Miraflores people made only "mushroom stones." These peculiar objects, one of which was found in an E-III-3 tomb, are of unknown use. Some see vaguely phallic associations. Others, such as the late Stephan de Borhegyi, connect them with the cult of the hallucinogenic mushrooms still to this day prevalent in the Mexican highlands, and it is claimed that the mortars and pestles with which the stones are so often associated were used in the preparatory rites.

But we have much more to go by than that, thanks to the devastation of

29 Broken Miraflores stela from Kaminaljuyu depicting Izapan gods (top) and a human figure in profile, associated with calendrical names in the 260-day count. The text below cannot yet be read.

Kaminaljuyu by modern real-estate entrepreneurs. It now appears that there were Miraflores artists capable of creating sculpture on a large scale, in an Izapan style that can only be called the forerunner of the Classic Maya. Moreover, the elite of this valley were fully literate at a time when other Maya were perhaps just learning that writing existed. Two of these monuments were encountered by accident in a drainage ditch. One is a tall, granite stela embellished with a striding figure wearing a series of grotesque masks of Izapan gods (the one over his face is the head of the bird-monster Wuqub' Kaqix), and carrying a chipped flint of eccentric form in one hand. On either side of him are spiked clay incense burners exactly like those found in Miraflores excavations. The other is even more extraordinary. It must have been of gigantic proportions before its deliberate breakage; the surviving fragments show that there were several Izapan gods, one bearded, surrounding a human figure with downpointing tridents in place of eyes, probably a precursor of a god who later appears at Tik'al; he too, wields an eccentric flint. The glyphs associated with these figures may be their calendric names,

28

29

for in ancient Mesoamerica, both gods and men were identified by the days on which they were born. A much longer text in several columns is incised below in a script which is otherwise unknown but which, in the opinion of the late Tatiana Proskouriakoff and others, may foreshadow Classic Maya writing, since there are strong similarities in form if not in specific characters. It cannot, however, yet be read.

Not only were stelae of major size carved by the Miraflores artisans, but also stone thrones; tenoned figures called "silhouette sculptures," which were perhaps originally meant to be stuck upright into temple and plaza floors; frog- or toad-effigy figures of all sizes; and many other forms. Once more, the pot-bellied figures are ubiquitous: did they represent a cult of the people, separate from the more aristocratic religion of the rulers? Or do they, as some believe, belong to an earlier horizon? Archaeology has unfortunately arrived on the scene too late to answer this.

The archaeologist Marion Hatch has recently encountered evidence for the existence of a sophisticated system of intensive agriculture at Kaminaljuyu. Connected with a now-extinct lake are various irrigation canals, one of which carried water to an artificial storage basin 52.5 ft (16 m) wide and 36 ft (11 m) deep; leading from the latter were small tributary channels which brought water to the fields, some of which were agricultural terraces on the sides of the ravines.

The astonishing wealth of the Miraflores people, their artistic and architectural capabilities, their obvious relation to the Classic Maya in matters of style, iconography, and script – all these things lead one to believe that the Izapan culture of the highlands must have had a good deal to do with the adoption of civilized life in the Central and Northern Areas. While the pre-eminence of Kaminaljuyu during the Late Preclassic period is plain to see, its star began to sink by the second and third centuries AD, and most of it was left in ruin at the close of the Late Preclassic. It was not until the Mexican invasions of the Early Classic that this great center regained its former splendor.

Elsewhere in the Guatemalan highlands, the French archaeologist Alain Ichon has excavated the mound site of La Lagunita, located in the Chixoy drainage some 25 miles (40 km) northeast of the K'iche' center of Chichicastenango. There he encountered a number of relief sculptures in a terminal Late Preclassic style related to the Izapan culture, but somewhat aberrant, including one representation of Wuqub' Kaqix. There were four stone sarcophagi, one containing two superimposed human skeletons with a wealth of offerings, including jade, variously colored obsidian, and white flint, along with a pottery effigy of a terrifying deity with long nose and gaping mouth revealing a lolling tongue and huge fangs.

The Peten and the Maya lowlands

While the Maya highlands and Pacific Coast were experiencing an extraordinary cultural efflorescence in the Late Preclassic, the Central and Northern Areas were hardly slumbering. Within the boundless forests, the agricultural

30 Usulutan ware bowl from Burial 85, Tik'al (Chikanel culture). Diam. *c.* 7 ¾ in. (20 cm).

economy and society had advanced to such a degree that massive temple centers were already rising in jungle clearings. But it is clear that from the very beginning the people of the lowlands were taking a somewhat different course from that of their kinsmen to the south, and it is their unique qualities which so distinguish them in the Classic period which was soon to be inaugurated.

Although there are minor differences from region to region, a single wide-spread culture, Chikanel, dominated the Central and Northern Areas at this time. Usulutan ware and vessels with wide, everted lips, elaborate rim flanges, or complex outline are, as in the Southern Area, hallmarks for the period. Most pottery is legless, and confined to a simple black or red mono-chrome, with thick glossy slips that feel waxy to the touch. It is strange that in most known Chikanel sites, figurines are not found, from which it may be supposed that there was a change in popular cults.

The most unusual feature of Chikanel culture, however, is the high elabo-ration of architecture. It must be remembered that the Peten-Yucatan shelf is blessed with an inexhaustible supply of easily cut limestone, and with abundant flint for tools with which to work it. Moreover, the Maya of the lowlands had discovered as far back as Mamom times that if limestone frag-ments were burnt, and the resulting powder mixed with water, a white plaster of great durability was obtained. And finally, they quickly realized the structural value of a concrete-like fill made from limestone rubble and marl.

With these resources at hand, the Maya temple architect was able to create some massive constructions at a very early date. At the great Peten sites of Waxaktun, Tik'al, El Mirador, and Nak'be, deep excavations have shown that major pyramids, platforms, and courts were already taking shape by Chikanel times. There is general agreement, for instance, that the E-VII-sub pyramid at Waxaktun, excavated by the Carnegie Institution of Washington in the

30

31

73

1930s, was built in the Chikanel phase; beautifully preserved by the overlay of later structures, this truncated temple platform is faced by brilliantly white plaster and rises in several tiers, each having the apron moldings which are so distinctive a feature of Maya architecture in the lowlands. On all four sides are centrally placed, inset stairways flanked by great monster masks which apparently represent the Jaguar God of the Underworld (the night sun), as well as sky-serpents. Postholes sunk into the floor show that the superstructure was a building of pole and thatch.

Although Group H at Waxaktun was discovered by Carnegie as long ago as 1935, it was only in 1985 that excavations under Juan Antonio Valdés of Guatemala's Institute of Anthropology and History revealed that its major constructions were almost entirely Late Preclassic, with hardly any Classic period overburden. The South Plaza, the focus of Valdés' research, is essentially a great platform supporting on the east a high, truncated pyramid (H-sub-3) with a central stairway; flanking it are two buildings with rooms which were once spanned by the corbel vault, or so-called "false arch," while three other buildings faced it on the west, all of them enclosing a small plaza.

Most of the South Plaza structures have huge, perfectly preserved masks and friezes formed of stucco over a stone core, and these were polychromed. On each side of the central stairway of H-sub-3 are two superimposed masks, each 8.7 ft (2.65 m) high. The iconography of the South Plaza is complex, with several deities represented, some of them with quite Olmecoid characteristics.

31 The north side of Pyramid E-VII-sub, Waxaktun, a Late Preclassic substructure belonging to the Chikanel culture. On top of this stucco-faced pyramid had once been a pole-and-thatch temple. Ht 26 ft 4 in. (8 m).

32 A greenstone mask, with shell-inlaid teeth and eyes, from Burial 85, Tik'al. Ht 5 in. (12.7 cm).

Even more advanced temples have been uncovered at Tik'al, which lies only a half-day's walk south of Waxaktun. Two late Chikanel structures, for instance, had superstructures with masonry walls, and it is possible, though certainly not proved, that the rooms were corbel-vaulted. Some quite extra-ordinary paintings embellished the outer walls of one of these temples, showing human figures standing in a background of cloud-like scrolls, carried out by a sure hand in black, yellow, red, and pink. Another set of murals, this time in black on a red background, was found inside a late Chikanel burial chamber at Tik'al. The subject matter comprises six richly attired figures, probably both human and divine. The two sets, which are thought to date from the last half of the first century BC, are pretty clearly in the Izapan style characteristic of Kaminaljuyu.

Some of the Late Preclassic tombs at Tik'al prove that the Chikanel elite did not lag behind the nobles of Miraflores in wealth and honor. Burial 85, for instance, like all the others enclosed by platform substructures and covered by a primitive corbel vault, contained a single skeleton. Surprisingly, this individual lacked head and thigh bones, but from the richness of the goods placed with him it may be guessed that he must have perished in battle and been despoiled by his enemies, his mutilated body being later recovered by his subjects. The remains were carefully wrapped-up in textiles, and the

32 bundle placed in an upright position. A small, greenstone mask with shell-inlaid eyes and teeth seems to have been sewn onto the bundle to represent the head. A sting-ray spine, the symbol of self-sacrifice among the Maya, and a spondylus shell were added to the gruesome contents. Packed around the burial chamber were no fewer than twenty-six vessels of the late Chikanel period, one of which contained pine-wood charcoal dated by the radiocarbon process to AD 16 ± 131.

The towering achievements of the Classic Maya in building and maintaining their enormous centers have blinded us to the equally remarkable florescence of Late Preclassic Maya culture. Two sites in Belize have provided exciting new data shedding light on this phenomenon. The first is Cerros, a relatively compact site located on a small, narrow peninsula near the mouth of the New River, on the southern edge of Chetumal Bay. Excavations and mapping carried out by David A. Freidel of Southern Methodist University have shown that this Late Preclassic center, with four primary pyramidal structures along with a host of other buildings, was surrounded by a moat-like canal which may have been connected with raised agricultural fields. One such pyramid was a two-tiered temple platform; its central stairway was flanked by four elaborate plaster-sculpture masks. Freidel interprets this as an elaborate cosmological diagram involving four important gods, and its relationship to the huge platform masks found at Waxaktun and on early buildings at Tik'al is obvious.

Far up the New River, a considerable distance to the southwest of Cerros, is the important site of Lamanai (known as "Indian Church" on older maps of Belize), which has been excavated by David M. Pendergast of the Royal Ontario Museum during a series of field seasons beginning in 1974. Lamanai lies on a long lake formed by the river, and its 718 mapped structures are stretched out in strip form along its shore. There is even an ancient harbor in the northern part of the site, testifying to its entrepreneurial importance in the regulation of ancient Maya trade. While it was occupied from earliest times right into the post-Conquest period, much of its importance lies in the large, imposing, Late Preclassic temple-pyramids which usually underlie Early Classic constructions, including one with a plaster-work mask closely resembling those from Cerros.

pl. III But the full scope of this Late Preclassic achievement in the southern Maya lowlands has only come to light at the sites of Nak'be and El Mirador, located in the northernmost Peten in a region with extensive swamps or *bajos*. We have already seen that Nak'be had a precocious development of monumental architecture during the Mamom phase of the Middle Preclassic. El Mirador, some 8 miles (13 km) northwest of Nak'be and connected to it by a causeway which crosses the intervening *bajos*, has turned out to be the oldest Maya capital city, far in advance of Tik'al, which it dwarfs by its size and lessens by its antiquity. The investigations and mapping carried out initially by Bruce Dahlin and Ray Matheny, and later by Richard Hansen, have shown that El Mirador is almost entirely of Late Preclassic (Chikanel) date; it was abandoned throughout the Early Classic, but there is a shoddy, Late Classic reoccupation which had little importance.

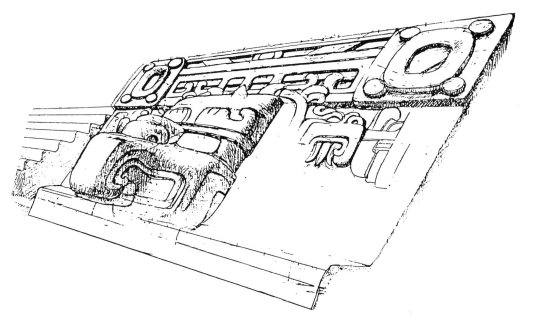

33 Giant stucco mask, Nak'be, Guatemala.

There are two groups of monumental construction, connected by a causeway, and in fact a whole network of causeways radiates out from El Mirador across the surrounding swampy landscape. The East Group is dominated by the Danta pyramid and its associated platforms, which cover an area of 18 hectares; the pyramid and the structure upon which it sits reach a height of 230 ft (70 m), and thus with its smaller superstructures must comprise an overall bulk which may be the largest in Mesoamerica, if not the New World. The Tigre pyramid in the West Group is no less than 180 ft (55 m) high, with an estimated volume of 380,000 cubic meters.

As at Cerros, Lamanai, Waxaktun, and Tik'al, gigantic stucco masks of deities flanked stairways at El Mirador; one excavated structure has huge masks of Wuqub' Kaqix, the great bird deity typical of the Late Preclassic. Typical also of this intriguing period in Maya culture history is the "triadic" pattern of architecture found here and at other similarly early lowland sites: this consists of a principal pyramid, plus two other ones which face each other, with all stairs leading from a central plaza. Richard Hansen suggests a mythological basis for the pattern, perhaps a triad of gods such as we find much later at the Classic city of Palenque.

The largest buildings at Nak'be were erected at the beginning of the Late Preclassic (c. 300 BC) over Middle Preclassic platforms. Dr Hansen has uncovered no fewer than nine monumental architectural masks and panels, including the largest yet known for the Maya – situated at the base of Structure 1, a vast relief of the Wuqub' Kaqix bird over 16 ft (4.9 m) high and 36 ft (11 m) wide, completely polychromed. Nak'be also has a stela,

33

reconstructed by the archaeologists from many fragments, which shows two important personages facing each other; details of costume link this relief in time and style to the Miraflores granite stela from Kaminaljuyu, which must have been exerting a potent influence on the lowlands during this era of nascent Maya civilization.

Such Late Preclassic splendor is found throughout the Peten-Yucatan peninsula wherever the spade has gone deep enough. Even in the seemingly less-favorable Northern Area, there are enormous constructions datable to this period, such as the great high mound at Yaxuna, a temple substructure having a ground plan of 197 by 427 ft (60 by 130 m). At the site of Etz'na in north-central Campeche, research carried out by Ray Matheny has shown that the Late Preclassic occupants had constructed a massive hydraulic system, consisting of 13.75 miles (22 km) of canals radiating out in all directions from the city's center, and even a moat surrounding a kind of "fortress'. The moat is obviously defensive, but Professor Matheny speculates that the canals could have been used to drain good agricultural land, to transport goods and people to the urban center, and to provide a habitat for game birds, fish, mollusks, and other food animals.

By the terminal Late Preclassic of the second and third centuries AD we are on the threshold of Classic Maya civilization. Temples arranged around plazas, construction with limestone and plaster, apron moldings and frontal stairways on pyramids, tomb building, and frescoes with naturalistic subjects – all had already taken shape by the end of the Late Preclassic. This brief epoch sees the intrusion of new ceramic traits which seem to have been first elaborated in El Salvador and later in Belize, the most important of these being the addition of hollow, breast-shaped supports to bowls, hour-glass shaped pot-stands, and polychrome. Maya polychrome is distinguished by a brilliant range of colors applied over a glossy, translucent orange underslip, but wherever it was first invented it certainly was not native to the Peten region. Corbeling of rooms must have evolved from methods employed in the construction of tombs, and by AD 250 began to be in universal use at *c.f.* 55,76 Peten sites. The principle is simple: above the springline of the walls, successive courses of stones were set in overlapping rows up to the vault summit, which was capped by flat stones. However, there is an inherent structural weakness, and the great thrust from above is taken up in Maya buildings by massive walls and by the strength of the rubble-cement fill. Nevertheless, once adopted it became the badge of Maya architecture in the lowlands, as opposed to the thatched or flat-beam roofs of Mexico.

The list is impressive, and one would think on the face of it that Maya civilization had emerged independently here in the lowlands, several centuries before the opening of the Classic era. But two items are missing or exceedingly rare: monuments with Long Count dates, and writing. These we know were present among the coeval Izapan centers of the highlands and Pacific Coast, and it is probable that they were derived from the even older Olmec civilization of the Gulf Coast. The Izapan style was spread from outside into the Central and Northern areas – a broken carving from a terminal Late Preclassic level of the Tik'al acropolis, the early Tik'al murals,

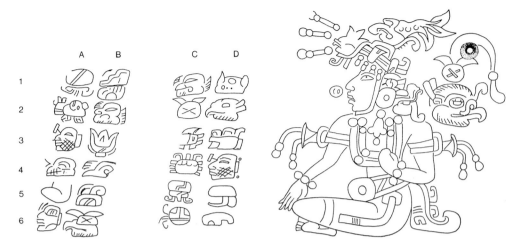

34 Incising on a greenstone pendant, Collection Dumbarton Oaks, Washington, DC. Late Preclassic period. The name of the ruler being "seated" (i.e. enthroned) appears at B6 and again behind his shoulder.

the Nak'be stela, and a human figure in relief on the walls of Loltun cave in Yucatan (associated with a Maya date which may fall in the year AD 100) all testify to this – but literacy and a concern with recording dates did not become prevalent in the lowlands until the eve of the Classic period.

It is entirely possible that this apparent lack of interest in written and dated records in the lowlands persisted because the Late Preclassic cities of the area were basically "acephalous', that is, they might not have been headed by a hereditary elite as they were to be in Classic times; we do know that the adoption of writing and the calendar in Mesoamerica goes hand in hand with the rise of elites. In this vein, it may be significant that archaeologists have thus far failed to find royal tombs or elite burials at El Mirador and Nak'be – or really outstanding ones at any other lowland site of the period, for that matter.

But towards the close of the Late Preclassic, writing had begun to appear sporadically, and it definitely celebrated the doings of great personages. A good example of this would be the greenstone pectoral at Dumbarton Oaks, said to be from Quintana Roo. A were-jaguar face on one side indicates that the object was originally Olmec; during the Late Preclassic, the reverse was delicately incised with the seated figure of a richly garbed ruler, facing four vertical columns of hieroglyphs. Next to the personage's shoulder is inscribed his name, almost surely to be read *Chan Muwan,* "Sky Owl." The same glyph combination appears twice in the text, once following a sign now known to be a very early form of the verb "to be seated." Epigraphers conclude that the pectoral reverse records the "seating," or accession to power, of the ruler in question.

By the time the Long Count calendar made its debut in the lowlands, at the opening of the Early Classic about AD 250, the life and times of the royal house had come to be the major preoccupation of the Maya state, and full Maya civilization had begun.

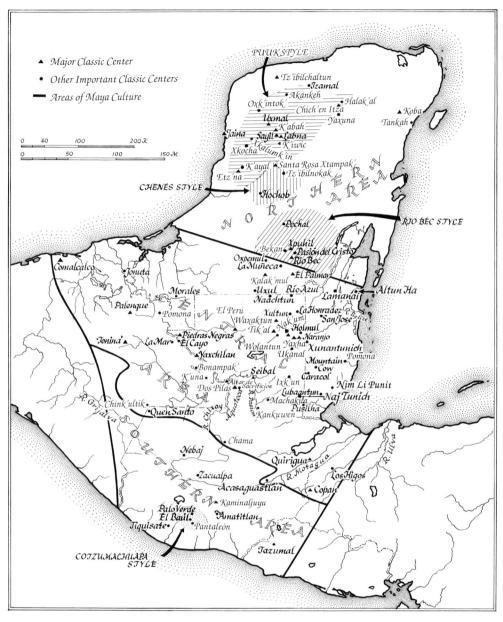

PUUK STYLE

▲ Major Classic Center
• Other Important Classic Centers
— Areas of Maya Culture

0   40   100   200 K
0   50   100   150 M

▲ Tz'ibilchaltun
• Izamal
• Akankeh
Oxk'intok' • Halak'al
Chich'en Itza ▲ Koba
Uxmal • Yaxuna Tankah •
K'abah
▲ Jaina Sayil ● Labna
Xkocha• K'iwic
Kalunk'in
K'ayal • Santa Rosa Xtampak
Etz'na • Tz'ibilnokak

CHENES STYLE →

NORTHERN AREA

• Hochob

• Pechal

RIO BEC STYLE ←

Xpuhil
Bekan • Pasion del Cristo
Oxpemul • Rio Bec
La Muñeca
• El Palmar

▲ Comalcalco
▲ Jonuta
• Morales
Palenque ▲
• Pomona
Kalak'mul
• Uxul Rio Azul
Naachtun
El Perú Xultun La Honradez
Waxaktun Tik'al Holmul San Jose
Nakum
Lamanai
▲ Altun Ha

Tonina ▲ La Mar • El Cayo
Piedras Negras
▲ Yaxchilan
• Bonampak
K'una • Seibal
Dos Pilas
Altar de Sacrificios
Wolantun Yaxha Naranjo
Ukanal Xunantunich
Mountain Pomona
Cow
IxK'un Caracol
Machakila • Nim Li Punit
Pusilha Lubaantun
Kankuwen Naj Tunich

Chink'ultik •
• QuenSanto
Chama

Nebaj

▲ Zacualpa
Quirigua
Los Higos
Acasaguastlan ▲ Copan

Kaminaljuyu
PaloVerde ▲
El Baúl •
Tiquisate• Amatitlan
Pantaleón

COTZUMALHUAPA STYLE

Tazumal

SOUTHERN AREA

35 Sites of the Classic period.

4· Classic Splendor:
the Early Period

During a span of six-and-a-half centuries, from about AD 250 to 900, the Maya, particularly those of the Central Area, reached intellectual and artistic heights which no others in the New World, and few in the Old, could match at that time. The Classic period was a kind of Golden Age, not only for them but for the rest of the Mesoamerican peoples. Large populations, a flourishing economy, and widespread trade were typical of the Classic, but although it was once thought to have been a period of relative peace and tranquillity in comparison with what followed, that notion has in the main been disproved. It is an equally unfounded assumption that the Classic peoples were ruled by priests. On the contrary, we shall see that the ancient Maya were just as warlike and had as thoroughly secular a government as the supposedly more bloodthirsty states of the Post-Classic.

The Classic in fact can only be defined accurately as that span during which the lowland Maya were using the Long Count calendar on their monuments. In 1864, workmen engaged in digging a canal near Puerto Barrios, on the steamy Caribbean coast of Guatemala, came across a jade plaque which subsequently found its way to Leiden, Holland. The Leiden Plate, possibly made at Tik'al, has engraved on one face a richly bedecked Maya lord at his accession, trampling underfoot a sorry-looking captive, a theme repeated on so many Maya stelae of later times. On the other side is inscribed the Long Count date 8.14.3.1.12, corresponding to 17 September AD 320. The style of the glyphs and the costume and pose of the person depicted call to mind the Late Preclassic monuments of the highlands and Pacific Coast, but in this case the date is preceded by the typical Maya Introductory Glyph, and the bar-and-dot numbers are followed by the signs for bak'tun and lesser periods. Until 1960 the Leiden Plate was considered the most ancient object dated in Maya fashion, but now we have Stela 29 from Tik'al, erected in 8.12.14.8.15 (AD 292).

The possibility that even earlier objects dated in the Maya system will some day be found in the Maya lowlands should be kept open, especially in the light of the Hauberg Stela, a miniature monument in the Princeton University Art Museum. This depicts a masked Maya lord in the act of a mystic bloodletting rite, and its very aberrant date (probably because of its antiquity) has been interpreted by the art historian Linda Schele and the German epigrapher Nikolai Grube as a day in the year AD 100. This important relief would thus be intermediate in time between dated inscriptions of the Izapan culture and the dawn of Classic Maya civilization.

Thus, the lowland Maya had definitely received the Long Count by the

36 The Leiden Plate, a jade plaque found in 1864, shows a Maya king trampling a captive underfoot and, on the reverse side, carries the date 8.14.3.1.12 1 Eb 0 Yaxk'in, corresponding to 17 September AD 320.

close of the third century AD. From this event until the Classic downfall, we have a very closely dated archaeological sequence governed by the carving of stelae and other monuments, which themselves have been tied at Waxaktun and other sites with the construction of floors, building stages, and tombs. The Classic very conveniently divides itself into an Early and a Late period at about AD 600; however, this division is not merely an invention of the archaeologist, for not only did a profound upheaval take place in part of the Central Area at that time, but there are considerable cultural differences between the two halves.

Teotihuacan: military giant

Two things set off the Early from the Late Classic: first, the strong Izapan element still discernible in Maya culture, and secondly, the appearance in the middle part of the Early Classic of powerful waves of influence and probably invaders from the site of Teotihuacan in central Mexico. This city was founded at about the time of Christ in a small but fertile valley opening onto the northeast side of the Valley of Mexico itself. On the eve of its destruction at the hands of unknown peoples, at the end of the sixth or beginning of the seventh century AD, it covered an area of over 8 square miles (20 square km) and may have had a population of between 100,000 and 200,000 people, living in over 2,000 apartment compounds. To fill it, Teotihuacan's ruthless early rulers virtually depopulated smaller towns and villages in the Valley of Mexico. It was, in short, the greatest city ever seen in the Pre-Columbian New World.

Teotihuacan is noted for the regularity of its two crisscrossing great avenues, for its Pyramids of the Sun and Moon, and for the delicacy and sophistication of the wall paintings which graced the walls of its luxurious palaces. In these murals and elsewhere, the art of the great city is permeated with war symbolism, and there can be little doubt that war and conquest were major concerns to its rulers. Repeated painted figures of jaguars, pumas, coyotes, and eagles bring to mind the warrior orders of the much later Aztecs, among whom the Eagle and Jaguar Knights played roles similar to the "Crazy Dog" warriors of the Great Plains. Teotihuacan fighting men were armed with atlatl-propelled darts and rectangular shields, and bore round, *c.f.* 47 decorated, pyrite mosaic mirrors on their backs; with their eyes sometimes partly hidden by white shell "goggles," and with feather headdresses, they must have been terrifying figures to their opponents.

At the very heart of the city is the massive Ciudadela, in all likelihood the compound housing the royal palace. Within the Ciudadela itself is the stepped, stone-faced temple-pyramid known as the Temple of the Feathered Serpent (TFS), one of the single most important buildings of ancient Mesoamerica, and apparently well known to the distant Maya right through the end of the Classic. When the TFS was dedicated about AD 200, at least 200 individuals were sacrificed in its honor. All of these were attired as Teotihuacan warriors, with obsidian-tipped darts and back mirrors, and some had collars strung with imitation human jawbones.

On the facade and balustrades of the TFS are multiple figures of the Feathered Serpent, an early form of the later Aztec god Quetzalcoatl (patron god of the priesthood). Alternating with these figures is the head of another supernatural ophidian, with retroussé snout covered with rectangular platelets representing jade, and cut shell goggles placed in front of a stylized headdress in the shape of the Mexican sign for "year"; Karl Taube of the University of California (Riverside) has conclusively demonstrated this to be a War Serpent, and has proved this to be a potent symbol wherever Teotihuacan influence was felt in Mesoamerica – and, in fact, long after the fall of Teotihuacan. Such martial symbolism extended even to the Teotihuacan prototype of the deity Tlaloc who, fitted with his characteristic "goggles" and year-sign, also functioned as a war god.

This was the mighty city that held dominion over large parts of Mexico in the Early Classic, as the center of a military and commercial empire that may have been greater than that of the much later Aztec. Drawing upon historical data on the Aztecs, the ethnohistorian Ross Hassig has suggested that Mesoamerican "empires" such as Teotihuacan's were probably not organized along Roman lines, with total replacement of local administrations by the imperial power; rather, they were "hegemonic," in the sense that conquered bureaucracies were pretty much left in place, but controlled and taxed through the constant threat of the overwhelming military force which could have been unleashed against them at any time. Thus, we can expect a good deal of local cultural continuity even in those regions taken over by the great city; but in the case of the lowland Maya, we shall also see outright interference in dynastic matters, with profound implications for the course of Maya history.

The Esperanza culture

The disintegration of Maya culture in the highlands began with the close of the Miraflores period, when building activity slackened at major sites. In fact, by the end of the Preclassic, the great ceremonial center of Kaminaljuyu, focal point of Maya cultural and political affairs in the Southern Area, appears to have been a virtual ruin.

Shortly after AD 400, the highlands fell under Teotihuacan domination. An intrusive group of central Mexicans from that city apparently seized Kaminaljuyu and built for themselves a miniature version of their capital. An elite class ruling over a captive population of Maya descent, they were swayed by native cultural tastes and traditions and became "Mayanized" to the extent that they imported from the Central Area pottery and other wares with which to stock their tombs. The Esperanza culture which arose at Kaminaljuyu during the Early Classic, then, is a kind of hybrid.

There are several complexes of Esperanza architecture at Kaminaljuyu, all built on a plan which is not in the least bit Maya. Essentially these are
37 stepped temple platforms with the typical Teotihuacan *talud-tablero* motif, in which a rectangular panel with inset (*tablero*) is placed over a sloping batter (*talud*). The good building stone which is so abundant in the Mexican highlands is missing at Kaminaljuyu, so that the architect, almost certainly a Teotihuacano himself, had to be content with clay faced with red-painted stucco. A single stairway fronted each stage of the platform, while on top a temple sanctuary was roofed either with thatch or with the more usual flat beam-and-mortar construction of Teotihuacan.

The foreign lords of the Esperanza phase chose the temple platforms themselves as their final resting-places. As with the earlier Miraflores people, each platform was actually built to enclose the ruler's tomb, a log-roofed chamber usually placed beneath the frontal staircase, successive burials and their platforms being placed over older ones. The honored deceased was buried in a seated posture upon a wooden bier and was accompanied to the other world not only by rich offerings of pottery and other artifacts, but also by one to three persons sacrificed for the occasion, generally children or adolescents. Surrounding him were rich funerary vessels, undoubtedly

37 Structure A-7 at Kaminaljuyu, a temple-pyramid of the Esperanza culture.

containing food and drink for his own use, as well as implements such as *metates* and *manos* needed to prepare them.

Jade ornaments, some in the process of manufacture, were recovered in quantity from the Esperanza tombs: beads, complex ear ornaments in the form of flared spools, pendants, and spangles are ubiquitous. Underneath one staircase was found a 200-lb (90-kg) boulder of jade from which V-shaped slices had been sawn, indicating that the Esperanza elite had access to a major source of this substance so precious to all the peoples of Mesoamerica. 38

Few of the pottery vessels from the Esperanza tombs are represented in the rubbish strewn around Kaminaljuyu, from which it is clear that they were intended for the use of the invading class alone. Some of these were actually imported from Teotihuacan itself, probably carried laboriously over the intervening 800 or 900 miles (1300–1450 km) on back racks such as those still used by native traders in the Maya highlands. The ceramic hallmarks of the Teotihuacan civilization are the cylindrical vessel with three slab feet and cover; a little jug with open spout and handle; the *florero,* so called from its resemblance to a small flower-vase; and Thin Orange ware, made to Teotihuacan taste in northern Puebla. All are present in Esperanza, but so are polychrome bowls from the Peten, with their peculiar "basal flanges." 39

Certain of the tripod vessels have been stuccoed and painted in brilliant colors with feather-bedecked Teotihuacan lords, or seated Maya personages 40 and both Maya and Teotihuacan deities, including the Butterfly Goddess (a symbol of the warrior cult) so popular in Mexico. One Peten Maya polychrome bowl had even been overpainted with processional figures in Teotihuacan style, speech scrolls curling from their mouths.

All sorts of other valuables were placed with the dead. That Esperanza pomp, perhaps the funeral itself, was accompanied by music is shown by shell trumpets and by large turtle carapaces used with deer-antler beaters as percussive instruments. On a large effigy incense burner from one grave, a seated person strikes a two-toned slit drum. Besides jade, the corpse was ornamented with pearls, cut-out pieces of mica, and rich textiles which have long since rotted away. Included in several tombs were pairs of jaguar paws, symbols of royal power among the highland Maya. The highest technical achievement is seen in the mirrors made up of pyrite plates cut into polygonal shapes and fitted to each other over a circular disk of slate, and could have been back mirrors for warriors. These are in all likelihood another import from Teotihuacan, but the reverse of one proved to have remarkable carving in an elaborate scrollwork style that is associated with the Classic Veracruz civilization then developing on the Gulf Coast of Mexico. The ability of the Esperanza rulers to amass luxurious objects from the most distant parts must have been considerable.

The Esperanza culture may have its spectacular side, but almost as striking are omissions. The Long Count calendar had disappeared from the Southern Maya Area for good, which is strange considering its ancient roots here. The figurine cult had utterly disappeared. Nor is there any sure indication of stone sculpture on any scale in Esperanza Kaminaljuyu. The evolution of Maya culture in the Southern Area, especially in the highlands, had come to a very abrupt end with the establishment of Teotihuacan hegemony, and apart from the imports of Peten products, Maya ways of doing things were replaced with Mexican from the Early Classic on. Were these intruders warriors or traders? They may well have been both. By Aztec times in central Mexico there was a special caste of armed merchants called *pochteca*, who journeyed into distant countries in search of rare manufactures and raw materials not available in the homeland, all of which were destined for the king. From representations of the *pochteca* god at Teotihuacan, we know that the institution is at least as old as the Early Classic. Thus, Kaminaljuyu may have been a southeasterly outpost of long-distance traders from that great city, established for the purpose of exporting Maya riches for the Teotihuacan throne. As will be seen, the presence of foreigners from Teotihuacan was felt through the Peten and as far north as Yucatan itself.

As for the vanquished Maya of the Guatemalan highlands, they must have continued on as before, rendering tribute to Mexican rather than native overlords, tillers of the land and laborers on public construction projects. The great public ceremonials of Kaminaljuyu may even have been forbidden to them. But one cult in which they were certainly allowed to participate was centered upon Lake Amatitlan, not far south of the Esperanza capital, where hot springs and fumaroles along the southern shore must have attracted annual processions rendering homage to the gods of water and fire.

The Esperanza Culture

38 (*Above left*) A long jade bead carved with a human figure wearing a crane headdress, from Tomb A-VI, Kaminaljuyu (Esperanza culture). L. 6 in. (15.6 cm).

39 (*Above*) Restored Thin Orange ware vessel in the form of a seated man, from Tomb X, Kaminaljuyu (Esperanza culture). This ware was manufactured to Esperanza taste in northern Puebla, and appears wherever Teotihuacan people had penetrated. Ht of vessel *c*. 11 ¾ in. (30 cm).

40 (*Left*) An Esperanza culture tripod vessel with cover, from Tomb B-II, Kaminaljuyu. The exterior had been stuccoed and painted in buff, red and light green. The warrior figures on the vessel are Mayoid, while the glyphs on the lid are Teotihuacanoid. H 12 ½ in. (32 cm).

41 Pottery incense burner with heads of the Death God and Xipe Totec, Mexican god of the springtime, from the Zarzal underwater site, Lake Amatitlan, Guatemala. Ht 9 ½ in. (24 cm).

41 Skindivers have brought up many hundreds of blackened vessels from the hot mud of the lake bottom, ranging from extraordinary incense burners to the pots and pans of the peasant household, all cast by devotees into the steaming waters.

In 1969 farm tractors plowing the fields in the Tiquisate region of the Pacific coastal plain of Guatemala, an area located south-southwest of Lake Atitlan that is covered with ancient (and untested) mounds, unearthed rich tombs and caches which contained a total of over 1,000 ceramic objects. These have been examined by Nicholas Hellmuth of the Foundation for Latin American Archaeological Research, and proved to consist of elaborate two-piece censers (according to Karl Taube symbolizing the souls of dead warriors), slab-legged tripod cylinders, hollow moldmade figures, and other objects, all in the Teotihuacan style. Numerous finds of fired clay molds suggest that these were mass-produced from Teotihuacan prototypes by military-merchant groups intrusive from central Mexico during the last half of the Early Classic.

Tzak'ol culture in the Central Area

Early Classic remains in the Central Area are burdened with towering constructions of Late Classic date, and it has only been since the 1960s that the elaboration of Maya civilization during this early period has been fully realized. The Tzak'ol culture, as the civilization of the Peten and surrounding regions is called, endures until about 9.8.0.0.0, or to round it off in Christian years, until AD 600.

Already Maya civilization is in full flower, with enormous ceremonial centers crowded with masonry temples and "palaces" facing onto spacious plazas covered with white stucco. Stelae and altars are carved with dates and embellished with the figures of men and perhaps gods. Polychrome pottery, the finest examples of which were sealed up in the tombs of honored personages, emphasizes stylized polychrome designs of cranes, flying parrots, or men, often on bowls with a kind of apron or basal flange encircling the lower part. Along with these purely Maya ceramics are vessels which show the imprint of distant Teotihuacan: again, the cylindrical vase supported by three slab legs, the small, spouted jug, and the *florero*.

There have been two schools of thought about the nature of the Teotihuacan presence in the Peten. Initially, following the discovery of royal tombs in Ti'kal's North Acropolis in the 1960s, and of associated stelae, some Mayanists, especially the late Tatiana Proskouriakoff and the art historian Clemency Coggins, argued for a takeover by rulers actually hailing from Teotihuacan. Subsequently, the majority opinion came to be that there was never an actual military intrusion of Teotihuacan people, but emulation by

42

c.f. 53

42 Pottery of the Tzak'ol phase at Waxaktun (Early Classic period). *a, b*, polychrome basal-flange bowls; *c*, spouted jug; *d, e*, tripod cylindrical vessels. *a*, 9 ⅜ in. (23.8 cm) wide; *b–e*, to scale.

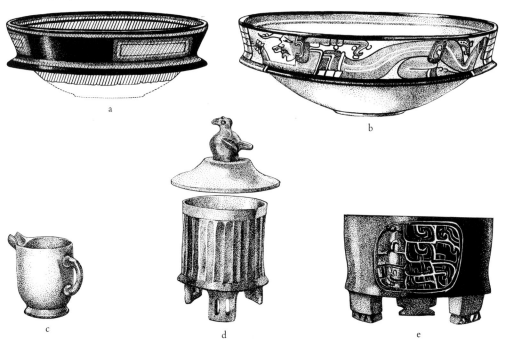

43 Polychrome two-part ceramic effigy from Burial 10 (the tomb of Nun Yax Ayin) at Tik'al. Tzak'ol culture. This represents an old god receiving a severed head as an offering.

the local Tik'al dynasty of the Teotihuacan cult of war, which the dynasts adopted for their own political ends; this is the scenario which appeared in the previous edition of this book. Which of these is the correct one? From the very latest epigraphic discoveries of David Stuart, it now appears that Proskouriakoff and Coggins were right all along.

Dynastic rule among the lowland Maya clearly has its deepest roots at Tik'al, the great city of the northern Peten whose Classic name was Mutul (the name "Tik'al" only appears in the nineteenth century). Later dynastic annals have retrospective reference to a putative founder, one Yax-Moch-Xoc, who may have lived in the third century AD. Waxaktun, less than a day's march north of Tik'al, is only slightly younger. According to these inscriptions, the eighth successor to the Tik'al throne was an individual known to epigraphers as "Great Jaguar Paw," but we know little about him other than his untimely end, which took place on 14 January AD 378; the Maya phrase referring to his demise states that "he entered the water," that is, the watery Underworld. On that very same day, according to the inscriptions, a figure named Siyah K'ak' ("Fire is Born") is laconically said to have "arrived from the west" at Tik'al and/or Waxaktun. Significantly, he had previously "arrived" at El Perú, a Peten center on the upper Río San Pedro – this would have been a natural route for an army marching between the Gulf Coast plain and Tik'al. The verb "arrive" is surely a euphemism for something more sinister.

These two events are probably intimately connected. Siyah K'ak' was in no way a member of the native Tik'al dynasty of "Jaguar Paw," but rather the liege and perhaps general of a strange figure whose very non-Maya hieroglyph is a spearthrower conjoined to an owl, a motif well known in the iconography of Teotihuacan, and Stuart hypothesizes that "Spearthrower Owl" could even have been a ruler of that fearsome capital. The "arrival" of Siyah K'ak' strongly suggests the sudden appearance of a Teotihuacan invasion force from the west, and the capture and immediate execution of the legitimate Maya ruler.

Whoever "Spearthrower Owl" might have been, within a year his own son, Nun Yax Ayin ("First Crocodile") – previously dubbed by archaeologists with the nickname "Curl Nose" – had been installed, presumably by Siyah K'ak', as the tenth ruler of Tik'al, thereby initiating a new dynasty of patently foreign extraction. Nun Yax Ayin was yet a boy when he succeeded to the throne: we have not one but two portraits of the young *ahaw* ("king") attired as a Teotihuacan warrior flanking Stela 31, the accession monument 47 of his own son Siyah Chan K'awil, along with a stela that records the death in AD 439 of the latter's grandfather, "Spearthrower Owl."

Burials of great richness, filled with luxury offerings of Teotihuacan and 43 local Maya origin, have been uncovered beneath the Tzak'ol temples of Tik'al's North Acropolis – not so much "acropolis" as the long-revered "necropolis" of the city's earliest kings; these include the tombs of both Nun Yax Ayin (who died in AD 420) and his son Siyah Chan K'awil. Burial 48 is 44 now generally accepted as the final resting place of the latter, following the suggestion by Clemency Coggins. The tomb chamber was cut from the soft underlying bedrock, and contained three interments: Siyah Chan K'awil himself and two adolescent victims sacrificed to accompany the dead king.

44 The tomb chamber of Siyah Chan K'awil (Burial 48) at Tik'al. Tzak'ol culture. On its walls is painted the date 9.1.1.10.10 4 Ok (20 March AD 457), together with other glyphs which probably represent flowers.

Tik'al and Teotihuacan

45 (*Left*) Fragmentary stela from Tik'al, showing a ruler attired as Tlaloc, the Teotihuacan war god.

46 (*Below*) Lid of a stuccoed bowl from the tomb of Nun Yax Ayin (Burial 10), Tik'al. Tzak'ol culture. The head and hands painted here belong to Xipe Totec, the Mexican god of the springtime.

47 (*Right*) Side view of Stela 31 at Tik'al, showing the youthful Nun Yax Ayin at the time of his accession. He is costumed as a Teotihuacan warrior: in one hand he carries an *atlatl* or spearthrower, and on his left arm a shield with the face of the Teotihuacan war god, Tlaloc.

The white, stuccoed walls had been covered with glyphs applied in black paint by a sure hand, including the Long Count date 9.1.1.10.10 (20 March AD 457), probably the date of the ruler's death or of his funeral.

During the 1960s and early 1970s, a period which saw the apogee (or nadir) of Maya tomb robbery in the southern lowlands, the modestly sized site of Río Azul in the northeasternmost Peten was heavily looted, and produced for the international market an extraordinary variety of elite objects of the utmost beauty, mainly but not entirely of Early Classic date. Three of these emptied tombs had Tzak'ol culture murals painted in red and black on the bare walls, including glyphic texts of dynastic nature, and a scene depicting the undulating surface of the Underwater world, a theme linked by Nicholas Hellmuth with Xibalbá, the Maya realm of the dead. A project led by R. E. W. Adams of the University of Texas, San Antonio has uncovered an intact tomb with further murals and Early Classic offerings, although not of the scale or magnificence of those already stripped of their finery.

If, as some scholars believe, Teotihuacanos were present in the Peten cities, might they have tried to impose the worship of their own gods upon the Peten Maya, substituting their own rain god for the native Chak? To this the upper part of a shattered stela from Tik'al, showing a large Tlaloc-like face exactly like that upon the shield of Stela 31, might be testimony; a more plausible interpretation is that this is a portrait of a foreign overlord attired as the Teotihuacan war god, who we know had Tlaloc characteristics. On finely 45, 47 stuccoed and painted vessels from the Tik'al tombs is the blue-faced Tlaloc 46 again, together with the Mexican god of spring, Xipe Totec, recognized by the open mouth and the pairs of vertical lines which pass through the eyes across the cheeks. Some of these vessels are Thin Orange ware manufactured in the Mexican highlands, another comes from the Tiquisate region on the Pacific Coast of Guatemala, while others represent hybrids in shape and decoration between Maya and Teotihuacan traditions.

There almost certainly was trade between the Peten and the Valley of Mexico. Tzak'ol sherds from basal flange bowls have been found at Teotihuacan, and green obsidian blades from central Mexico were placed with the Tik'al dead. However, of all the perishable products which must have traveled the same routes – textiles, quetzal feathers, jaguar pelts, wooden objects, and so forth – nothing at all remains.

The wonderful Maya mural art has its roots in the Chikanel wall paintings of Tik'al, but by Tzak'ol times it had reached a very high degree of elaboration. Destroyed since their discovery in the 1930s, the lovely Early Classic wall paintings of Temple B-XIII at Waxaktun were executed in muted tones of red, brown, tan, and black. The scene is one from real life: before a palace building sheltering three Maya ladies, two male figures, one painted a warlike black, are in conversation (which is undoubtedly recorded in several columns of indecipherable glyphs). At one side are two horizontal rows of figures, probably meant to be standing on two levels of a stepped platform, painted with a strong feeling for individual caricature; a few are chattering in excited discourse. Some are singers shaking rattles, while a small boy beats time on a skin-covered drum.

48 Early Classic jade plaque of the bird-monster god, Wuqub' Kaqix, from Copan, Honduras. Ht 4 ¼ in. (10.7 cm).

49 A jade object shaped like an ear flare from Pomona, Belize (early Tzak'ol culture). The four glyphs refer to gods. Diam. 7 in. (17.8 cm).

Not only in the northern Peten, but at many other places in the Central Area, major Maya centers were well established by the fifth century AD and even earlier. At these, Teotihuacan domination is less easy, or even impossible, to demonstrate, and one can suppose that this was restricted to the Tik'al-Waxaktun area alone. None the less, Yaxha, a small Maya city located southeast of Tik'al, has a stela in pure Teotihuacan style apparently depicting a warrior-goddess with Tlaloc mask, and a city plan which combines the amorphous Maya pattern with formal "streets" laid out in the central Mexican fashion. Yaxha, incidentally, is the only Classic Maya city to retain its original name.

Whatever might be the nature of Teotihuacan influence on the affairs, c.f. 45–47 both political and cultural, of the Peten Maya, in the last half of the sixth century a serious crisis shook Tik'al and Waxaktun. No more stelae were erected, and there are signs of widespread and purposeful mutilation of public monuments. It is not clear what all this means, but although none of the Peten sites actually seems to have been abandoned near the close of the Early Classic, there might have been fierce internecine warfare or perhaps even a popular revolt.

When the smoke clears, in the first decades of the seventh century, Classic Maya life is seen to have been reconstituted much as before, possibly with new rulers and new dynasties. But Teotihuacan was no longer a political and/or economic force in Peten Maya civilization. In some great event of which we have no written record, the central part of that city was destroyed, and the empire of which it was the capital came to an end. This took place by AD 600, and may have been a decisive factor in the Maya disturbances in the closing decades of the Early Classic. However, just as the memory of the achievements of Classical Greece and Rome has remained forever strong in Western civilization, so did the glories of Teotihuacan continue to live in the minds of Maya rulers right through the end of the Late Classic: a Maya king was always proud to take the field attired as a Teotihuacan-style warrior, fitted with the characteristic War Serpent headdress or helmet.

Copan in the Early Classic

Although relatively isolated in a remote valley on the southeastern perimeter of the Central Area, not even Copan escaped the heavy cultural grip of Teotihuacan. According to much later inscriptions, the Copan dynasty was founded in the early fifth century AD by Yax K'uk' Mo' ("Green [or First] Quetzal-Macaw"); this royal line was to persist essentially unbroken until the death of the sixteenth ruler in AD 820. Yet there must have been earlier chiefs or even kings who failed to be recorded in the annals of the Late Classic.

The key to the dynastic history of Copan is the square monument known as Altar Q, which celebrates an event in the life of the sixteenth king, Yax Pasah, that took place in AD 776. Around its four sides are seated this ruler and all of the previous fifteen kings in the succession, each on his own name glyph. Facing Yax Pasah is Yax K'uk' Mo' himself, handing him the baton of office. While all of these potentates wear the wrapped turban characteristic of

50 (Left) The finest Maya wood carving known, this seated figure from Tabasco, Mexico, represents a moustachioed lord with folded arms; traces of hematite remain on the piece. Ht 14 in. (35.5 cm).

Copan rulership, only the Founder is adorned with the goggles of the Teoti-huacan war god. As deciphered by David Stuart, the text on Altar Q's upper surface opens with the "arrival" and accession to office of Yax K'uk' Mo' in AD 426; this brings to mind the "arrival" of Siyah K'ak' in Tik'al during the previous century, and it must be more than coincidental that both are given the honorary title of "West *Kalomte* ('Paramount Ruler of the West')." Stuart interprets all this to mean that the Founder was another stranger coming in from the west, perhaps from Teotihuacan.

In an extraordinary marriage of epigraphy and dirt archaeology, Copan's modern excavators are beginning to confirm what was previously only known from the inscriptions.

Rather than destroy Late Classic buildings to get at earlier constructions, American and Honduran teams have been investigating Copan's huge Acropolis with several kilometers of tunnels, working in from the great face exposed by past ravages of the nearby Copan River. As shall be seen, the most spectacular discoveries have been made underneath Temple 16, a mighty pyramid now known to have been dedicated through the centuries to the cult of the royal Founder, Yax K'uk' Mo'. During the 1996 and 1997 field seasons, Robert L. Sharer and David W. Sedat of the University of Pennsylvania hit archaeological "pay dirt," the very earliest and most deeply buried structure of all in the Acropolis, nicknamed by them "Hunal"; this was a relatively small temple platform in the purest Teotihuacan architectural style, complete with *talud* and *tablero*. Intrusive into Hunal they found a vaulted masonry tomb containing a single raised burial slab, on which rested the cinnabar-covered bones of a male individual approximately fifty years of age, with jade-inlaid incisors; rich offerings of Teotihuacan-style and other ceramics lay nearby. There is every reason to believe that this is Yax K'uk' Mo' himself, the "stranger from the west."

Soon after this interment, Hunal was covered by another temple platform, this time in the familiar apron-molding style of the Peten, and faced with a fine stuccoed and polychromed panel of the Maya Sun God; and over this Copan's second ruler placed an even more splendid platform; known as "Margarita," this is adorned on its western face with an extraordinary stucco relief of two birds, a quetzal and a macaw – a full figure form of the Founder's name. And within Margarita was what is probably the richest tomb ever discovered at Copan, of an aged female whom Professor Sharer hypothesizes was the widow of Yax K'uk' Mo'. Among this noble lady's lavish offerings was what the excavators call the "Dazzler Pot," a stuccoed, slab-leg tripod brilliantly polychromed with a Teotihuacan temple from the doorway of which peeks a bird face with goggled eyes – could this be the Founder himself?

In the summer of 1992, the long-term project directed by William Fash of Harvard University encountered what appears to be Copan's oldest monument, in a deep, exploratory tunnel underneath the famous Hieroglyphic Stairway. This seems to be a marker set into a floor some time early in the fifth century AD, and depicts Yax K'uk' Mo' (probably posthumously) and his son and heir facing each other across a central pair of glyph columns. Both are

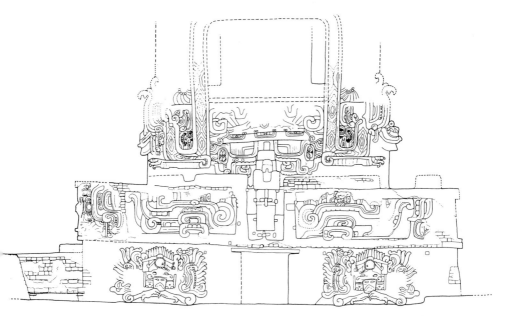

51 Elevation of the west side of the Rosalila Structure, Copan, showing the stuccoed facade sculpture uncovered in 1991.

completely attired in Maya style – here at Copan, on the southeastern periphery of the Maya lowlands, native culture proved to be stronger than the alien philosophy imported from central Mexico. Are these twin gods (we shall come across such later)? Or are they co-rulers of the Copan polity?

Previous tunneling into the mass supporting the Hieroglyphic Stairway has disclosed a fifth-century temple which may be contemporary with Yax K'uk' Mo'; while much destroyed by later building activities, enough has remained of the upper facade to see that it was covered with an enormous crocodile in stucco relief. At about the same time, Copan's first ball court was constructed, out in the open plaza to the northwest; this was to be the first of three successively built on the same spot, and already it had stone macaw heads as boundary markers, as in the final one seen by modern tourists.

One of the more exciting discoveries at Copan in recent years was made by Honduran archaeologist Ricardo Agurcia. Dubbed the Rosalila Structure, this is a temple dating to the close of the Early Classic which had been buried almost intact by later building, and gives Mayanists a good idea of what the splendid exterior of an intact stuccoed and polychromed temple looked like before time and the elements have done their work of destruction. Even part of the roof crest is preserved. On the front (facing west) is the Principal Bird Deity, Wuqub' Kaqix in all his glory. His huge head with Sun God eyes is on the second story, and his serpent-bird wings are spread out on the upper facade of the lower one. An archaeological bonus was the find of sacred objects left on the floor of Rosalila, including nine eccentric flints which had been wrapped in blue cloth, some of which still adhered to the flints.

51, pls. IV–V

95

Unlike in the northern Peten, there is no "hiatus," no gap at Copan between the Early and Late Classic: the eleventh ruler, Butz' Chan, spans the gap, dying peacefully in the year AD 628. Although war was eventually to bring temporary reverse to Copan's fortunes, being on the periphery of great civilizations sometimes has its rewards.

The Northern Area

There is abundant pictorial and glyphic evidence for warfare across the Maya area during the Early Classic, but proof of warfare is remarkably difficult to derive from "dirt" archaeology. A vivid exception to this rule is provided by Bekan in the Chenes region just north of the Peten, which was completely surrounded by massive defensive earthworks some time between the second and fourth centuries BC. These consist of a ditch and inner rampart, with a total height of 38 ft (11.6 m), and would have been formidable, according to David Webster of Pennsylvania State University, if the rampart had been surmounted by a palisade. It would be tempting to see this as a consequence of a putative Teotihuacan invasion of the Chenes, but it is a purely Maya matter as the earthwork was built before the appearance of strong Teotihuacan influence at Bekan.

52 A double-chambered pottery vessel of the Tzak'ol culture, possibly from Río Azul, northeastern Peten, Guatemala. On the right, the Hero Twin Hunahpu aims his blowgun at the giant bird-monster Wuqub' Kaqix, rising up on the left. Ht 11 in. (30.3 cm).

53 The stuccoed figure of a monkey, a speech scroll issuing from its mouth, is shown in Teotihuacan style on the upper facade of an Early Classic building at Akankeh, Mexico.

A good deal less is known about the Early Classic in the stony land of Yucatan and Campeche than in the south. In both ceramics and architecture, these Maya adhered closely to Peten standards. One of the earliest centers is Oxk'intok' in the scrubby plain of western Yucatan, with a stone lintel carved in the fifth century AD, and some contemporary but aesthetically inferior reliefs.

A more interesting site is Akankeh, southeast of Mérida, the present-day capital of Yucatan. On the one hand, there is a stepped pyramid-platform with inset stairway of apron moldings of straightforward Peten Maya type. On the other, there is an extraordinary platform with a *talud-tablero* facade, stuccoed with relief figures in Teotihuacan style: anthropomorphic bats, birds of prey, a squirrel, and a representation of the central deity of Teotihuacan, known as the Feathered Serpent or Quetzalcoatl. Apart from the bats (unknown in Teotihuacan iconography), there is little or nothing Maya about this building. On the contrary, it may be evidence that the dynamic people of Teotihuacan had established outposts not only in the Southern and Central Areas, but also here in the Northern Area, foreshadowing the great Mexican invasions that were to take place in Yucatan five centuries later.

52

53

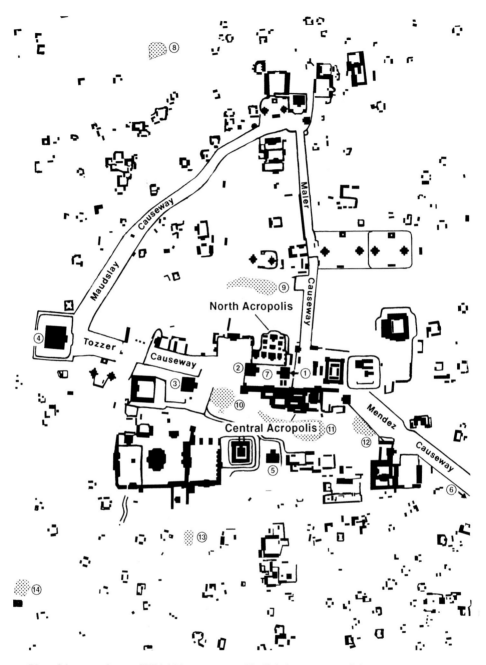

54 Plan of the central part of Tik'al (the area covered is slightly over 1 sq. mile). *1–5* Temples I–V; *6* Temple of Inscriptions; *7* Great Plaza; *8–14* Reservoirs: *8* Bejucal, *9* Causeway, *10* Temple, *11* Palace, *12* Hidden, *13* Madeira, *14* Perdido.

5· Classic Splendor: the Late Period

The great culture of the Maya lowlands during the Late Classic period is one of the "lost" civilizations of the world, its hundreds of cities and towns often buried under an almost unbroken canopy of tropical forest. At one time it could be said that we did not know who lived in these now-decayed centers, and how the Maya realm was then governed. It was even thought that the major sites which are often called "cities" were nothing of the sort.

Large masonry buildings are easy to map, but, curiously enough, so are the simple huts of the common people, for the ancient Maya conveniently raised their houses on low, rectangular mounds of earth and stone to avoid the summer floods. Topographic surveys of large Maya sites like Tik'al and Seibal in the Peten, or Tz'ibilchaltun (Dzibilchaltún) in northern Yucatan, reveal a very amorphous pattern of structures ranging from great temple-pyramids and so-called "palaces" down to individual house mounds arranged around tiny plazas (these were probably family compounds). This pattern is a far cry from the neat gridiron layout of Teotihuacan in central Mexico, which conforms far more to our idea of what a city should be. An earlier generation of archaeologists considered the great sites to be nothing more than relatively empty ceremonial centers, staffed only by the putative priest-rulers and their retinues, and bustling with populace only during great rituals and times of corvée labor.

The intellectual tide has changed in the light of new data and new concepts. While it is true that, with the exception of Caracol in Belize and the Teotihuacan-influenced Yaxha in the Peten, there are no streets to be discerned in lowland sites during the Classic, these nevertheless functioned as cities, since they were the administrative and ritual centers for small states and had populations as large as many post-Roman cities of the Old World. In early, pre-industrial cities and towns of the Eastern Hemisphere, we are used to seeing city walls, but these are not found at Classic Maya sites. Because of the seemingly unplanned nature of the settlement pattern, the boundaries of Maya cities are difficult to determine. Bekan in the Río Bec region is surrounded by a moat, the Petexbatun site of Punta de Chimino is isolated on its peninsula by a deep moat, and Waxaktun and Tik'al are separated by a defensive earthwork, but these are exceptions to the rule. When city walls are found, as at Dos Pilas and Uxmal, they seem to date to the Terminal Classic, when Maya civilization was generally on the decline.

The late Sylvanus G. Morley once classified all known Maya centers, both Classic and Post-Classic, according to their supposed degrees of relative importance, ranging from Class 1 giants like Tik'al and Copan down to Class

4 centers such as Bonampak' and Akankeh. In 1946 he listed a total of 116 sites in the Northern and Central Areas, but explorations since then suggest that the figure could probably be doubled.

54   How large were the great cities in terms of size and population? Tik'al and Kalak'mul are the largest of all Classic Maya sites and have been completely mapped down to the last house mound, although in view of the difficulty of drawing boundaries around any settlement of the lowlands it is hard to say exactly where they end. At Tik'al, within a little over 6 square miles (15.5 square km), there are about 3,000 structures, ranging from lofty temple-pyramids and massive palaces to tiny household units of thatch-roofed huts. Estimates of the total Tik'al population in Late Classic times vary all the way from 10,000 to 90,000 persons. If one accepted the latter figure, which many Mayanists think is the most likely, this would mean a density higher than that of an average city in modern Europe or America. A glance at the Tik'al layout will show that this is a concentration of a basically dispersed population, with a slight increase in frequency and size of houses as one moves closer to the heart of the site itself, where the dwellings of aristocrats and bureaucrats alike would have been more splendid.

The same somewhat "colloidal" appearance is typical of all other known Classic centers, which in the northeast Peten were always placed on low ridges so that they could be easily seen for several miles, if the trees around them were cut. They look, in fact, rather like artificial mountains. Water was scarce in the Peten, and at huge centers like Tik'al there are several artificial reservoirs of some size, surrounded by embankments, which provided sufficient water to the inhabitants over the winter dry season.

Opposite
XI Lintel 24 from Yaxchilan, Mexico. In a bloodletting ritual that took place on 28 October AD 709, the ruler "Shield Jaguar" holds a torch, while his wife Lady Xok draws a thorn-studded rope through a hole in her tongue. Screenfold books rest in the basket at her knees. Late Classic period.

Overleaf
XII Jaina figurine of a beautiful, barebreasted woman who may be the young Moon Goddess. The pigment on her skirt and body is the famous Maya Blue, a unique combination of indigo and a special clay. Late Classic period. Ht. 22.5 cm.

XIII Jade mosaic vase with portrait head of the Maize God, from Burial 196, a royal interment of the Late Classic period at Tikal, Guatemala. The pieces once adhered to a wooden interior, which has long since disintegrated. The grotesque head protruding from the front is a symbol of rulership.

XII

XIV

XIV Rollout of a Late Classic polychrome vase, with the ballgame in progress. The participants wear large "yokes," the left-hand figure has dropped to one knee to propel the large ball with his hip. The text at the top is the Primary Standard sequence, and names both the artist and the contents of the vase (chocolate).

XV

XV A stylized battle is taking place in this rollout scene from a Late Classic chocolate vase said to come from Nebaj, Guatemala. Several captives are being taken by noble warriors armed with spears; the names of some of the figures are revealed in accompanying texts. Below the rim is a Primary Standard Sequence inscription naming the patron or owner of the vase.

XVII The Hero Twin Hunahpu, a scribal patron, is writing in an open codex on a Late Classic polychrome plate from the Peten. Repeated twice below the rim is the hieroglyph of his father, the Maize God (an appropriate symbol, since plates of this shape were used to hold cooked maize tamales).

Previous two pages

XVI In this rolled-out palace scene from a Late Classic polychrome vase, an enthroned ruler brandishes a rattle, while his kneeling wife performs a dance to the rhythm. The king wears the insignia of a scribe in his headdress. His spouse is clad in a semi-transparent overgarment and skirt; her names and titles are given in the text to the left.

Classic sites in the Central Area

A Classic Maya center typically consists of a series of stepped platforms topped by masonry superstructures, arranged around broad plazas or court-yards. In the really large sites such as Tik'al there may be a number of building complexes interconnected by causeways. Towering above all are the mighty temple-pyramids built from limestone blocks over a rubble core. Although the temples themselves contain one or more corbeled and plaster-covered rooms, these are so narrow that they could only have been used on the occasion of ceremonies meant to be kept from plebeian eyes. Tall they are, but the Maya architects were not content and almost always added a further extension to the upper temple, a so-called roof comb, which along with the temple facade was highly embellished with painted stucco reliefs.

The bulk of the construction at a Maya site, however, is taken up by the palaces, single-storied structures built on similar principles to the temple-pyramids, but on much lower platforms and containing more plastered rooms, sometimes up to several dozen in the same building. Occasionally, there may be one or two, or even more, interior courtyards within the palaces. Evidence from the Central Acropolis of Tik'al, excavated by archaeologist Peter Harrison, along with graphically detailed scenes painted on Late Classic vases, shows that the palaces were the administrative centers of the

55

55 A room in the Five-Story Palace at Tik'al, a part of the Central Acropolis group. From a photograph taken by Teobert Maler. These "palaces" are believed to have served both as royal residences and as adminis-trative centers. As seen here, there are usually one or more plastered benches along the back wall of the rooms.

city, and were in many cases built up over several centuries, as each new ruler in a dynasty added his own palace to what became a single, large complex. Seated on benches backed by large cushions covered with jaguar pelts, the *ahaw* ("king") or *kalomte* ("paramount ruler") dispensed justice, received tribute, entertained ambassadors, feasted, and otherwise acted royally in rooms draped with swagged curtains. In the great courtyards took place less private activities, such as dances, ritual bloodletting from the penis and tongue on calendrically important days, and almost certainly sacrifice of high-ranking prisoners by beheading.

From the ceramics we get an idea of the palace staff. All rulers would have had their own palace orchestras; among the instruments depicted are long, wooden trumpets, conch shell trumpets, standing drums, turtle-carapaces beaten with antlers, rattles, and end-flutes. There also seem to have been royal dancers, but the ruler himself was often shown dancing in Maya art. Serving the *ahaw* was a host of underlings wearing headdresses resembling fancy starched napkins, and often seated in an honored position near the throne was a court dwarf. Above all of these courtiers, however, were the artists and scribes, a subject that will be treated in more detail in Chapter 9.

Of course, if the rulers, their families, and the courtiers actually *did* live in the vaulted rooms of these masonry palaces, and not in perishable pavilions of wood and thatch, then there would have to have been royal cooks and royal kitchens, royal chocolate-makers, and a vast staff of other menials, with a rigid division of labor; such staffs are known for historically documented cultures elsewhere in Mesoamerica, particularly for the Aztecs and for the Tarascans of Michoacan.

In any Classic center in the Central Area with a claim to importance, standing stelae were placed in the stucco floors of the plazas, usually fronting certain important temples but sometimes palaces as well. At times the stelae appear on platforms supporting temple-pyramids, but the rule seems to have been that certain stelae were always associated with specific structures, for reasons which until recently were something of a mystery. Generally a stela will have a low, round, flat-topped "altar" standing before it. The subject-matter of the relief carvings on one or both stela faces seems always the same: a richly attired Maya ruler, generally a male, carrying peculiar emblems such as the so-called ceremonial bar or manikin scepter, or else a similarly garbed person with spear and shield, trampling a captive underfoot. We shall examine these reliefs and the Long Count dates and glyphs which are inscribed on them in Chapter 9, for the story that they tell is now unfolding.

56

Ball courts seem to be present at many sites in the Central Area, but they are more frequent and better made in the southeast, at sites like Copan. These courts are of stucco-faced masonry, and have sloping playing surfaces. At Copan, three stone markers were placed on each side, and three set into the floor of the court, but the exact method of scoring in the game is obscure. Toward the western part of the Central Area, in centers along the Usumacinta River, sweat baths are known, possibly adopted from Mexico where such structures can still be found in many highland towns.

58

Awe-inspiring though the great Maya cities are, there is little overt indica-

56 Stela 4, Machakila, Guatemala (Late Classic period). The ruler holds a "manikin scepter" representing the god of rulership, K'awil.

tion of any overall planning in their arrangement. Rather, the typical center seems to have grown by accretion as temples, palaces, and entire complexes were rebuilt over and over again through the centuries. There was a gradual accumulation of architectural features that seem to have had social and political functions of a special (but still largely undetermined) nature. Nothing could be more alien to the Maya center than the kind of grid plan seen in some of the great urban sites of Mexico, such as Teotihuacan.

Copan and Quiriguá
Certainly one of the loveliest of all Classic Maya ruins is Copan, situated   57
above a tributary of the Río Motagua in a section of western Honduras famed for its tobacco. Stephens, who explored the site in 1839 (and bought it for 50 dollars!) called it "a valley of romance and wonder, where . . . the genii who attended on King Solomon seem to have been the artists." The principal temple-pyramids rest on an artificial acropolis which has been partly carried away by the Copan River, but many of the structures remain intact. Among them is the Temple of the Hieroglyphic Stairway (Temple 25), completed in the eighth century AD, with a magnificent frontal staircase every one of whose sixty-three steps is embellished on the risers with an immense dynastic text of about 2,500 glyphs; this is certainly the longest one known

57 A restoration drawing of the site of Copan, Honduras, by Tatiana Proskouriakoff. To the right is the Acropolis, to the left the Great Plaza. The bulk of the construction shown here is of the Late Classic period.

58 The Ball Court at Copan from the south (Late Classic period).

59 Monkey-man scribal god, from Copan. He holds a brush pen in one hand, and a conch-shell inkpot in the other.

60 Stone bust of the Young Maize God, from Temple 22, Copan, one of the wonderfully baroque carvings from this site. Ht 28 in. (71 cm).

The glories of Copan

61 Stela D and its "altar", north side of the Great Plaza at Copan, from a lithograph published by Frederick Catherwood in 1844. The "altar" represents the Death God. The stela was erected by the ruler Waxaklahun Ubah K'awil to commemorate the *tun* ending date 9.15.5.0.0 (26 July AD 736). Ht of stela 11 ft 9 in. (3.6 m).

for the Maya, but since most of it was found in extremely jumbled condition, it is far from easy to reconstruct. Most of the Hieroglyphic Stairway was built by Copan's unlucky thirteenth ruler (of whom more anon), but it was completed in the mid-eighth century by the fifteenth ruler, "Smoke Shell," with a strange "bilingual" inscription, one part Maya, and the other a matching text in what some local artist must have imagined to be Teotihuacan hieroglyphs. Even at this late date, a century and a half after the fall of the great Mexican city, memories of Teotihuacan remained strong.

The ball court at Copan is the most perfect known for the Classic Maya, with tenon sculptures in the shape of macaw heads as its markers. But it is the wonderfully baroque qualities of its carving in the round which distinguish this site from all others, for the Copan artists worked in a greenish volcanic tuff superior to the limestone in use among the Peten centers. Not only were doorways, jambs, and facades of the major temples ornamented with stone figures of the Rain God, young Maize God, and other deities, but no fewer than sixty-three stelae were carved and erected in Early and Late Classic times, together with fourteen "altars." Many of these were placed on the north end of the site, in a broad court bounded by narrow stepped platforms from which the populace could gaze upon the spectacles involved with the stela cult.

59, 60
61

The thirteenth ruler of Copan was the man usually known as "18 Rabbit" (his real name has been shown by epigrapher David Stuart to be Waxaklahun Ubah K'awil, "18 are the bodies(?) of K'awil"), a great but ultimately unfortunate monarch, who took power on 9 July AD 695. During his reign, the Acropolis and ceremonial precinct began to take on their present form; and to him may be attributed the marvelous Temple 22, a structure symbolizing the "Mountain of Sustenance" well known in the mythology of the later Aztecs, from which all the crops which sustain the human race – above all, maize – are derived. Rising up the corners of the temple's substructure are monstrous faces representing *witz* or mountains, and adorning the temple itself were numerous busts of the young Maize God, sculptures which are among the finest ever produced by the Classic Maya.

Like all Classic kings, Waxaklahun Ubah K'awil was something of an egoist, and the Great Plaza is crowded with his monuments, including Stela H which depicts him in the jade-bedecked costume of the Maize God. On the fateful day 9.15.6.4.16 6 Cimi 4 Tzec (3 May AD 738), shortly after he had dedicated the final version of the ball court, Waxaklahun Ubah K'awil' was ignominiously captured and beheaded by "Kawak Sky" of Quiriguá, a nearby city (see below) which had largely been under Copan's thumb in past centuries.

This sudden downturn in Copan's fortunes, however, was short-lived, and the fourteenth successor, "Smoke Monkey," took office the following month. This man was responsible for a remarkable building identified by artist-archaeologist Barbara Fash as a *Popol Na* ("Mat House"), the council chamber of the city. On its upper facade, both front and back, are cut-stone mats; interspersed with them are eight figures seated cross legged over hieroglyphs, most probably names of places within the Copan polity. In apparent

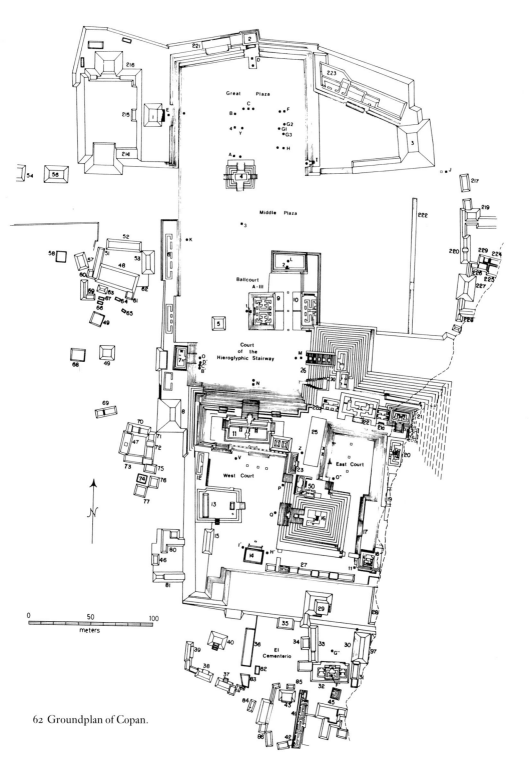

62 Groundplan of Copan.

63 (*Left*) Stela D at Quiriguá, Guatemala, from a photograph taken by A. P. Maudslay in 1885. This monument was erected on 9.16.15.0.0, or 19 February AD 766. Ht 19 ft 6 in. (5.9 m).

64 (*Right*) Altar of Zoomorph O at Quiriguá. On the left of this enormous monument, which was dedicated on the *k'atun* ending 9.18.0.0.0 (11 October AD 790), is the figure of the rain god Chak dancing in an S-shaped cloud. L. 12 ft 4 in. (3.8 m).

corroboration of William Fash's suggestion that the building functioned as a meeting chamber for local chiefs, a nearby midden seems to hold the remains of banquets held within it.

Copan's final well-attested ruler was the sixteenth, Yax Pasah, seemingly a weak and ineffective lord who allowed the nobility to expand in number and in power; David Stuart has found that one of these even had the temerity to style himself a *ch'ul ahaw,* "holy king." This state of affairs may explain the splendor of the suburban palace complex known austerely as Structure 9N-82, dedicated in AD 781. Devoted to the Monkey-Man Scribes of the Classic Maya, this palace may well have been inhabited by a high-ranking noble scribe and his family (see Chapter 9).

Quiriguá lies only 30 miles (48 km) north of Copan; it is a far humbler Classic center that seems on the testimony of the inscriptions to have been one of the latter's suzerainties, at least at certain times of its history. Recent hieroglyphic evidence suggests that in fact it was founded by Copan. Situated not far from the western bank of the Rio Motaguá, in its lush lower reaches, Quiriguá contains a few architectural groups of no great distinction. Its enormous sandstone stelae and carved zoomorphic stones, however, are quite another matter; indeed Stela E, erected late in the eighth century, might claim to be the greatest stone monument of the New World, its shaft measur-

63

ing 35 ft (10.7 m) in height. On the front face it is carved with the figure of a bearded ruler holding a small hand shield and a "manikin scepter" in either hand, while the sides are covered with texts containing several Long Count dates. The great skill of the Quiriguá sculptors can be seen in the grotesque full figures which take the place of cycle glyphs in the inscriptions of several other stelae, in the stone "zoomorphs" representing crouching earth monsters or sky deities with humans seated among their snake-like coils, and in the richly embellished boulders ("altars") associated with them.

64

Eventually, however, the worm turned: in AD 725, "Kawak Sky" ascended the Quiriguá throne and pursued a policy of rebellion against the domination of Copan. As we have seen, this culminated sixteen years later with Copan's defeat, and the humiliating capture and execution of its king.

Tik'al

It is more than likely that the ruins of Tik'al, in the very heart of the Peten, were first encountered by the brave Father Avendaño and his companions in 1695. Lost and starving among the swampy *bajos* and thorny forests of

65 Temple I at Tik'al. This is the funerary pyramid of Hasaw Chan K'awil.

66 A carved wooden lintel from Temple IV at Tik'al. Beneath the body of a double-headed serpent the ruler Yax K'in is seated on a war palanquin during a celebration of a great military victory on 26 July AD 743. He carries a spear in one hand and a shield on the left wrist. L. in greatest dimension 6 ft 9 in. (2.1 m).

northern Guatemala, they came across a "variety of old buildings, excepting some in which I recognized apartments, and though they were very high and my strength was little, I climbed up them (though with trouble)." Tik'al has now been partly restored by the University of Pennsylvania and the Guatemalan government; a giant among Maya centers, it is one of the largest Classic sites in the Maya area and one of the greatest in the New World. Particularly impressive are its six temple-pyramids, veritable skyscrapers among buildings of their class. From the level of the plaza floor to the top of its roof comb, Temple IV, the mightiest of all, measures 229 ft (70 m) in height. The core of Tik'al must be its great plaza, flanked on west and east by two of these temple-pyramids, and on the north by the acropolis already mentioned in connection with its Late Preclassic and Early Classic tombs, and on the south by the Central Acropolis, a palace complex. Some of the major architectural groups are connected to the Great Plaza and with each other by broad causeways, over which many splendid processions must have passed in the days of Tik'al's glory. The palaces are also impressive, their plastered rooms often

67 Two incised bones from the Temple I tomb, Tik'al. *Top*, three Chaks (Rain Gods) are catching fish. *Above*, seven Maya deities travel in a canoe into the Underworld. In the middle is the Maize God; to the left and right are the old Paddler Gods.

68 (*Left*) Incised bone of the Late Classic period from Hasaw Chan K'awil's tomb, Tik'al. A hand holding a brush pen appears from the jaws of Itzamna, inventor of writing, in his serpentine form.

still retaining in their vaults the sapodilla-wood spanner beams which had only a decorative function.

Tik'al is not particularly noteworthy for its stone sculptures. Among the many limestone stelae lined up in the Great Plaza before the acropolis, the best are of the Early Classic period. Nonetheless, there were great artists in the service of Tik'al's rulers, for the fortunately preserved wooden lintels above the doorways of the temple-pyramids are covered with lovely reliefs of Maya rulers in various poses accompanied by lengthy glyphic texts. Artistry of a different sort can be seen in the remarkable offerings accompanying the splendid tomb underneath Temple I, discovered in 1962 by Aubrey Trik of the University of Pennsylvania. In it, a very great ruler named Hasaw Cha'an K'awil had been laid to rest with his riches – his ornaments of jade and shell – and with vessels filled with food and drink, and a mighty pyramid built over his remains. But what was really unusual was a large collection of bone tubes and strips which had been delicately incised with scenes of gods and men carried out with the most extreme sophistication. According to David Stuart, some of these appear to relate episodes of Early Classic Tik'al history around the time of the "arrival" event (see Chapter 4). The fine drawing and calligraphy displayed on these bones give us some idea of what a Classic Maya codex may have looked like, none of these bark-paper books having survived except in the most fragmentary form in tombs at sites like Altun Ha and Waxaktun.

There are ten reservoirs at Tik'al from which the Maya obtained their drinking water, one of which was perforce refurbished by the modern archaeologists in lieu of any other potable source. These are often surrounded by artificial earthen levees, and contain sufficient water throughout the dry season. Some of them no doubt began as quarries, although the latter are known in many other places around the site, where outcrops and half-worked blocks of limestone still bear the marks of the crudely chipped tools with which they were hewn by the stone-masons of over one thousand years ago.

Yaxchilan, Piedras Negras, and Bonampak'

The many dozens of Classic Maya centers scattered over the Peten and Belize – such as Waxaktun, Nakum, Naranjo, Xunantunich, Caracol and Altun Ha – are witnesses to the importance of this region before its abandonment. Maya sites are as numerous along the banks of the Usumacinta and its tributaries, in the southwestern part of the Central Area. Yaxchilan is a major center strung out along a terrace of the Usumacinta, with some of its components perched on the hills above. While its temple-pyramids reach no great height, their upper facades and roof combs were beautifully ornamented with figures in stucco and stone. Yaxchilan is famous for its many stone lintels, carved in relief with scenes of conquest and ceremonial life, with which are associated dates and glyphic texts providing clues to the real meaning of the Classic Maya inscriptions. All this must wait, however, until Chapter 9. Further downstream is Piedras Negras, which has also produced similar data. This site is more extensive than Yaxchilan, and has a large number of particularly fine stelae set in place before its temples, as well as eight sweat baths, complete with stone-built hearths lined with potsherds, masonry benches for the bathers, and drains to carry off water used in the baths.

69, pl. XI

70

Few discoveries in the Maya area can rank with that of Bonampak', politically important during the Early Classic, but by the Late Classic an otherwise insignificant center clearly under the cultural and political thumb of Yaxchilan. Bonampak', which lies not far from the Río Lacanha, a tributary of the Usumacinta system, was first stumbled across in February 1946 by two American adventurers who were taken there by Lakandon Indians among whom they had been living. Three months later, the photographer Giles Healey was led by a group of Lakandon to the same ruins, and he was the first non-Maya to gaze at the stupendous paintings which covered the walls of three rooms in one of the structures.

The Bonampak' murals, which can be dated to shortly before AD 800 on the basis of Long Count texts and stylistic considerations, obviously relate a single narrative, a story of a battle, its aftermath, and the victory celebrations. Against a background of stylized jungle foliage, a skirmish takes place among magnificently arrayed Maya warriors, while musicians blow long war trumpets of wood or bark. The scene shifts to a stepped platform in Bonampak' itself; the miserable prisoners have been stripped, and are having the nails torn from their fingers. An important captive sprawls on the steps, perhaps tortured to exhaustion, and a severed head lies nearby on a bed of leaves. A naked figure seated on the platform summit pleads for his life to the central figure, the great lord Chan Muwan, king of Bonampak', clad in

73

69 Lintel 25, Yaxchilan, Mexico. The scene depicts a bloodletting rite which took place on 23 October, AD 681, the accession day of Itzamna Balam II ("Shield Jaguar the Great"). Shown here is the kneeling figure of his wife, Lady Xok, holding a bowl in which a stingray spine and bloodied paper have been placed. Before her rises a double-headed snake from whose mouths appear a warrior and a head of Tlaloc, the Teotihuacan god of war. Ht 4 ft 3 in. (1.3 m).

70 (Right) Stela 14, from Piedras Negras, Guatemala. The monument marks the accession to the throne in AD 761 of the young lord seated in the niche. At the foot of the platform stands a middle-aged woman, perhaps the new king's mother. Ht 9 ft 3 in. (2.8 m).

71 A detail of one of the remarkable wall paintings in Room 1 at Bonampak', dating to *c.* AD 790. Musicians sing and beat time, while to the left a group of mummers perform, masked as water gods.

72 (*Below*) A Maya king is seated on a dais above three lesser figures on this engraved stone from Bonampak', Mexico. One hands him the "Jester God" diadem of rulership. Dedicated AD 692. Ht 38 ½ in. (98 cm).

Lords of Bonampak' and Yaxchilan

73 A wall painting in Room 2 at Bonampak', *c.* AD 790. On a terraced platform stands Chan Muwan, king of Bonampak', and his subordinates. Below, captives taken in a jungle battle are being tortured by having their fingernails removed.

jaguar-skin battle-jacket and surrounded by his subordinates in gorgeous costume. Among the noble spectators is a lady in a white robe, holding a folding-screen fan in one hand. Chan Muwan's principal wife, she is identified by the glyphic text as coming from Yaxchilan. One of the final ceremonies includes a group of mummers fantastically disguised as water gods, accompanied by an orchestra of rattles, drums, turtle carapaces (struck with antlers), and long trumpets. Perhaps the culminating scene is the great sacrificial dance performed to the sound of trumpets by lords wearing towering headdresses of quetzal plumes; in preparation for it, white-robed Maya ladies seated on a throne draw blood from their tongues, and a strange, pot-bellied, dwarf-like figure standing on a palanquin is carried on-stage. 71

No verbal description could do justice to the beautiful colors and to the skill of the hand (or hands) which executed these paintings. Suffice it to say Bonampak' has thrown an entirely new light on the warlike interests of the Maya leaders, upon social organization and stratification in a Maya center, and upon the magnificence of Late Classic Maya culture in general, before time destroyed most of its creations. Bonampak' was abandoned before the murals were finished, and the artists dispersed, as Maya civilization in the Peten went into eclipse.

Dos Pilas, Toniná, and Palenque

A Vanderbilt University project under the direction of Arthur Demarest has investigated a particularly important group of sites, all located atop an escarpment overlooking the shallow Lake Petexbatun, south of the Río Pasión which forms one of the main branches of the Usumacinta. These are Tamarandito, Arroyo de Piedra, Punta de Chimino, Aguateca, and Dos Pilas; the last-named city seems to have dominated the rest, and, in fact, to have begun putting together a large-scale state as early as the seventh century AD, when a noble lineage arrived from Tik'al and established a royal dynasty. So powerful had Dos Pilas become that, on 3 December AD 735, its ruler had the audacity to attack Seibal, a far larger and more ancient city located on a bluff above the Pasión; the next day, Seibal's king fell captive to Dos Pilas; instead of being executed, he continued to live as a vassal lord under the Dos Pilas ruler.

By the mid-eighth century, warfare had in fact become a real problem to all the major Petexbatun sites, and a system of defensive walls topped by wooden palisades was constructed around and within them, often with little regard for the functions which particular structures had once served. Aguateca, in spite of its placement on the edge of an escarpment with a wide view over the countryside to the east, was attacked and burned to the ground, probably at the beginning of the ninth century. For Yale archaeologist Takeshi Inomata, this was a godsend, as he has found a vast quantity of artifacts *in situ* on the floors of houses abandoned by their occupants, a "Pompeii-like" situation that has enabled him to identify specialized areas, such as a house which was probably that of the chief scribe of the city.

As with Copan on the southeast Maya frontier, the cities of the far south-western lowlands often display considerable innovation in art and architecture, as compared with the more staid central Peten sites. Comal-calco, for instance, out on the alluvial plains of Tabasco, is unique in the pre-Conquest New World for its use of fired brick in construction, an adaptation to a virtually stoneless environment, while Toniná specialized in sculpture-in-the-round to an extent not seen since the demise of the Olmec civilization. In 1991, Mexican archaeologists uncovered an extraordinary stucco relief at Toniná, in which the skeletalized Death God brandishes the severed head of an important captive who is apparently Hunahpu, one of the Hero Twins of Maya mythology. This city, in the hill country of central Chiapas, must have been a feared military power, for its ruler managed to capture "K'an-Xul," king of the great city of Palenque and second son of the renowned Palenque *ahaw* Hanab Pakal.

The late Sylvanus Morley considered Palenque to be the most beautiful of all the Maya centers, albeit in comparison with a giant like Tik'al it is of no great size – but as yet it has not been mapped in full. The setting is incomparable: Palenque lies at the foot of a chain of low hills covered with tall rain forest, just above the green flood plain of the Usumacinta. Parrots and macaws of brilliant plumage fly at tree-top level; on rainy days the strange roar of howler monkeys can be heard near the ruins. A small stream runs through the site and is carried underneath the principal complex, the

74 The Palace and Tower at Palenque, viewed southwest from the Temple of the Inscriptions. In the distance is the floodplain of the Río Usumacinta.

Palace, by a corbel-vaulted aqueduct. A veritable labyrinth, the Palace is about 300 ft long and 240 ft wide (91 by 73 m), and consists of a series of vaulted galleries and rooms arranged about interior courtyards or patios, dominated by a unique four-story square tower with an interior stairway. It has been suggested that the tower was used as an observatory, but it commands a wide view and could also have served as a watch-tower. Arranged along the sides of two of the patios are grotesque reliefs, almost caricatures of prisoners showing submission by the usual means, one hand raised to the opposite shoulder, and it could have been in these courts that the captured enemies of Palenque were arraigned, tortured, and sacrificed. 74

The Palenque artists excelled in stucco work, and the exteriors of the pilasters ranged along the galleries of the Palace are marvelously embellished in that medium with Maya lords in relief, carrying the symbols of their authority, while lesser individuals sit cross-legged at their side. All these stuccoes were once painted, and the noted Palenque authority Merle Greene Robertson has found a definite color code: for instance, the exposed skin of humans was painted red, while that of gods was covered with blue. 75

75 Stucco-decorated pier on the Palace, Palenque. Hanab Pakal, attired as the Maize God, dances on the left; both figures grasp a fantastic serpent.

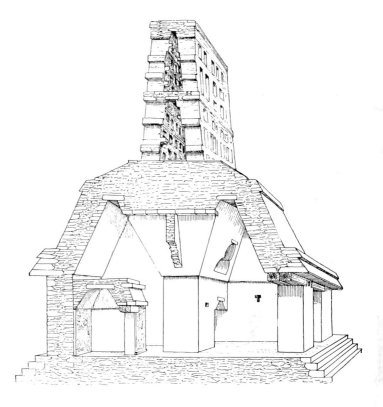

76 Cross-section of the Temple of the Cross at Palenque, showing the construction of the roof comb, vaults, and inner sanctuary.

Of the temple-pyramids of Palenque, three were constructed on more or less the same plan, and must have served somewhat the same function. These are the Temples of the Sun, the Cross, and the Foliated Cross, arranged   76, 77 about three sides of a plaza on the eastern side of the site. Each temple rests on a stepped platform with frontal stairway, each has a mansard roof with comb, and each has an outer and an inner vaulted room. Against the back wall of the latter is a "sanctuary," a miniature version of the larger temple; in its rear is set up a magnificent low relief tablet carved with long hieroglyphic texts and exhibiting the same motif: two individual males, one taller than the other, face each other on either side of a ceremonial object. In the case of the Temple of the Sun, the most perfect of all Maya buildings, this central object is the mask of the Jaguar God of the Underworld, the sun in its night aspect, before two crossed spears. The two other temples have in its place a branching world tree (which bears an astonishing resemblance to the Christian cross) surmounted by a monstrous quetzal bird. The exterior pilasters of the sanctuaries also bear stone reliefs of standing figures, the one on the right side of the Cross "sanctuary" unusual in that it shows God L, the patron of warriors and traders, smoking a cigar.

Today's archaeologists may call the inner structures of these three buildings sanctuaries, but epigrapher Stephen Houston has found that the Maya called them something else: *pibnal*, meaning "sweatbath." We know from modern ethnology and ethnohistoric accounts that the Mesoamerican peoples administered such baths to women before and after childbirth, and Houston's interpretation of this strange name is that it was symbolic of the birth of the god to whom each building in the Cross Group was dedicated. We will touch upon this "Palenque Triad," and the inscriptions in the "sanctuaries," in Chapter 9.

Linda Schele and David Freidel have shown us that there is a further, deeper meaning to the three structures of the Cross Group: they symbolize the Maya Creation itself (see Chapter 9). At the northern apex of the triangle that they form, the inscription of the Temple of the Cross records the events of the Creation and the history of the Palenque dynasty, surrounding the world tree in the form of a cross. On the eastern side, the panel of the Temple of the Foliated Cross celebrates the Tree of Maize and the Mountain of Sustenance; while the Temple of the Sun on the western side was consecrated to the birth of war.

Thanks to some remarkable advances in our understanding of the Palenque inscriptions, we now know why these three temples are so similar: the tablets in their sanctuaries all record the accession in AD 684 of the king known as Kan Balam (or "Snake Jaguar"), and the two flanking figures are *both* his portraits, but at different ages – as a six-year-old boy, and at his accession at the age of forty-nine.

From time to time over the past sixty years that excavations have been carried out at Palenque, finds have been made of fairly well-stocked tombs that were intruded into temple platforms and into the Palace itself. But these are nothing compared with the remarkable discovery made in June 1952 by

pl. VI the Mexican archaeologist Alberto Ruz. The Temple of the Inscriptions rests on a 65-ft-high (19.8-m) stepped pyramid approached by a noble frontal stairway. On the walls of its portico and central chamber are three panels containing a total of 620 hieroglyphs with many dates, the latest of which corresponds to AD 692. The floor of the temple itself is covered by large stone slabs, but Ruz was particularly curious about one which had a double row of holes provided with removable stone stoppers; on removing this it was clear that he had hit upon a vaulted stairway leading down into the interior of the pyramid, but intentionally choked with rubble. In four field seasons he had completely cleared the stairs, which changed direction half-way down, finally reaching a chamber on about the same level as the base of the pyramid. It too had been filled, but on its floor were encountered the skeletons of five or six young adults, probably all sacrifices. At its far end, the passage was blocked by a huge triangular slab which filled the entire vault.

It was on removing this slab that Ruz first looked into the great Funerary

79 Crypt, a discovery rivaling that of Bonampak' in importance. The chamber is 30 ft long and 23 ft high (9 by 7 m), and its floor lies underneath the frontal stairway but below the level of the plaza, some 80 ft (24 m) down from the floor of the upper temple. Around its walls stride stucco relief figures of men in very archaic costume, perhaps the Nine Lords of the Night of Maya theology, but it is equally possible that they were meant to be distant ancestors of the deceased. In all events, it was they who gave the Temple of the Inscriptions its original Maya name, *Bolon Ete Na*, "Nine Figures

77 (*Right*) View from the northeast of the Temple of the Sun, Palenque, dating from the late seventh century AD.

Lord Pakal
of Palenque

78 Life-sized jade mosaic mask of Hanab Pakal, from the Funerary Crypt, Temple of the Inscriptions, Palenque, and dated to AD 683. The eyes are fashioned of shell and obsidian, and all the pieces were once affixed to a wooden backing, now rotted away.

79 (*Below*) Funerary Crypt in the Temple of the Inscriptions, Palenque, dated to AD 683. The sarcophagus of the great king Hanab Pakal lies below and supports the carved stone slab. Around the walls of the corbelled chamber are nine stuccoed figures.

80 Relief carving on the upper surface of the Sarcophagus of the Temple of the Inscriptions, Palenque. The youthful-appearing K'inich Hanab Pakal (the 80-year-old king interred within the tomb) falls through gigantic fleshless jaws into the Underworld; above him rises the World Tree, surmounted by the bird-monster Wuqub' Kaqix. Surrounding the scene is a band depicting celestial bodies and ancestral figures. AD 683.

80 House." A huge rectangular stone slab, 12.5 ft (3.8 m) long and covered with
relief carvings, was found to overlie a monolithic sarcophagus within which
an ancient Maya ruler had been put to rest. A treasure-trove of jade accom-
78 panied the corpse: a life-sized mosaic mask of jade was placed over the face,
jade and mother-of-pearl disks served him as ear spools, several necklaces of
tubular jade beads festooned the chest, and jade rings adorned his fingers. A
large jade was held in each hand and another was placed in the mouth, a
practice documented for the late Yucatec Maya, for the Aztecs, and for the
Chinese. Two jade figures, and two sensitively modeled heads in stucco were
placed on the floor of the funerary chamber.

Epigraphic detective work has revealed that the man in the Funerary
Crypt was the mightiest of all of Palenque's rulers: Hanab Pakal ("Flower
Shield"), the father of Kan Balam; he had ascended the throne when he was
twelve years old and had died in AD 683 at the venerable age of eighty. It is
immediately evident that this great man had the Crypt built to contain his
own remains; further, that he might have had the entire temple-pyramid
above it raised in his own lifetime. Thus it seems that the Temple of the
Inscriptions was a funerary monument with exactly the same primary
function as the Egyptian pyramids. And this, of course, leads one to look
upon most Maya temple-pyramids as sepulchral monuments, dedicated to
the worship of deceased kings.

Such a conclusion is backed up by many finds in the Central Area, and not
just at the really large sites. Altun Ha, for example, is a relatively small center
– perhaps qualifying only as a Maya town – in northern Belize, with an
antiquity reaching back into Preclassic times. It has no stelae, and thus played
no great role on the Classic political stage, but some fairly spectacular finds
have been made there by David M. Pendergast of the Royal Ontario
Museum. One of these was the famous "Sun God's Tomb" constructed in a
modestly sized funerary pyramid. Before the interment of the honored
deceased (an adult male), virtually the entire crypt had been draped in cloth.
The corpse had then been placed on a wooden platform, and accompanied by
the skins of jaguars or pumas, by matting and cordage, and by necklaces and
pendants of jade and *Spondylus* (thorny oyster) shell. The *pièce de résistance*
was the largest carved jade ever found in Mesoamerica, a 5.9-inch-high (14.9
cm) effigy head of the monstrous bird-deity Wuqub' Kaqix, according to the
Popol Vuh epic the "sun" of the era preceding our own.

Classic sites in the Northern Area: Río Bec, Chenes, and Koba

The deserted forests of southern Campeche and Quintana Roo form the
wildest part of the Maya region, but scattered through them are many ruined
centers which have as yet been untouched by pick or spade. Our knowledge
of these sites, as Tatiana Proskouriakoff pointed out, is owed "to the gum-
chewing habit of our sedentary city-dwellers," for it is the chicle hunters who
have come across them while searching for the sapodilla trees from which the
gum is extracted. Several share in an aberrant architectural style named after
the large site of Río Bec. Here showiness rather than function is what was

81 North facade of Structure V at Hormiguero, Mexico (Río Bec culture), from a photograph taken by Karl Ruppert in 1933. The figure stands before the doorway of the one-room temple, entered through the jaws of a monstrous mask. On the west side are the remains of a false tower.

apparently sought, for characteristic of this style of the Late Classic is the decoration of perfectly ordinary small "palaces" with high towers imitating the fronts of temple-pyramids; these towers are solid, however, the steps being impossibly narrow and steep, and the "doorway" at the summit leading to nothing. It is as though the Río Bec architects wished to imitate the great Tik'al temples without going to any trouble. In the Río Bec sites, such as Xpuhil and Hormiguero, we begin to see on facades and roof combs the elaborate ornamentation emphasizing masks of the sky-serpent and the w*itz* ('mountain') monster, which become of increasing concern to Maya architects as one moves further north into the Yucatan Peninsula. To today's "functionalists," the fakery of the Río Bec style is somewhat repellent, but no one could help but be awed by these mysterious sites crumbling in their jungle fastness.

    Between the Río Bec area and the Puuk Hills of Yucatan is the Chenes, a well-populated zone of northern Campeche. Like those of Río Bec, with whom they must have been in close contact, the Chenes architects lavishly ornamented facades with sky-serpent masks and volutes, but the false towers of the former are missing. And, as at the Puuk sites to the north (see Chapter

81, 82

82 Palace at Xpuhil (Río Bec culture), from a reconstruction drawing by Tatiana Prosk-ouriakoff. The three towers are completely solid and served no other function than decoration.

6), the ornamentation consists of hundreds of small sculptural elements set into the buildings. One enters the front room through fantastic jaws, and is faced with tiers of masks, one over the other, on the corners.

While the two sub-areas that we have been discussing are clearly intermediate in space and style between the Peten and the terminal Late Classic Puuk styles, there are centers in the wild eastern half of the peninsula which are obviously direct extensions of central Peten ideas and perhaps peoples. One of these is Koba, a name implying something like "ruffled waters," a fitting epithet since it was built among a small group of shallow, reedy lakes in northern Quintana Roo; until the middle of this century the zone was frequented only by Maya hunters who occasionally burned incense before the stelae scattered among its ruins. Koba is not a single site but a whole group linked to a central complex by long, perfectly straight masonry causeways usually called by the Maya term *sakbe* ("white road"). There are more than sixteen of these, but what the idea was behind their construction we cannot even guess, for quite often a *sakbe* several miles in length will reach a ruin of very paltry dimensions. *Sakbe* No.1 is the strangest of all, for it continues west from Koba in a generally straight direction for no less than 62 miles (100 km), finally reaching the site of Yaxuna, some 12 miles (19 km) southwest of Chich'en Itza. Some have claimed that the Maya *sakbeob* were arteries of commerce, but a purely ceremonial function is far more plausible.

The buildings of Koba are in a sorry state of preservation, but there appear to have been temple-pyramids and palaces like those of the Peten. It continued to be inhabited into Post-Classic times, for there are a few structures like those of Tulum (a very late town on the east coast of the peninsula), and there are references to Koba in late Maya legends in which the center is associated with the Sun God.

Art of the Late Classic

Late Classic Maya art evolves directly out of that of the early half of the period, but excepting the demonstrably Terminal Classic sculpture of the Puuk, there is very little outside influence still to be seen. Maya artists now were free to go their own way, developing a remarkably sophisticated style as introspective as that of Asia and almost as "naturalistic" as that of Europe and the Mediterranean. But the Maya were not always interested in three-dimensionality, although they could when they wished give depth to a scene by foreshortening, and to figures by backlighting. Their art is essentially a painterly one, narrative and baroque, tremendously involved with ornament and grotesques but preserving what Proskouriakoff has called "order in complexity." Finally, the Late Classic Maya were, with their predecessors the Olmecs and their contemporaries the Moche of Peru, the only American Indians interested in rendering the uniqueness of individual characters through portraiture.

The Maya artists excelled in low-relief carving, and that is what most Maya sculpture is, whether on stelae, lintels, or panels. By the eighth century AD, they had achieved a complete mastery of this medium, posing their figures in such a manner that in place of the rigid formality prevalent in earlier monuments, a kind of dynamic imbalance among the different parts of the composition was sought which leads the eye restlessly along. A lintel from K'una, a site only a few miles from Bonampak', provides a magnificent 83 example of artistic contraposition, the goateed Maya resting on one leg and leaning forward clasping a ceremonial bar; but surely the perfection of relief carving was attained on the Late Classic tablets from Palenque, particularly 85 the Tablet of the Slaves which shows Chak Zotz' ("Great Bat") seated upon 84 the backs of two barbaric-looking captives. Naturally, over such a wide area there were specializations, real schools of carvers at various sites. Copan, as has been mentioned, had a notable development of three-dimensional sculpture (as did Toniná in the Chiapas hills), while Palenque, at the other end of the Central Area, concentrated on reliefs carried out with extremely sophisticated use of carved and engraved lines.

Pottery objects of Late Classic manufacture run the gamut from crude, mold-made figurines and the ordinary pots and pans of everyday life to real works of art. Among the latter are the fantastic incense burners common at Palenque and in some of the caves of Chiapas and Tabasco, consisting of tall, 86 hollow tubes modeled with the figures or heads of gods, particularly the

83 Stone lintel from the Late Classic site of K'una (Lakanha), Mexico. The protagonist is a *sahal*, an official subordinate to the king of Bonampak'; he holds a "ceremonial bar," a stylized, double-headed sky-serpent. In the text is carved the *tun* ending 9.15.15.0.0 (4 June AD 746). Ht 27 ¼ in. (68.8 cm).

84 Detail from the Tablet of the Slaves, dated to AD 730. Shown here is the head of Chak Zotz', a high-ranking subordinate lord, who sits cross-legged on the backs of two crouching captives. On either side of him are his parents, his mother handing him the "flint-shield" symbol of war.

85 Stone tablet incised with the head of Chak, the Maya god of rain, from the Late Classic period at Palenque.

Jaguar God of the Underworld, sometimes placed one on top of the other like Alaskan totem poles. Vertical flanges were placed on either side, and the whole painted in reds, ochers, blue, and white, after firing.

Jaina, a small limestone island just off the coast of Campeche and separated from the mainland by a tidal inlet, is one of the most enigmatic archaeological sites in the Maya area. For some reason known only to themselves, the ancients had used it as a necropolis, and it is close enough to the Puuk sites inland (Chapter 6) for it to have been their rulers and nobles who were buried there. Certainly the puniness of the temples constructed on the island is not in keeping with the great number of graves or with the magnificence of the offerings found in them. It is from these that archaeologists and looters have recovered the delicate, sophisticated figurines for which Jaina is famous. All objects are hollow and fitted with whistles at their backs; the faces were usually made in molds, but these and other details were embellished by the fingers of the artist. At one level of comprehension the emphasis is upon portraiture of real persons, perhaps the occupants of the graves: haughty nobles and armed warriors, some with tattooed or scarified faces, beautiful young women and fat old matrons. But at another level, these

87–89, pl. XII

143

The potters' art

86 (*Left*) Large pottery censer, probably from a cave in Chiapas or Tabasco, Mexico. The main face is that of the Jaguar God of the Underworld, the guise of the Sun on his nightly journey beneath the earth. Censers of this form were especially popular at Palenque. Ht 23¾ in. (60.3 cm).

87 (*Right*) Pottery figurine of a woman sheltering a man, Jaina, Mexico. Ht 8 in. (20.3 cm).

88 (*Below*) Pottery figurine, probably from Jaina. The subject is the Fat God, wearing feathered war costume and carrying a shield. Ht 11½ in. (29.2 cm).

89 (*Below right*) Pottery figurine from Jaina. A seated man holds an unidentified object, possibly a celt. Like all the finest pieces from Jaina, this figurine was made partly with a pottery mold and partly with the fingers, and was painted after firing. Ht 4½ in. (11.4 cm).

might also represent deities. For example, of two common, rather Freudian motifs, one depicts a woman sheltering a grown man as though he were her child, and might well be some kind of mother goddess; while the other, an ugly old man making advances to a handsome female must be an aged underworld divinity and his consort, the young Moon Goddess. Another common supernatural in Jaina collections is the Fat God, who seems to have been popular among the Maya of Campeche.

At some point in the Late Classic the lowland Maya invented a brilliant blue pigment which can often be seen on Jaina figurines, on effigy incense burners, and in the murals of Bonampak'. This is the famous Maya Blue, now proven through physical and chemical analysis to have been produced by mixing indigo (a vegetable dye) with a special clay, and heating the combination. The resulting pigment is extraordinarily stable, and – unlike modern blue pigments – highly resistant to the effects of light, acids, and time. Because this particular clay is found only at a place in Yucatan called Sakalum, it was probably there that Maya artists made their extraordinary discovery. Maya Blue continued to be manufactured right through the Spanish Conquest, and has even been found in Colonial murals in central Mexico.

Maya potters achieved chromatic effects of great brilliance in their vessels by firing them at low temperatures, sacrificing durability for aesthetic effect. Late Classic polychromes, generally deep bowls, cylindrical vessels, or footed dishes, are sometimes painted with the same narrative skill as the wall paintings. One vessel is a 10-inch-high (25-cm) vase from an otherwise run-of-the-mill grave at Altar de Sacrificios in the Central Area. Justifiably described as "a ceramic masterpiece," six strange figures, all of them dead or wearing the attributes of death and darkness, are painted on its exterior along with glyphs including a Calendar Round date corresponding to AD 754. The figure of an aged supernatural with closed eyes apparently dancing with a sinister, grossly fat snake is so well done that it suggests the employment of artists of genius in decorating pottery (this figure is now known to be a *way*, a subject which will be considered in more detail in Chapter 9). Vessels could also be carved when leather-hard, just before firing, some excellent vases in this style from Yucatan depicting God GI – one of the Maya pantheon's more enigmatic gods – seated among swirling volutes.

It is natural that the Maya lavished upon jade, the most precious substance known to them, their full artistry. That these jades were traded over considerable distances is evident from Late Classic Usumacinta-style pieces which were tossed into the Sacred Cenote at Chich'en Itza during the Post-Classic period, and some from the lowland Maya even found their way to Oaxaca and the Valley of Mexico. Most are very thin plaques with low relief carving on one face, probably executed by tubular drills of cane used with jade sand. A fine plaque from Nebaj in the Southern Area must be a product of a Central Area artist, and shows a recurrent theme, a richly dressed noble seated upon a throne, leaning forward to chat with a dwarf, perhaps a court buffoon.

Not only jade, but marble as well was worked by the lowland Maya lapidaries; but it must have been a rare substance, for objects made from it are

Ceramic masterpieces

90 Polychrome pottery vase of the Tepeu culture from Altar de Sacrificios, Guatemala. This side shows an old *way* supernatural, apparently dead, dancing with a boa constrictor. Five other supernaturals appear on the vase. In the text is a Calendar Round date probably corresponding to AD 754. Ht 10 in. (25.4 cm).

91 (*Below*) Black pottery jar from the Chochola area of northwestern Yucatan, Mexico. The vessel has been deeply carved with the figure of the enigmatic deity "GI", against a swirling background, and red pigment rubbed into the cut-away areas. Ht 5 ½ in. (14 cm).

92 Incised pottery bowl (Slate ware) from the Northern Area. The design, a modified step-and-fret pattern, is carried out in a negative smudging technique. Ht 4 ½ in. (11.4 cm).

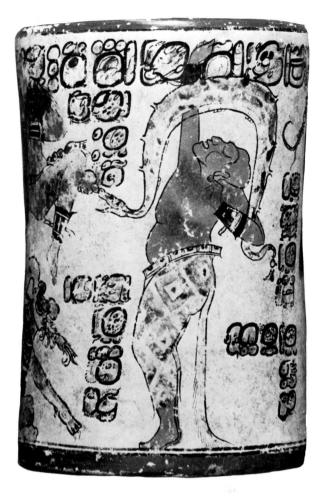

93 This carved jade plaque from Nebaj, Guatemala, is emerald green with white clouding, and represents a Maya lord in conversation with a palace dwarf. W. 5 ¾ in. (14.6 cm).

94 Travertine marble bowl, said to be from the state of Campeche, Mexico. A row of incised glyphs encircles the rim. Below, on the fluted sides, are incised a ruler (shown here), his wife, and his chief scribe or *ah k'uhun*. Each figure holds a symbolic object.

**Maya
mastercarvers**

95 (*Left*) Three deity heads with the forehead "smoke curl" of the god K'awil are visible in this tour-de-force of the flint-chipper's art from Copan. Ht 13 in. (33 cm).

96 (*Above*) Carved shell pendant, probably from Jaina. A young man with the flattened head so highly esteemed by the Maya appears above a fantastic fish, the body of which is covered with unreadable glyphs. The cut-away areas were once inlaid with jade. Ht 3⅛ in. (7.9 cm).

97 (*Below*) Incised obsidians from an offering placed beneath a stela at Tik'al (Tepeu culture). The flat side of a crude flake has in each instance been engraved with the figure of a deity or with a simplified mat design. The god K'awil appears at upper left and right; the Sun God K'inich Ahaw at lower right.

94 infrequent. A fluted vase of translucent onyx marble, with incising in Late Classic style, is a fine example of the genre. It is somewhat doubtful whether the well-known marble vessels from the Ulua region of western Honduras are to be considered as Maya at all, but fragments from them have been found in deposits assigned to the Terminal Classic in Belize and Peten sites. That the Maya could impose their artistic conventions on any medium is apparent

95
97 in the "eccentric" flint blades chipped to include divine faces in profile, and small blades of obsidian incised with the gods of the Maya pantheon; these were favorite objects for placing in caches under stelae or beneath temple floors in Central Area sites. Along the coast of Campeche, above all at Jaina, art in carved shell reached a high level, the Maya typically painting the lily by

96 inlaying these lovely objects with small pieces of apple-green jade.

It should always be borne in mind, however, that almost all Maya art that survived the vicissitudes of time is in imperishable materials. Classic murals and pictorial ceramics testify that the vast majority of it consisted not of stone, jade, and pottery, but of carved wood and woven and painted textiles. Every temple, every palace room was probably festooned with curtains and wall hangings. Virtually all of this has disappeared without a trace in the tropical environment. It is a certainty that there must have been many thousands of Classic Maya books written on bark-paper, but not a single one has come down to us (although unsalvageable traces are occasionally found in elite graves). All of this, and more, perished in the great cataclysm described in the next chapter.

6· The Terminal Classic

Maya civilization in the Central Area reached its full glory in the early eighth century, but it must have contained the seeds of its own destruction, for in the century and a half that followed all its magnificent cities had fallen into decline and ultimately suffered abandonment. This was surely one of the most profound social and demographic catastrophes of all human history. Yet ironically, during the terrible era that saw the Classic collapse in the southern lowlands, the Maya exerted an altogether unprecedented influence over the Gulf Coast and even the central highlands of Mexico. And it is clear that there was no similar decline in the Northern Area: quite the contrary, in the Puuk region and at Chich'en Itza, cities achieved a remarkable florescence – including some of the finest architecture ever seen in the pre-Conquest New World – that was only snuffed out by what may have been foreign invasion.

The Terminal Classic, from about AD 800 until 925, was therefore a time of tragedy and triumph, in which old thrones toppled in the south as a new political order took shape in the north, in which southern cities fell into the dust as northern ones flourished. It was an era marked by widespread movements of peoples, during which the destinies of central Mexico and the Maya area became as closely intertwined as they had been in the days of Teotihuacan's hegemony, and in which the stage was set for the rise of a new power in Mexico: the Toltecs.

The Great Collapse

The collapse of Maya civilization in the southern lowlands at the end of the Late Classic is indisputable, being abundantly documented in the archaeological record. What *is* in dispute is the "why?" Generations of scholars have tried to account for the Great Collapse, and explanations have included just about everything from epidemic diseases, invasion by foreigners from Mexico, social revolution (championed by Eric Thompson and still a plausible hypothesis), lowering of the water table, and even earthquakes and hurricanes. Unfortunately, the latest Classic inscriptions throw little light on the problem, since their parsimonious texts never deal with such mundane matters as censuses or agricultural production figures.

From 751 to about 790, long-standing alliances began to break down, interstate trade declined, and conflicts between neighboring city-states increased (the battle of 792 commemorated by the Bonampak' murals illustrates this situation). From 790 to 830, the death rate of cities outstripped the birth rate, while after 830 construction stopped throughout the Central Area, with the exception of peripherally located sites like Lamanai. The k'atun ending date 10.3.0.0.0 (AD 889) was celebrated by inscriptions at only five sites; the k'atun ending 10.4.0.0.0 (AD 909) appears only on a monument at Tonina, and incised on a jade from a site in southern Quintana Roo. And the very last Maya date from the Peten was carved on a stela at Itzimte, and corresponds to 15 January 910. One by one the lights of Classic urban civilization had winked out.

We know from the downfall of past civilizations such as the Roman and Khmer empires that it is fruitless to look for single causes. But most Maya archaeologists can now agree that three factors were paramount in the downfall: 1) endemic internecine warfare, 2) overpopulation and accompanying environmental collapse, and 3) drought. All three probably played a part, but not necessarily all together in the same time and in the same place. Warfare seems to have become a real problem earlier than the other two. Rulers and their entourages had conducted military campaigns against their rivals as far back as the Preclassic, but by the late eighth century in the Petexbatun region, these activities intensified and began to destroy the prevailing social contract, going far beyond the mere taking of a few royal captives for sacrifice. The system of palisaded walls encountered by Arthur Demarest and his associates at sites like Dos Pilas and Aguateca is datable between AD 760 and 830, by which time many of the palaces and temple superstructures had been reduced to rubble, and the inhabitants (probably augmented by refugee villagers from the rural hinterlands) lived a fearful existence in mere thatched huts huddled within the walls. As Demarest writes, there was a real devolution from cities involved in regional alliances, to warring centers, to minor sites, to tiny villages, all within half a century.

Other cities in the Central Area eventually followed suit. What had happened to Classic Maya society? Demarest lays it to an intensification of inter-elite competition, showing itself in different ways: not only in "wasteful architectural extravagance," in balkanization of political authority, and in senseless regional wars, but also in ecological over-exploitation. This last factor has found recent confirmation in research undertaken by Kevin Johnston at the site of Itzan, on a small tributary of the Río Pasión. Thanks to a long road bulldozed through a residential part of the site, Johnston has determined that about a half of all domestic house floors were *not* located on top of house mounds, and thus would have been invisible to the usual archaeological surface survey. What this means is that we may have to double our previous population estimates for the Central Area, which already run into the many millions.

One can only conclude that by the end of the eighth century, the Classic Maya population of the southern lowlands had probably increased beyond the carrying capacity of the land, no matter what system of agriculture was in use. There is mounting evidence for massive deforestation and erosion throughout the Central Area, only alleviated in a few favorable zones by dry slope terracing. In short, overpopulation and environmental degradation had advanced to a degree only matched by what is happening in many of the poorest tropical countries today. The Maya apocalypse, for such it was, surely had ecological roots.

The final factor in the Great Collapse may have been drought; in Chapter 1 we described the recent, highly convincing, geochemical evidence that there had been a major episode of droughts in the Maya lowlands which lasted from AD 800 to 1050. Given the kinds of social, political, and ecological stresses already in effect in the Central Area, this might have been the final blow which finished off Classic culture in the Peten once and for all. Year after year the increasingly desperate peasantry may have planted their dwindling supply of seed corn, only to see it wither as soon as it sprouted from the parched earth. With the Maya ruling elites no longer able to call down the rains from Chak, they would soon have lost "the mandate of heaven"; the revolutions hypothesized by Eric Thompson could have been the final act in the tragedy.

It was not just the "stela cult" – the inscribed glorification of royal lineages and their achievements – that disappeared with the collapse, but an entire world of esoteric knowledge, mythology, and ritual. Much of the elite cultural behavior to be described in Chapter 9, such as the complex Underworld mythology and iconography found on Classic Maya funerary ceramics, failed to re-emerge with the advent of the Post-Classic era, and one can only conclude that the royalty and nobility, including the scribes who were the repository of so much sacred and scientific knowledge, had "gone with the wind." They may well have been massacred by an enraged populace, and their screenfold books consumed in a holocaust similar to that carried out centuries later by Bishop Landa.

New investigations have shown that at least some of the Central Area population survived the debacle, for instance in the valleys of the Belize and New Rivers, finally to succumb to diseases introduced by the Spanish invaders of the sixteenth and seventeenth centuries. Nonetheless these dwindling groups would have known little about the glories of the Classic past, and some would have been wanderers among the now-empty centers, camping out like savages, or archaeologists, in the rooms of forgotten palaces – peoples like the Lakandon, burning copal incense before the strange depictions of mortal men and women who had now become gods.

But what happened to the bulk of the population who once occupied the Central Area, apparently in the millions? This is one of the great mysteries of Maya archaeology, since we have little or no evidence allowing us to come up with a solution. The early Colonial chronicles in Yucatec Maya speak of a "Great Descent" and "Lesser Descent," implying two mighty streams of refugees heading north from the abandoned cities into Yucatan, and Linda Schele and Peter Mathews, like Sylvanus Morley before them, believe that this account reflects historical fact (we shall return to this theory in the next chapter). Some may have migrated in a southerly direction, particularly into the Chiapas highlands. So far, however, this putative diaspora seems to have left no real traces in the archaeological record.

Seibal and the Putun Maya

The great city of Seibal on the Río Pasión apparently recovered from its defeat at the hands of the far smaller Dos Pilas, but during the Terminal Classic it seems to have come under the sway of warriors (or warrior-traders) from further afield. The evidence is to be found in the part of the site known as Group A; in its south plaza sits an unusual four-sided structure with four stairways. In front of each stairway is a stela, and a fifth stands inside the temple. All five record the k'atun ending 10.1.0.0.0 (1 December AD 849), and have as their protagonist an individual with the name "Wat'ul." Two of them show him as an obvious foreigner, with clipped moustache and pageboy haircut, but wearing Classic Maya regalia. There are even more "foreign"-looking stelae at Seibal which belong to this period, with non-Maya calendrical glyphs, and one figure wearing the bird mask of the central Mexican wing god, Ehecatl, with a Mexican speech scroll curling from the beak.

Who were these people? We have much to learn about the ninth century in the southern Maya lowlands, but could Eric Thompson have been right in thinking that the Putun or Chontal Maya of the Tabasco and southern Campeche plains had begun taking over some of the more important sites in the southern Peten, such as Seibal, perhaps moving into a power vacuum? These somewhat Mexicanized merchant-warriors controlled the great Gulf Coast entrepot of Xicallanco where Mexican and Maya traders met, and were known to the later Aztecs as "Olmeca-Xicallanca." There is now incontrovertible evidence that the Putun had not only penetrated into the lowland Maya "heartland," they had reached the central highlands of Mexico. In recent years, excavations at the hilltop site of Cacaxtla, tradition-ally ascribed to the Olmeca-Xicallanca, have uncovered a ninth-century palace with brilliant polychrome murals in Maya style. Among other things, these show dignitaries in Maya costume bearing Maya "ceremonial bars," which are in the style of the Putun-influenced stelae of Seibal, and a great war going on between two contending factions, which immediately recalls the battle scene of Bonampak'.

pl. x

Recently, Linda Schele and Peter Mathews have given a different interpretation of Wat'ul; according to the texts on his monuments, he was not a foreigner from the west, but had been placed in Seibal by the ruler of Ukanal, a city of the eastern Peten; but that does not answer the question of the patently Mexican hieroglyphs on other Seibal monuments. And regardless of what these texts tell us about who sent him from the east, the Fine Orange ceramics typical of this period at Seibal and other Terminal Classic sites in the Peten definitely originated in the west – on the Gulf Coast plain, in Putun country. One of the stelae in question records that a ceremony involving Wat'ul was "witnessed" by a visitor from "Puh," or Place of the Reeds. While Schele and Mathews believe this to have been Chich'en Itza, it is equally possible that this was Tollan/Tula, the Toltec capital in far-off central Mexico; this is a matter still in dispute.

The question remains, if these were Olmeca-Xicallanca or Putun Maya, what were they doing there, almost 500 miles (800 km) from their homeland? For that matter, why are there bas-reliefs showing seated figures in Maya style on the ninth-century Temple of the Feathered Serpent at Xochicalco in Morelos, just south of the Valley of Mexico? It is now evident that the ninth century was a time of turmoil over much of Mesoamerica, with the power of Teotihuacan long since gone, and the old order in the Maya lowlands breaking down. In this power vacuum, the Putun, seasoned businessmen with strong contacts ranging from central Mexico to the Caribbean coast of Honduras, must have played a very aggressive role in a time of troubles, and their presence in the Mexican highlands may have played a formative role in what was to become the Toltec state.

Terminal Classic sites in the Northern Area: the Puuk

"If Yucatan were to gain a name and reputation," wrote Bishop Landa in 1566, "from the multitude, the grandeur and the beauty of its buildings, as other regions of the Indies have obtained these by gold, silver and riches, its glory would spread like that of Peru and New Spain." Landa was not exaggerating, for ruins there are by the hundreds. Sylvanus Morley saw this as evidence for what he called a "New Empire" founded by refugees from the derelict civilization of the Central Area, his so-called "Old Empire," and he claimed to find references in the late Maya chronicles to a double-pronged migration from the south. However, ceramics recovered from excavations, along with a better reading of the ethnohistoric sources, led Eric Thompson and George Brainerd to the view that many of the Yucatecan sites were coeval with the Peten centers which were claimed to pre-date them. Modern scholarship has found that both schools were partly right and partly wrong: the great era of Yucatecan culture was the Terminal Classic, when many Peten cities had fallen into ruin, but there never was a real "empire" among the Maya, as Morley had believed.

It will be remembered that a group of very low hills, the Puuk, is to be found in southwestern Yucatan, a region, as Nicholas Dunning and Jeff Kowalski tell us, that has deep and fertile soils, in fact the best in the northern part of the peninsula. Perhaps by the Late Preclassic the Maya of the region had learned how to construct *chultunob* or bottle-shaped cisterns to provide scarce drinking water over the dry season, and populations began to expand. During the Late Classic itself, the Puuk was fragmented into many relatively small major centers controlling domains that included pockets of particularly productive soil.

It is in the Puuk that the dominant Terminal Classic style of the peninsula took form, by the end of the Late Classic. The problem of dating is acute, for some of these centers are mentioned in the chronicles by late upstart lineages who claimed to have founded them, but there are truncated Long Count dates painted on capstones in the late ninth and early tenth bak'tun; the very latest reads 10.3.17.12.1, or AD 905, but Thompson believed that the Puuk style may have lasted until 10.8.0.0.0 (AD 987), when Toltec invaders usher in the Post-Classic.

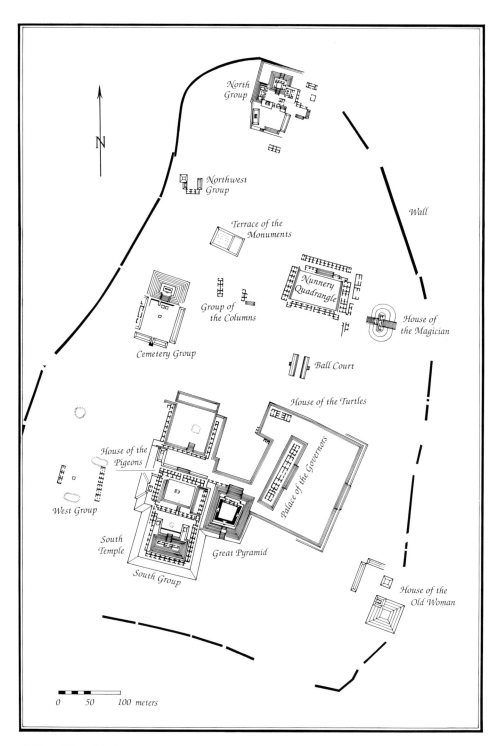

98 Plan of Uxmal, by far the largest Puuk site.

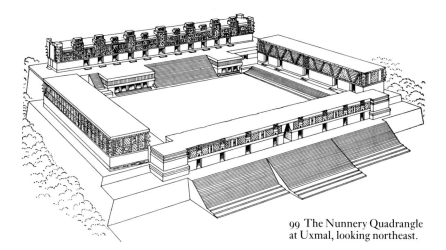

99 The Nunnery Quadrangle
at Uxmal, looking northeast.

Characteristic of Puuk buildings are facings of very thin squares of limestone veneer over the cement-and-rubble core; boot-shaped vault stones;
decorated cornices; round columns in doorways; engaged or half columns
repeated in long rows; and the exuberant use of stone mosaics on upper
facades, emphasizing the usual monster-masks with long, hook-shaped
snouts, as well as frets and lattice-like designs of criss-crossed elements. In
the perfection of architectural facades, the Puuk is far ahead of the more
sloppy Peten style.

Uxmal is by far the largest Puuk site, and one of the triumphs of Maya
civilization. Traditionally, this was the seat of the Xiu family, but this was a
johnny-come-lately lineage of Mexican origin that could not possibly have
built the site. The archaeological and epigraphic evidence testifies that
Uxmal had emerged as the capital of a large, Terminal Classic state centered
in the eastern Puuk between AD 850 and 925. Uxmal is dominated by two
mighty temple-pyramids, the Great Pyramid and the House of the
Magician, the upper temple of the latter entered through a monster-mask
doorway like those of the Chenes. Next to the Magician is the imaginatively
named Nunnery, actually a palace group made up of four separate rectangular buildings arranged around an interior court; although the group could be
entered from the corners, the principal gateway with its corbel arch lies on
the south side. The mosaic elements making up the masonry facades of the
Nunnery Quadrangle are particularly interesting; they include miniature
representations of the thatched-roof huts of the ordinary folk of the time.

An iconographic study by Jeff Kowalski suggests a cosmological layout for
the Nunnery. The higher placement of the North Building, with its 13
exterior doorways (reflecting the 13 layers of heaven), and the celestial
serpents surmounting the huts identify it with the celestial sphere. The
iconography of the West Building, with 7 exterior doorways (7 is the mystic
number of the earth's surface), and figures of Pawahtun – the earth god as a
turtle – indicate this to be the Middleworld, the place of the sun's descent

98, pl. VIII

99, pl. I

100 West wing of the Palace at Sayil, Mexico (Puuk culture). Seemingly three-storied, each row of rooms actually rests on a solid rubber core. The vaults have collapsed in the lower "story."

Puuk architecture

101 Arch at Labna, a Puuk culture site in Mexico, from a view published by Frederick Catherwood in 1844.

102 East wing of the Nunnery (Puuk culture) at Chich'en Itza, Mexico, from a lithograph by Frederick Catherwood.

103 The five-storied structure at Etz'na, Campeche (Terminal Classic period).

into the Underworld. The East Building has mosaic elements reflecting the old war cult of Teotihuacan, where tradition had it that the sun was born; thus, this may also be Middleworld, the place of the rising sun. Finally, the South Building has 9 exterior doorways (the Underworld or Xibalba had 9 layers), and has the lowest placement in the complex; it thus seems to be associated with death and the nether regions.

Below the Great Pyramid, on its own artificial terrace, is the House of the Governor, the finest structure at Uxmal and the culmination of the Puuk style. The upper facade or frieze of the three long interconnected structures of this building is covered by a fantastically elaborate mosaic of thousands of separate masonry elements set into the rubble core, a symphony of step-and-fret, lattice-work, and monster-mask motifs combined into a single harmonious whole.

There are only a handful of carved stelae at Uxmal; not only are they sloppily executed, but they are in a sorry state of preservation. Nevertheless, Kowalski has been able to work out a partial dynastic history dominated by the figure of Lord Chak, during whose reign the House of the Governor was built, probably as his administrative headquarters.

A causeway or *sakbe* 11 1/4 miles (18 km) long runs southeast from Uxmal through the small site of Nohpat to K'abah, so presumably the three centers were connected ceremonially if not politically. K'abah is noted for its Kotz' Po'op palace, with an extraordinary facade made up of hundreds of monster masks, and for its freestanding arch. Sayil, to the south of K'abah, is dominated by a magnificent three-story palace. It has the additional distinction of being thus far the only Puuk site to be completely and intensively mapped; Jeremy Sabloff of the University of Pennsylvania, who headed the project, estimates that about 10,000 people lived in an urban core of 1.7 square miles (4.5 square km), with an additional 7,000 in the zone around this core. To the east of Sayil is Labna, another sizeable Puuk city, with an elaborate freestanding arch (far more impressive than K'abah's), a palace group, and a lofty temple-pyramid.

Etz'na is the southernmost of the Puuk sites, and is best known for its five-storied structure which combines features of pyramids and palaces. Presumably its Late Preclassic canal-and-moat system, described in Chapter 2, remained in use throughout the Terminal Classic.

The Terminal Classic at Chich'en Itza

That the Puuk style reached east as well as north is evident at the great site of Chich'en Itza in east-central Yucatan, where a number of buildings at this otherwise Toltec-Maya center closely resemble those to the west, with the proviso that Puuk veneer masonry is seldom present. These are largely located in the southern zone of the city, and include the three-storied Nunnery, the Ak'ab Tz'ib ("dark writing," so-called from the reliefs containing glyphic texts on one of the doorways), the Casa Colorada, the Temple of the Three Lintels, and the Temple of the Four Lintels.

Lintels in the Nunnery and other buildings contain quite extensive hieroglyphic texts, which have been analyzed by David Kelley, Ruth Krochok, Michel Davoust, and other epigraphers. They were inscribed within a very brief period spanning only the second half of the ninth century, and celebrate not the dynastic history of individual kings, as in the southern lowlands, but rather temple dedication rituals carried out by groups of lords, such as bloodletting and drilling of new fire. Many scholars now believe that Chich'en Itza was then governed by what the later Maya chronicles call *mul tepal*, "joint rule," seemingly by at least two groups of three (or perhaps four) brothers.

One of these brothers is named K'ak'upakal, "Fiery Shield"; the Colonial sources mention a K'ak'upakal who is described as a valiant Itza captain, and this raises the question of whether these are the same persons. If so, then the *mul tepal* brothers might have been Itza Maya, but we will defer the treatment of these enigmatic people until the next chapter. Could the rulers of Terminal Classic Chich'en have been Putun? This also is a possibility, since there are distinct iconographic links between the late monuments of Seibal and those of Chich'en (even in the Toltec-Maya period), and it will be recalled that there is a strong hint of joint rule in the stelae surrounding Seibal's four-sided temple.

One of the strangest and most intriguing structures ever raised by the Maya is the Caracol (Spanish for "snail"), located in the Puuk section of Chich'en. Once stigmatized by Eric Thompson as a "two-decker wedding cake on the square carton in which it came," it is nevertheless one of the outstanding monuments of the Terminal Classic. The Caracol has long been described in the popular literature as an observatory, and this has been proved beyond a shadow of a doubt by measurements taken by the archaeoastronomers Anthony Aveni, Sharon Gibbs, and Horst Hartung. The ancient Maya used lines of sight taken from its platforms and door and window jambs to plot the rising and setting positions of the sun, the moon, and, above all, the planet Venus. As will be seen in Chapter 9, Maya astronomers had a remarkably accurate knowledge of the apparent motion of Venus, and it may be that at least some of that learning came from observations carried out in the Caracol.

pl. VII

The Cotzumalhuapa problem

The Pipil have always been an enigmatic people. Their language is Nahuat, a close relative of Nahuatl, the official tongue of the Aztecs, differing mainly from the latter by a substitution of *t* in place of *tl*. Having intruded into the Maya area at some unknown time from an equally unknown region in Mexico, by the Spanish Conquest the Pipil had established a major settlement in a small zone within the well-watered Piedmont zone just above the Pacific plain of Guatemala. From traditions recorded in Colonial times, however, it is known that their domain had once extended somewhat to the west into lands later claimed by the Kaqchikel Maya.

This once-Pipil territory is the locus of a vanished civilization which was indisputably Mexican, centering upon the town of Santa Lucía Cotzumal-

The Cotzumalhuapa style

104 (*Above*) A stone relief of a figure emerging from the carapace of a crab, from El Baúl (Cotzumalhuapa culture). On either side are the Mexican dates 2 Monkey and 6 Monkey. Ht 3 ft 3 in. (1 m).

105 (*Right*) A thin stone head (*hacha*) from El Baúl (Cotzumalhuapa culture). Objects of this sort were probably ball-court markers. Ht *c*. 1 ft (30.5 cm).

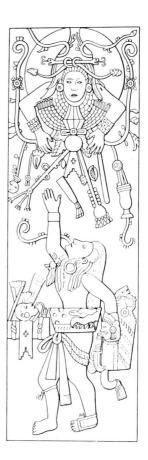

106 A ball-player salutes the Moon Goddess. Monument 4 from Santa Lucía Cotzumalhuapa (Cotzumalhuapa culture, Terminal Classic period).

huapa, in a region which once was famed for its production of cacao, the chocolate beans used not only for drink but as currency. There are only about a half-dozen Cotzumalhuapan sites known, or perhaps just one large one, for all lie within a tiny area of only 20 square miles (52 square km). Each is a compact ceremonial center consisting of temple substructures arranged on a single large platform measuring only a few hundred yards on its long axis; structures have earthen cores faced with river cobbles, but stairways and some courts were occasionally covered with dressed stone.

From the evidence of art style and pottery, the Cotzumalhuapan culture must have flourished in the Terminal Classic. A more hard, cruel, and unsympathetic sculptural style can hardly be imagined, or one less Maya in 104 its general aspect. As Eric Thompson noted, the Cotzumalhuapan sculptors showed "a haunting preoccupation with death." Reliefs of skulls and manikin figures of skeletons are not uncommon. Their second obsession was the rubber ball game. Secure evidence for the game comes from certain stone objects that are frequent in the Cotzumalhuapan zone and in fact over much of the Pacific Coast down to El Salvador. Of these, most typical are the U-shaped stone "yokes" which represented the heavy protective belts of wood and leather worn by the contestants; and thin heads or *hachas* with human faces, grotesque carnivores, macaws, and turkeys, generally thought 105 to be markers for the zones of the court, but worn on the yoke during post-game ceremonies. Both are sure signs of a close affiliation to the Classic cultures of the Mexican Gulf Coast, where such ballgame paraphernalia undoubtedly originated.

Among the relief and in-the-round sculptures of the Cotzumalhuapan sites are representations of some purely Mexican gods: Xipe Totec; the Wind God Ehecatl, shown as a horrifically snouted monster with one extruded eyeball; Tlaloc; Tlalchitonatiuh, god of the rising sun; the Old Fire God, Huehueteotl; and Quetzalcoatl as Feathered Serpent. On some magnificent stelae, ball players wearing "yokes" and protective gloves reach up to celestial deities, usually the Sun or Moon. From the bodies of gods and men may sprout the fronds and pods of cacao, the apparent source of Cotzumalhuapan wealth.

Not only their religion, but their very calendar was Mexican. The majority of the glyphs on the monuments are recognizable as the kind of day-names prevalent among the peoples of southern Mexico, while the numbers and coefficients are expressed in the Mexican fashion by dots or circles only, without the use of the bar for "five" so characteristic of the Maya. Again, as in Mexico, individuals (and perhaps gods, too) were identified by the day of their birth.

The creators of the Cotzumalhuapan civilization, then, were not Mayan but Mexican, most likely the Pipil themselves. There are suggestive connections with the Gulf Coast plain, where there is a similar concentration upon the ballgame, death, human sacrifice, and the cultivation of cacao. If these were the Pipil, then there might have been an ancient center of Nahuat speakers in southern Veracruz who, as another *pochteca* group, could have invaded the southern Maya area across the Isthmus of Tehuantepec. But the Cotzumalhuapa problem is very far from solved.

The end of an era

Beyond the continuing mystery which surrounds the demise of civilization in the Peten and neighboring regions, there is still much to be learned about the Terminal Classic. In many respects, what transpired in the Puuk area was a replay of the great collapse which had taken place a century earlier in the southern lowlands: for reasons which are yet unclear (but which may also include overpopulation and a growing inability of the Puuk rulers to feed their people), all of its cities and lesser centers were virtually abandoned by the end of the tenth century; when first encountered by the Spaniards, they were in ruins.

There was one great exception to this second collapse. To the east of the Puuk, Chich'en Itza was to gather new strength, and to become the largest and perhaps even the most powerful Mesoamerican city of its day, as the transition was made from Classic to Post-Classic.

7·The Post-Classic

By the close of the tenth century the destiny of the once proud and independent Maya had fallen into the hands of grim militarists from the highlands of central Mexico, where a new order of men had replaced the supposedly more intellectual rulers of Classic times. About the events that led to the conquest of Yucatan by these foreigners, and the subsequent replacement of their state by a resurgent but already decadent Maya culture, we know a good deal, for we have entered into a kind of history, albeit far more shaky than that which was recorded on the monuments of the Classic Period. The traditional annals of the peoples of Yucatan, and also of the Guatemalan highlanders, which were transcribed into Spanish letters early in Colonial times apparently reach back as far as the beginning of our Post-Classic era and are very important sources.

But such annals should be used with much caution, whether they come to us from Bishop Landa himself, from statements made by the native nobility, or from native lawsuits and land claims. These are often confused and often self-contradictory, above all since native lineages seem to have deliberately falsified their own history for political reasons. Our richest and most treacherous sources are the K'atun Prophecies of Yucatan, contained in the so-called Books of Chilam Balam which derive their name from a Maya savant said to have predicted the arrival of the Spaniards from the east. The "history" which they contain is based upon the Short Count, a cycle of 13 k'atuns (13 × 7,200 days or 256¼ years), each k'atun of which was named from the last day, always Ahaw, on which it ended. Unfortunately, the Post-Classic Maya thought in purely cyclic terms, so that if certain events had happened in a K'atun 13 Ahaw, they would recur in the next of the same name. The result is that prophecy and history are almost inextricably entwined in these documents that sometimes read like divine revelation; one such history, for example, begins:

> This is the record of how the one and only god, the 13 gods, the 8,000 gods descended, according to the words of the priests, prophets, Chilam Balam, Ah Xupan, Napuk Tun, the priest Nahaw Pech, and Ah K'awil Ch'el. Then was interpreted the command to them, the measured words which were given to them.

The Toltec invasion and Chich'en Itza

Into the vacuum created by the collapse of the older civilizations of central Mexico moved a new people, the Nahua-speaking Toltecs, whose northern

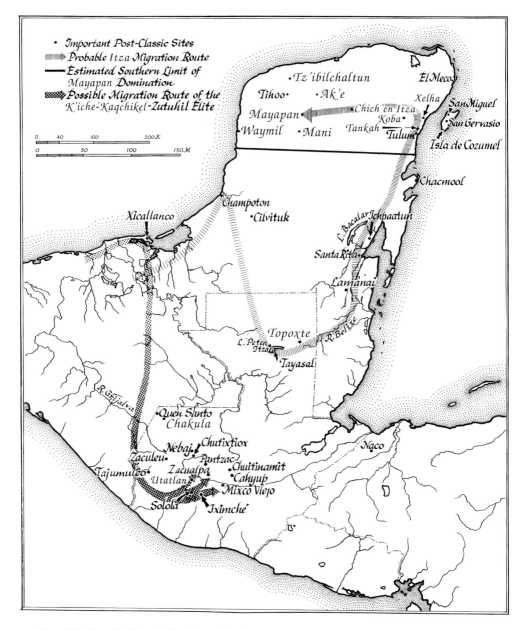

107 Sites of the Post-Classic period and late migration routes.

origins are proclaimed by their kinship with the non-agricultural barbarians called the Chichimec. Shortly after AD 900 they had settled themselves at the key site of Tula ("Tollan" in Nahuatl, or "Place of the Reeds"), under the leadership of a king named Topiltzin, who also claimed the title of Quetzal-coatl or "Feathered Serpent" (the culture hero of Mexican theology). Prominent among these people were the military orders that were to play such a significant role in later Mexican history, and whom we have already seen in Early Classic Teotihuacan – the Eagles, the Jaguars, and the Coyotes – and which paid homage to the war god Tezcatlipoca ("Smoking Mirror") rather than to the more peaceable Quetzalcoatl. According to a number of quasi-historical accounts of great poetic merit, a struggle ensued between Topiltzin Quetzalcoatl and his adherents on the one hand, and the warrior faction on the other. Defeated by the evil magic of his adversary Tezcatlipoca, the king was forced to leave Tula with his followers, most probably in AD 987. In one version well known to all the ancient Mexicans, he made his way to the Gulf Coast and from there set across on a raft of serpents for Tlapallan ("Red Land"), some day to return for the redemption of his people.

Wracked by further internal dissensions and deserted by most of its inhabitants, the Toltec capital was finally destroyed by violence in AD 1156 or 1168, but its memory was forever glorious in the minds of the Mexicans, and there was hardly a ruling dynasty in Mesoamerica in later days which did not claim descent from the Toltecs of Tula. The city, which was certainly the administrative center of an empire spanning central Mexico from the Atlantic to the Pacific, has been securely identified as an archaeological site in the state of Hidalgo, some 50 miles (80 km) northwest of Mexico City, so that a good deal is known about Toltec art and architecture in its place of origin. Everywhere the Toltec went, they carried with them their own very unsym-pathetic style, in which there is an obsession with the image of the Toltec warrior, complete with pillbox-like headdress with a down-flying bird in front, a stylized bird or butterfly on the chest, and carrying a feather-decorated *atlatl* in one hand and a bunch of darts in the other. Left arms were protected by quilted padding, and the back by a small shield shaped like a round mirror. Prowling jaguars and coyotes, and eagles eating hearts dominate the reliefs which covered their principal temple-pyramid, a testimony to the importance of the knightly orders among these militarists.

Now, it so happens that the Maya historical sources speak of the arrival from the west of a man calling himself K'uk'ulkan (*k'uk'ul*, "feathered," and *kan* 'serpent') in a K'atun 4 Ahaw which ended in AD 987, who wrested Yucatan from its rightful owners and established his capital at Chich'en Itza. According to the late Maya scholar Ralph Roys, the accounts of this great event are seriously confused with the history of a later people called the Itza, who moved into the peninsula during the next K'atun 4 Ahaw, in the thirteenth century, and gave their name to the formerly Toltec site of Chich'en. In any case, the Maya credited K'uk'ulkan and his retinue with the introduction of idolatry, but the impressions left by him were generally good, for Bishop Landa states:

108 Wall painting from the Temple of the Warriors, Chich'en Itza. Canoe-borne Toltec warriors reconnoiter the Maya coast.

They say he was favorably disposed, and had no wife or children, and that after his return he was regarded in Mexico as one of their gods and called Quetzalcoatl; and they also considered him a god in Yucatan on account of his being a just statesman.

The goodwill contained in these words is almost certainly due to most of the ruling houses of later times being of Mexican rather than Maya descent, for surely the graphically rendered battle scenes of Chich'en Itza tell us that the conquest of Yucatan by the supposedly peaceful Topiltzin Quetzalcoatl and his Toltec armies was violent and brutal in the extreme. The murals found in the Temple of the Warriors at Chich'en Itza, and the reliefs on some golden disks fished up from the Sacred Cenote at the same site, tell the same story. The drama opens with the arrival of the Toltec forces by sea, most likely 108 along the Campeche shore, where they reconnoiter a coastal Maya town with whitewashed houses. In a marine engagement in which the Maya come out in rafts to meet the Toltec war canoes, the former suffer the first of their defeats. Then the scene moves to the land, where in a great pitched battle (commemorated in the now-ruined murals of the Temple of the Jaguars) fought within a major Maya settlement the natives are again beaten. The final act ends with 109 the heart sacrifice of the Maya leaders, while the Feathered Serpent himself hovers above to receive the bloody offering.

The Yucatan taken over by the Toltec exiles was then in its Puuk phase, but following the invasion, Uxmal and most other important Puuk centers

109 Repoussé gold disk from the Sacred Cenote, Chich'en Itza. Two Toltec men-at-arms attack a pair of fleeing Maya. Diam. 8 ¾ in. (22.2 cm).

must have been abandoned under duress. Chich'en Itza, which in those days may have been called Uukil-abnal ('Seven Bushes'), became, under the rule of Topiltzin Quetzalcoatl, the supreme metropolis of a united kingdom, a kind of splendid recreation of the Tula which he had lost. New architectural techniques and motifs were imported from Toltec Mexico and synthesized with Puuk Maya forms. For instance, columns were now used in place of walls to divide rooms, giving an air of spaciousness to halls; a sloping batter was placed at the base of outside walls and platforms; colonnades of pure Tula type were built, which included low masonry banquettes covered with processions of tough Toltec warriors and undulating feathered serpents; and walls were decorated with murals in bands. And everywhere the old Maya monster-masks were incorporated in these new buildings.

For not only was there a synthesis of styles at Chich'en Itza, but also a hybridization of Toltec and Maya religion and society. Jaguar and Eagle knights rub elbows with men in traditional Maya costume and Mexican astral deities coexist with Maya gods. The old Maya order had been overthrown, but it is obvious that many of the native princes were incorporated into the new power structure.

110, 111

112

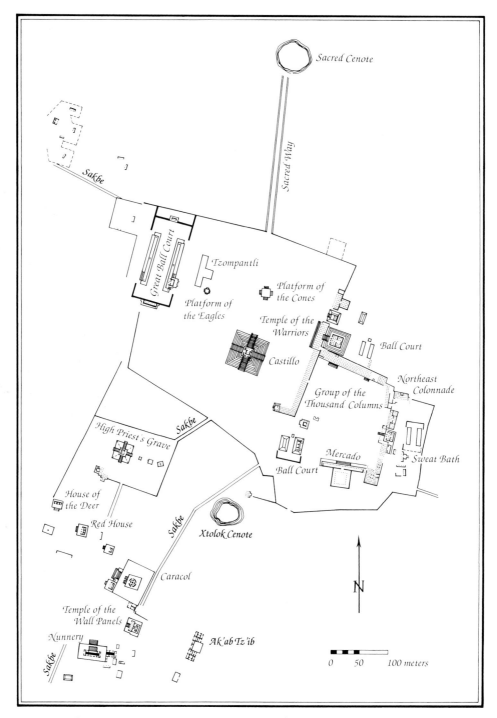

Sacred Cenote

Sacred Way

Sakbe

Great Ball Court

Tzompantli

Platform of
the Cones

Platform of
the Eagles

Temple of the
Warriors

Ball Court

Castillo

Northeast
Colonnade

Sakbe

Group of the
Thousand Columns

High Priest's Grave

Mercado

Sweat Bath

House of
the Deer

Ball Court

Red House

Sakbe

Xtolok Cenote

Caracol

N

Temple of the
Wall Panels

Nunnery

Ak'ab Tz'ib

Sakbe

0   50   100 meters

110 Plan of Chich'en Itza.

111 View of the main monuments at Chich'en Itza, looking northeast from the Nunnery. In the foreground is the Caracol; beyond it to the left, the Castillo or Temple of Kukulcan; and to the right, the Temple of the Warriors.

112 Toltec warrior emerging from the jaws of a cloud-serpent, detail from a gold disk from the Sacred Cenote, Chich'en Itza.

At the hub of Toltec Chich'en stands its most important structure, the so-called "Castillo," a great four-sided temple-pyramid which Landa tells us pl. IX was dedicated to the cult of K'uk'ulkan. The corbel-vaulted temple at the summit of the four breathtaking stairways is a curious mixture of indigenous and foreign, monster masks embellishing the exterior, reliefs of tall war captains from Tula being carved upon the jambs of its doors. Inside the Castillo has been discovered an earlier Toltec-Maya pyramid, with beautifully preserved details, such as the chambers of the superstructure which contain a stone throne in the form of a snarling jaguar, painted red, with eyes and spots of jade and fangs of shell; atop the throne rested a Toltec circular back-shield in turquoise mosaic. Before it is one of the sculptures called "chacmools," reclining figures with hands grasping plate-like receptacles held over the belly, perhaps for receiving the hearts of sacrificed victims. Chacmools are ubiquitous at Tula and at Chich'en, and are a purely Toltec invention.

From the Castillo may be seen the Temple of the Warriors, a splendid building resting upon a stepped platform, surrounded by colonnaded halls. 113 It is closely planned after Pyramid "B" at Tula, but its far greater size and the

113, 114 The Toltec Temple of the Warriors, Chich'en Itza (*opposite*) from a doorway of the Castillo. The building is a grandiose replica of Pyramid B at Tula in Mexico, and a symbol of Toltec ascendancy over Yucatán. (*Below*) A "chacmool" figure at the head of the stairs. Reclining figures of this sort were introduced by the Toltec, and are thought to be connected with the cult of heart sacrifice. Ht 3 ft 6 in. (1.1 m).

115 The Toltec-Maya Ball Court at Chich'en Itza. With walls 27 ft (8.2 m) high, and an overall length of about 490 ft (149 m), this is the largest court in Mesoamerica. The rings set high on either wall were used in scoring the game.

excellence of the workmanship lavished upon it suggest that the Toltec intruders were better off in Yucatan, where they could call upon the skills of Maya architects and craftsmen. The building is approached on the northwest through impressive files of square columns, which are decorated on all four faces with reliefs of Toltec officers. At the top of the stairs a chacmool gazes stonily out upon the main plaza, while the entrance to the temple itself is flanked by a pair of feathered serpents, heads at the ground and tails in the air. Beyond them can be seen the principal sanctuary with its table or altar supported by little Atlantean Toltec warriors. All interior walls had been frescoed with lively scenes related to the Toltec conquest of Yucatan.

In 1926, just as restoration of the Temple of the Warriors by the Carnegie Institution staff was near completion, another such structure came to light underneath it, and from this, the Temple of the Chacmool, were recovered relief-carved columns still bearing the bright pigments with which they were painted. Two benches in the temple interior had been painted in a most interesting fashion, one with a row of Toltec leaders seated upon jaguar thrones identical to that in the interior of the Castillo, but the other with Maya nobles seated upon stools covered with jaguar skin, bearing manikin scepters in Maya fashion. Could these have been quisling princes?

114

The splendid Ball Court of Toltec Chich'en is the largest and finest in all   115
Mesoamerica. Its two parallel, upright walls measure 272 ft long and 27 ft
high (82.6 by 8.2 m), and are 99 ft (30 m) apart. At either end of the I-shaped
playing field is a small temple, the one at the north containing extensive bas-
reliefs of Toltec-Maya life. That the game was played Mexican-style is
shown by the two stone rings set high on the sides of the walls, for a Spanish
chronicler tells us that among the Aztecs whichever team managed to get the
ball through one of these not only won the game and the wager but the clothing of the onlookers. Above the east wall of the court is placed the important
Temple of the Jaguars, whose inner walls were once beautifully painted with   116
Toltec battle scenes, so detailed and convincing that the artist must have been
a witness to the Toltec invasion. Decades of neglect have resulted in their
almost total ruin.

Landa describes "two small stages of hewn stone" at Chich'en, "with four
staircases, paved on the top, where they say that farces were represented, and
comedies for the pleasure of the public," surely to be identified with the two
Dance Platforms which have their facings covered with themes directly
imported from Tula, such as eagles and jaguars eating hearts. Human sacri-   117
fice on a large scale must have been another gift of the Toltecs, for near the
Ball Court is a long platform carved on all sides with human skulls skewered
on stakes. The Aztec name given to it, Tzompantli ("skull rack"), is certainly   118
apt, for in Post-Classic Mexico such platforms supported the great racks
upon which the heads of victims were displayed. Each of the six Ball Court

116 Doorway of the
Temple of the
Jaguars, overlooking
the Ball Court,
Chich'en Itza. Shown
here are one of two
Feathered Serpent
columns which
support the lintel, and
a door jamb with a
relief figure of a
Toltec warrior.

reliefs depicts the decapitation of a ball player, and it is entirely possible that the game was played "for keeps," the losers ending up on the Tzompantli.

Chich'en Itza is most renowned not for its architecture, but for its Sacred Cenote, or Well of Sacrifice, reached by a 900-ft-long (274-m) causeway leading north from the Great Plaza. From Landa's pen comes the following:

> Into this well they have had, and then had, the custom of throwing men alive as a sacrifice to the gods, in times of drought, and they believed that they did not die though they never saw them again. They also threw into it a great many other things, like precious stones and things which they prized.

Shortly before the Spanish Conquest, one of our Colonial sources tells us that the victims were "Indian women belonging to each of the lords," but in the popular imagination the notion has taken hold that only lovely young virgins were tossed down to the Rain God lurking below its greenish-black waters. The late Earnest Hooton, who examined a collection of some fifty skeletons fished up from the Sacred Cenote, commented that "all of the individuals involved (or rather immersed) may have been virgins, but the osteological evidence does not permit a determination of this nice point." A goodly number of the skulls turned out to be from adult males, and many from children, while pathology showed that "three of the ladies who fell or were pushed into the Cenote had received, at some previous time, good bangs

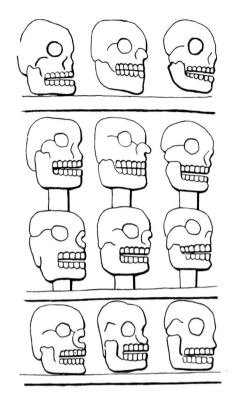

117 (*Left*) Toltec relief panel of a jaguar eating a heart, from the Dance Platform of the Eagles, Chich'en Itza. Such a theme is also known at Tula in the Toltec homeland, and is symbolic of the military order of the Jaguars.

118 (*Right*) Bas-relief of skulls skewered on a rack, from the Tzompantli, Chich'en Itza.

on various parts of the head . . . and one female had suffered a fracture of the nose"!

As the great Mayanists Ralph Roys and A. M. Tozzer stressed, the peak of the sacrificial cult at the Sacred Cenote was reached after the decline of Toltec Chich'en, and continued into Colonial times and even later. None the less, many of the objects dredged from the muck at the bottom of the Cenote are of Toltec manufacture, including some marvellously fine jades and the gold disks already mentioned. For metals had now appeared in the Maya area, although probably all casting and most working was done elsewhere and imported, the many copper bells and other objects from the well being of Mexican workmanship. From places as far afield as Panama the local lords brought treasures of gold to offer to their Rain God.

109, 112

The Rain God's cult is also strikingly evident in the underground cavern of Balank'anche, located 2½ miles (4 km) east of Chich'en Itza. In a deep, hot, and humid chamber which they later sealed, the Toltec priests had placed almost 100 incense burners of pottery and stone, most of them at the base of an enormous stalagmitic formation – in appearance like some great World Tree, as Nikolai Grube notes – in the center of the chamber. Twenty-six of these censers are hour-glass in shape, and had been modeled with the goggle-eyed visage of the Mexican Rain God, Tlaloc, and polychromed. Off to one side they had made an offering of miniature *metates* with their *manos*, and it is tempting to speculate whether there might once have been 260 of these, the number of days in the sacred calendar. David Freidel, Linda

119

119 Chamber in the cave of Balank'anche, Yucatan. In the center, stalactite and stalagmite have united in an immense pillar resembling a world tree; around it were placed Toltec incense burners of pottery and stone.

Schele, and Joy Parker have suggested that the priests may have associated these tiny implements with the hunchbacks and dwarfs of the last creation.

This Toltec occupation has been detected at other places in the Yucatan Peninsula, and is everywhere marked by the presence of the glazed pottery called Plumbate ware, produced in kilns along the Guatemala-Chiapas border area near the Pacific shore. Plumbate vessels must have been made to Toltec taste, for they often take the form of Toltec warriors, but many are simple, pear-shaped vases supported on hollow legs, very much like the carved and painted vessels also associated with the Toltec period in Yucatan.

In 1984 and 1985, a team led by Anthony Andrews and Fernando Robles C. mapped and excavated the tiny island called Isla Cerritos, in the mouth of the Río Lagartos estuary on the north coast of Yucatan. This has proved to be the port of Chich'en Itza, with a seawall pierced by entryways on the exposed side, and with ceramics virtually identical to those of the great Toltec-Maya capital. It will be remembered from Chapter 1 that Yucatan's greatest resource was its coastal salt beds, and Isla Cerritos was certainly strategically located to exploit production and trade in this necessity. But other items were moving along these trade networks, for the excavators encountered obsidian from the mines in central Mexico, turquoise which had probably originated

120, 122

Toltec-style pottery

120 A Toltec effigy jar (Plumbate ware) in the form of the god Itzamna, from Guatemala. Ht 6 in. (15.2 cm).

121 (*Below left*) Hands are depicted in black paint on this X–Fine Orange ware jar from coastal Campeche. Together with Plumbate ware, pottery of this kind is a marker for the Toltec presence in the Maya area. Ht *c.* 7 in. (17.8 cm).

122 (*Below*) A Toltec tripod jar (Plumbate ware) from coastal Campeche, Mexico. Produced on the Pacific slopes of Chiapas and Guatemala in Toltec style, this glazed ware was widely traded over much of southern Mesoamerica. Ht 7½ in. (19 cm).

in the American Southwest (a luxury item prized by the Toltecs and their cultural heirs the Aztecs), and gold from lower Central America.

What finally happened to the Toltecs? All indications are that their mighty capital, Chich'en Itza, was abandoned in a K'atun 6 Ahaw which ended in AD 1224, and they are heard of no more. Another people now take the stage for a brief moment and Maya culture lives a little while longer.

A word of caution should be inserted here, for we are in the midst of a great scholarly controversy. The version of Toltec-Maya history given above is that worked out by the late Ralph Roys, the leading student of Maya ethno-history of his time, but it is by no means accepted by all Mayanists. The basic problem of dealing with the Short Count chronological system has already been described; this means that other interpretations are possible, but not necessarily probable. A dissenting view that has often cropped up in recent years is that the Toltecs of Tula, and the Toltec-Maya of Chich'en Itza, at least in part were contemporary with the terminal Late Classic Maya of the southern lowlands prior to their collapse, and that Tula was more influenced by the Maya than the reverse. An even more extreme theory is that the Toltecs never really existed (see below). Only modern excavations at Chich'en Itza, a site which – despite years of excavations – is still poorly known, will tell us whether these views are tenable, or ill-founded. Some of the revisionists have gone so far as to suggest that the 11.16 or Thompson correlation should be abandoned for one which would make all Classic period Long Count dates $256\frac{1}{4}$ years later, but this is impossible on astronomical and ethnohistoric grounds, and on the evidence of radiocarbon dating.

And just to add to the problem presented by the Early Post-Classic in Yucatan, Drs. Andrews and Robles suggest that it was not the Toltecs who established their capital at Chich'en as Puuk power waned, but the Itza themselves, a people they see as emerging from a mosaic of "westerners" – peoples from the lower reaches of the Usumacinta and Grijalva river systems, like Eric Thompson's Putun Maya. These would have monopolized the salt beds and the coastal trading routes, eventually consolidating their control over most of the northern peninsula. This theory would not, however, explain the extremely close iconographic links between Chich'en Itza and Toltec Tula, and would relegate most of the ethnohistoric accounts which we have of the Toltec from peoples as diverse as the Aztecs and the highland Maya to little more than fiction. The problem remains.

The Itza and the city of Mayapan

The Toltecs may finally have been accepted by the natives of Yucatan, but the Itza were always despised. Epithets such as "foreigners," "tricksters and rascals," "the lewd ones," and "people without fathers or mothers" are applied to them by the Maya chronicles; and the title carried by the Itza war leader K'ak'upakal, "he who speaks our language brokenly," shows that they could not have been Yucatec in origin. Some scholars have suggested that at the beginning of their history the Itza were a group of Mexicanized Chontal-Maya (that is, Putun) living in Tabasco, where commercial connections with central Mexico were deep-rooted, but more recently it has been demonstrated that they actually had been native to the Peten, moving out with the Great Collapse. At any rate while the Toltecs lorded it over Yucatan, the Itza were settled in a place called Chak'anputun ("Savannah of the Putun"), probably Champoton on the coast of Campeche. About AD 1200 they were driven from this town and wandered east across the land, "beneath the trees, beneath the bushes, beneath the vines, to their misfortune," migrating through the empty jungles back to the region of Lake Peten Itza, and to the eastern shores of Belize. Finally, this wretched band of warriors found their way up the coast and across to Chich'en Itza, where they settled as squatters in the desolate city, in K'atun 4 Ahaw (AD 1224–44).

Leading the Itza diaspora to northern Yucatan was a man who also claimed the title of K'uk'ulkan, like his great Toltec predecessor of the tenth century, and he must have consciously imitated Toltec ideas, such as the cult of the Sacred Cenote, which now reached a peak of intensity. And yet another cult was initiated, that of the Goddess of Medicine (and childbirth), one of the several aspects of the old lunar goddess Ix Chel, with pilgrims from all over the Northern Area voyaging to her shrine on the island of Cozumel.

In K'atun 13 Ahaw (AD 1263–83) the Itza founded Mayapan, some of the tribe remaining behind at Chich'en Itza, which now had lost its old name of Uukil-abnal and taken on its present one (meaning "mouth of the well of the Itza"). The wily K'uk'ulkan II populated his city with provincial rulers and their families, thus ensuring a dominion over much of the peninsula. However, after his death (or departure), troubles increased, and it was not until about 1283 that Mayapan actually became the capital of Yucatan, after a revolt in which an Itza lineage named Kokom had seized power, aided by Mexican mercenaries from Tabasco, the Kanul ("guardians"). It may have been this sinister Praetorian Guard which introduced the bow-and-arrow to Yucatan.

Mayapan, which is situated in the west central portion of the peninsula, is a residential metropolis covering about 2½ square miles (6.5 square km) and completely surrounded by a defensive wall testifying to the unrest of those days. There are over 2,000 dwellings within the wall, and it is estimated that between 11,000 and 12,000 persons lived in the city. At the center of Mayapan is the Temple of K'uk'ulkan, a pitifully shoddy imitation of the Castillo at Chich'en Itza. The colonnaded masonry dwellings of important persons were near this, just as Landa tells us, but dwellings become poorer as one moves away from the center. Each group of thatched-roof houses probably sheltered a family and is surrounded by a low property wall. The city "pattern" is completely haphazard: there are no streets, no arrangement to be discerned at all, and it seems as if the basically dispersed Maya had been forced by the Itza to live jam-packed together within the walls in a kind of urban anarchy. No city like it had ever been seen before in the Maya area. On what did the population live? The answer is tribute, for Father Cogolludo tells us that luxury and subsistence goods streamed into the city from the vassals of the native princes whom the Kokom were holding hostage in their capital.

Of supreme importance to the residents of Mayapan, living in such a stony and relatively dry environment, was the location of *cenotes* within the walls, which archaeologist Clifford Brown has discovered were constructed so as to enclose the maximum number of these natural wells. But some *cenotes* may have served for more than drinking water, for Brown has found a tunnel leading off from one right under the Temple of K'uk'ulkan, bringing to mind the tunnel and secret chamber below the Pyramid of the Sun in Teotihuacan. And deliberately excluded from the walled city is a large *cenote* which is still held in awe by the local people as a holy place inhabited by a monster (one old man has seen a feathered serpent going in and out!).

By this time, the Maya were thorough-going idolaters, and the excavators of Mayapan found a proliferation of shrines and family oratories, in which were placed brightly painted pottery incense burners of little artistic merit, representing Mexican gods such as Quetzalcoatl, Xipe Totec (the God of Spring), and the Old Fire God, side-by-side with Maya deities such as Chak the Rain God, the Maize God, and Itzamna (the Maya version of the Old Fire God of central Mexico).

123, 124

In an ill-omened era, K'atun 8 Ahaw (1441–61), fate began to close in upon the Itza. Hunak Ke'el was then ruler of Mayapan, an unusual figure who achieved prominence by offering himself as a sacrifice to be flung into the Sacred Cenote at Chich'en, and living to deliver the Rain God's prophecy given him there. The ruler of Chich'en Itza was a man named Chak Xib Chak. According to one story, by means of sorcery Hunak Ke'el drove Chak Xib Chak to abduct the bride of the ruler of Izamal, whereupon the expected retribution took place and the Itza were forced to leave Chich'en. Next it was the turn of the Kokom, and a revolt broke out within the walls of Mayapan, stirred up by an upstart Mexican lineage named Xiw which had settled near the ruins of Uxmal. The Maya nobles of Mayapan joined the Xiw, and the Kokom game was up; they were put to death and the once great city was destroyed and abandoned for all time.

Those Itza who were driven from Chich'en Itza were to be in evidence for several centuries more, however. Once again they found themselves as outcasts in the deserted forests, this time wandering back to the Lake Peten Itza which they had seen in a previous K'atun 8 Ahaw. On an island in the midst of its waters they established a new capital, Tayasal (a Spanish corruption of *Tah Itza)*, now covered by the city of Flores, chief town of northern Guatemala. Safe in the fastness of an almost impenetrable wilderness, their island stronghold was bypassed by history. Tayasal was first encountered by Hernán Cortés in 1524, while that intrepid conqueror was journeying across the Peten with his army to punish a rebellious insubordinate in Honduras, and he was kindly received by king Kanek', whose name was borne by a long line of Itza rulers. It was not until the seventeenth century that the Spaniards decided something must be done about this last, untamed Maya kingdom, and several missionaries were sent to convert Kanek' and his people – to no avail.

One of the very last to make the attempt was Fray Andrés de Avendaño y Loyola. In 1988 an extraordinary manuscript came to light in Mexico; this is

123 Pottery incense burner from a shrine at Mayapan. This effigy of God B, the Rain God Chak, carries a small bowl in one hand and a ball of flaming incense in the other. The censer was painted after firing with blue, green, black, red, white, and yellow pigments. Ht 21½ in. (54.6 cm).

124 Upper part of pottery incense burner from Mayapan, Mexico. God M, Ek' Chuah, who was the patron of merchants, is shown here, identifiable from his partly broken, Pinnochio-like nose. Red, blue, and yellow paint had been applied to the censer. Ht 9½ in. (24.1 cm).

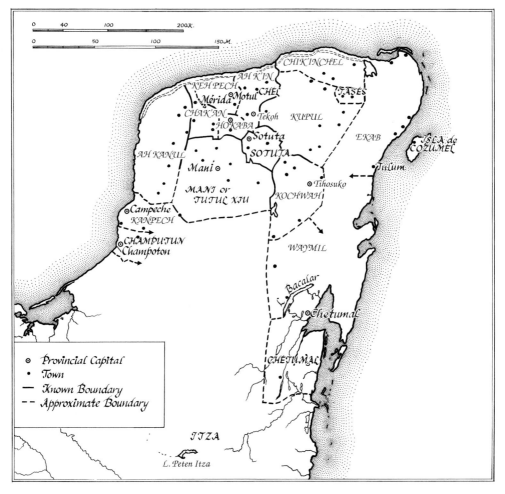

125 The independent states of the Northern Area on the eve of the Spanish Conquest.

a fragment of a longer document in a rather Italianate Spanish that describes the visit by Avendaño, two Franciscan companions, and ten converted Maya to Kanek's domain, probably early in 1695. As they waited in a hut in the hostile town of Chak'an, on the lake's western shore, a breathtaking sight met their eyes. From the east came a great, wedge-shaped flotilla of canoes,

> all of them adorned with many flowers and playing much music with sticks and with drums and wooden flutes. And seated in one larger than all was the king of the Itzas, who is the Lord Canek [Kanek'], which means the star twenty serpent.

The last of the Maya kings wore a crown of gold, and gold disks in his ears from which golden pendants hung down to his shoulders. He had bands of pure gold on his arms and golden finger-rings, and his blue sandals were covered with golden bells. Over his blue tunic he wore a long, white cape, also edged with blue, emblazoned with the hieroglyph of his name.

Kanek' did not succumb to the Franciscans' arguments. But two years later, Spanish arms succeeded where peaceful missions had repeatedly failed. It seems almost beyond belief that Tayasal fell to the Spaniards only in 1697, and that while students at Harvard College had been scratching their heads over Cotton Mather's theology, Maya priests 2,000 miles away were still chanting rituals from hieroglyphic books.

The independent states of Yucatan

With Mayapan gone, the whole peninsula reverted to the kind of political organization that had been the rule in Classic times, six centuries earlier. In place of a single, united kingdom were now sixteen rival states, each jealous of the power and lands of the other, and only too eager to go to war in asserting its claims. The culture of the times, for whatever it was worth, was Maya, for much of what the Mexicans had brought was already forgotten and traditional Maya ways of doing things were substituted for imported habits. 125

There are few archaeological sites which can be assigned to this final phase, although the life of the times is well described by Landa and other early post-Conquest writers who were able to question natives who had actually participated in that culture. We are sure that there were one or more major towns within each province, but these were chosen by the Spaniards for their settlements and most are buried under centuries of Colonial and more recent constructions.

One site which was untouched, however, is Tulum, a small town in the province of Ekab founded in the Mayapan period. Spectacularly placed on a 126

126 Plan of the walled town of Tulum, on the Caribbean coast of the Yucatan Peninsula. *A*, Castillo; *B*, Temple of the Frescoes; *C*, Temple of the Diving God.

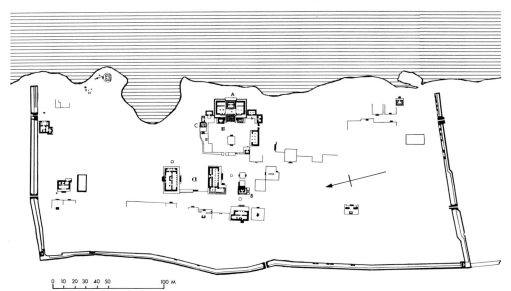

0 10 20 30 40 50   100 M

127 Temple of the Frescoes, Tulum, from the west, a photograph taken prior to 1923, before the walled site had been cleared. The temple is noted for its wall paintings carried out in a hybrid Mixtec-Maya style. Inset panels over the doorways contain stucco "diving god" figures, while stuccoed faces at the corners of the lower story suggest its dedication to the god Itzamna.

128 Detail of a wall painting in the Temple of the Frescoes at Tulum. An aged goddess, probably Ix Chel, carries two images of the god Chak

cliff above the blue-green waters of the Caribbean, Tulum is surrounded by a defensive wall on three sides and by the sea on the fourth. Probably no more than 500 or 600 persons lived there, in houses concentrated on artificial platforms arranged along a sort of "street." The principal temple, a miserable structure called the Castillo, and other important buildings are clustered together near the sea. On the upper facades of many of these dwarfish structures, which are of strikingly slipshod workmanship, are plaster figures of winged gods descending from above. Wall paintings have been found on both the interior and outer surfaces of some temples, but the best-preserved are in the two-storied Temple of the Frescoes. Like the 127 murals of the Late Post-Classic center of Santa Rita in northern Belize (discovered by Thomas Gann in 1894 and subsequently destroyed), the style of these is less Maya than Mixtec, undoubtedly influenced by the pictorial manuscripts of that gifted people from the hilly country of Oaxaca. Yet the content of the Tulum frescoes is native Maya, with scenes of gods such as Chak and various female divinities performing rites among bean-like 128 vegetation. In one, the Rain God sits astride a four-legged beast, for which there can be but one explanation: they had seen, or heard tell of, Spaniards riding on horseback. Not only Tayasal, then, but also Tulum must have lived for a while beyond the Conquest, protected by the dense forests of Quintana Roo.

The Central Area in the Post-Classic

As was mentioned in the last chapter, not all of the lowland Maya centers and populated regions suffered total decline and abandonment with the Classic collapse, although most certainly did. In fact, Koba in the northeast had a virtual renaissance in the Post-Classic, as Tulum-style superstructures were built on top of Classic pyramids. In the Central Area certain towns, including Tayasal, were founded and flourished after AD 1200 on islands in the chain of lakes that extends across the eastern Peten almost to the Belize border. Lamanai, the ancient port town on the New River, saw much construction during the Post-Classic, and was occupied well into the Colonial era, as a church built in the sixteenth century (and abandoned in the next) testifies.

Maya-Mexican dynasties in the Southern Area

In the mountain valleys of highland Guatemala, there were numerous independent nations on the eve of the Conquest, but the K'iche' and Kaqchikel were the greatest of these. All indications are that they and their lesser neighbors, the Tzutuhil and Pokomam, had been there since very early times. And yet they claimed in their own histories that they had come from the west, from Mexico. As the Annals of the Kaqchikels relate:

> From the setting sun we came, from Tula, from beyond the sea; and it was at Tula that arriving we were brought forth, coming we were produced, by our mothers and fathers, as they say.

129 Group C, Chuitinamit, Guatemala, looking west; restoration drawing by Tatiana Proskouriakoff. The K'iche' built an impressive stronghold here after driving out the Pokoman Maya. A typically Mexican feature of the late highland centers is the double pyramid in the middle of the group. In the background can be seen a ball court.

This claim may have been pure wishful thinking, similar to that of many Americans who would have liked their forebears to have stepped off the *Mayflower* in 1620. The noted authority on K'iche' Maya culture and history, Robert Carmack, traces the *actual* origin of the K'iche' elite not to the Toltec diaspora of the late tenth and eleventh centuries, but to a much later incursion of Toltecized Chontal-Nahua speakers (in other words, Putun Maya) from the Gulf Coast border region of Veracruz and Tabasco. These "forefathers" would have arrived as small but very formidable military bands similar to the Japanese samurai, and terrorized the native K'iche' and Kaqchikel highlanders. Gradually they established an epi-Toltec state, complete with a ruling line claiming descent from Quetzalcoatl. Many of the elite's personal names, as well as names of early places, objects, and institutions, seem to be Chontal rather than K'iche'; and they introduced into the Guatemalan highlands many Nahua words for military and ritual matters.

129   The *conquistadores* have described the splendor of their towns, such as Utatlan, the K'iche' capital which was burned to the ground by the terrible Pedro de Alvarado, or the Kaqchikel center Iximche. These sites were placed in defensive positions atop hills surrounded by deep ravines, and are completely Mexican down to the last architectural detail. Typically, the principal building is a large double temple with two frontal stairways, much like the Great Temple of the Aztecs in Tenochtitlan, and there usually is a

well-made ball court nearby, for we know from the Popol Vuh that the highlanders were fond of that game. Lastly, all buildings are covered in Mexican fashion with flat beam-and-mortar roofs, the corbel principle being unknown here.

Best preserved of these late highland centers is Mixco Viejo, capital of the   130
brave Pokoman nation; the almost impregnable site, surrounded by steep gorges, fell to Alvarado and two companies of Spanish infantry only through treachery.

Utatlan (this Nahuatl name is "Q'umaraq aj" in K'iche' Maya) is the best known of these highland capitals, both archaeologically and ethnohistorically. In it, there was a fundamental social cleavage between the lords and their vassals: these were castes, in the strictest sense of the term. The former were the patrilineal descendants of the original warlords; they were sacred, and surrounded by royal emblems. The vassals served as foot-soldiers to the lords, and while they could and did receive military titles through their battlefield prowess, they were still subject to sumptuary laws. Merchants had a privileged status, but they had to pay tribute. In addition, the free population included artisans and serfs (a growing class of rural laborers). Slaves comprised both sentenced criminals and vassal war captives; in general, only captive lords were considered fit for sacrifice, or for consumption in cannibalistic rites.

130 Group B, Mixco Viejo, Guatemala, looking east. The ruins of the Pokoman capital are surrounded on all sides by tremendously precipitous ravines. To take the town from its defenders, Alvarado's Spanish army had to advance up a steep path along which only two abreast could move, under a hail of rocks and poisoned arrows. This is the main group of the site, dominated by the usual double temple.

There were twenty-four "principal" lineages in Utatlan, closely identified with the buildings or "Big Houses" in which they (the lords) carried out their affairs. The functions carried out in them were ceremonial lecturing; the giving of bride-price; and eating and drinking associated with marriages between the lineages. The K'iche' state was headed by a king, a king-elect, and two "captains," but there was also a kind of quadripartite rule (known also in Yucatan) embodied in four chiefs, one from each of the four major Utatlan lineages.

Documentary evidence unique for the ancient Maya enables us to associate specific ruined temples at Utatlan with gods revered by the K'iche'. The major cult structures faced each other across a plaza, and were dominated by the Temple of Tojil, a Jaguar deity connected with the sun and with rain. In the same plaza was the circular temple dedicated to the Feathered Serpent, while the Ball Court of Utatlan represented the Underworld. There was a palace elaborating the idea of the Big Houses in honor of Utatlan's ruling lineage, the Kawek ("Rain") dynasty; other Big Houses can be identified as the range structures so typical of highland towns. Perhaps we have a clue here to the functions played by the "palaces" in Classic sites of the southern lowlands.

The Spanish Conquest

"The raised wooden standard shall come!" cried the Maya prophet Chilam Balam, "Our lord comes, Itza! Our elder brother comes, oh men of Tantun! Receive your guests, the bearded men, the men of the east, the bearers of the sign of God, lord!"

The prediction came true in 1517, when Yucatan was discovered by Hernández de Córdoba, who died of wounds inflicted by Maya warriors at Champoton. The year 1518 saw the exploratory expedition of Grijalva, and that of the great Hernán Cortés in 1519, but Yucatan was for a while spared as the cupidity of the Spaniards drew them to the gold-rich Mexico. The Spanish Conquest of the northern Maya began only in 1528 under Francisco de Montejo, on whom the Crown bestowed the title of Adelantado. But this was no easy task, for unlike the mighty Aztecs, there was no overall native authority that could be toppled, bringing an empire with it. Nor did the Maya fight in the accepted fashion. Attacking the Spaniards at night, plotting ambushes and traps, they were jungle guerrillas in a familiar modern tradition. Accordingly, it was not until 1542 that the hated foreigners managed to establish a capital, Mérida; even so revolt continued to plague the Spaniards throughout the sixteenth century.

The reduction of the Southern Area was largely the accomplishment of the resourceful but cruel Pedro de Alvarado, who arrived in Guatemala in 1523 fresh from his Mexican triumphs with cavalry, footsoldiers, and native auxiliaries. By 1541, the year of his death, the K'iche' and Kaqchikel kingdoms had fallen under the Spanish yoke, and indigenous resistance was largely at an end.

But the Maya are, for all their apparent docility, the toughest Indians of

Mesoamerica, and the struggle against European civilization has never once halted. In 1847 and again in 1860 the Yucatec Maya rose against their white oppressors, coming very close the first time to taking the entire peninsula. As late as 1910 the independent chiefs of Quintana Roo were in rebellion against the dictatorial regime of Porfirio Diaz, and only in the last few decades have these remote Maya villagers begun to accept the rule of Mexico. Likewise the Tzeltal of highland Chiapas have repeatedly risen, most notably in 1712 and 1868, and both they and the Tzotzil Maya form the backbone of the Zapatista National Liberation Army which has challenged the Mexican authorities since the initial uprising of 1994. The Cholan-speaking regions west of Lake Izabal in Guatemala were feared by missionaries and soldiers alike as "The Land of War," and the pacification of these Maya took centuries. The survival of the Itza on their island Tayasal is a case in point; another is that of the Lakandon, still relatively independent. No, the Maya were never completely conquered, but their civilization and spirit were seemingly broken – and went underground. As a poem from one of the books of Chilam Balam puts it:

> Eat, eat, thou hast bread;
> Drink, drink, thou hast water;
> On that day, dust possesses the earth;
> On that day, a blight is on the face of the earth,
> On that day, a cloud rises,
> On that day, a mountain rises,
> On that day, a strong man seizes the land,
> On that day, things fall to ruin,
> On that day, the tender leaf is destroyed,
> On that day, the dying eyes are closed,
> On that day, three signs are on the tree,
> On that day, three generations hang there,
> On that day, the battle flag is raised,
> And they are scattered afar in the forests.
> On that day, the battle flag is raised,
> And they are scattered afar in the forests.

8· Maya Life on the Eve of the Conquest

While we have until this moment been dealing mainly with the pots, jades, and ruins of a once great people, we actually know a good deal more than this about the daily life of the Maya, particularly of the natives of Yucatan on the eve of the Conquest. For it is our good fortune that the early Spanish missionaries were accomplished scholars, and that owing to their eagerness to understand the nations they wished to convert to the Cross they have left us with first-class anthropological accounts of native culture as it was just before they came. So it is upon this foundation that we must interpret the archaeological remains of the Post-Classic Maya – and the Maya of the Classic as well.

The farm and the chase

Maya agriculture, which has been described in some detail in Chapter 1, was the foundation of their civilization. Maize, beans, squashes, chile peppers, cotton, and various kinds of root crops and fruit trees were cultivated. That the pre-Conquest lowlanders usually prepared their plots by the slash-and-burn method is certain, but exactly how large trees were felled prior to the adoption of copper axes in the Post-Classic (and of steel ones in Colonial days) is unclear; perhaps they were merely ringed and left to die. The times of planting were under the control of a kind of farmer's almanac of which we apparently have examples in two of the codices. According to Landa, fields were communally owned and jointly worked by groups of twenty men, but this may not be very close to the real picture, as we shall see.

In Yucatan, the Maya stored their crops in above-ground cribs of wood, but also in "fine underground places" which might well be the *chultunob* so common in Classic sites. The Spanish sources consistently fail to mention tortillas or flat cakes *(pek wah)* for the lowland Maya; while a few clay griddles have been found in Post-Classic occupations in sites like Lamanai, these may have been used to toast cacao beans rather than tortillas. However, other ways of preparing maize are mentioned in the sources. These include *saka'*, a corn-meal gruel which was taken with chile pepper as the first meal of the day; *k'eyen*, a mixture of water and sour dough carried in gourds to the fields for sustenance during the day; and the well-known tamales *(keehel wah)*, which turn up in food offerings found painted on Late Classic ceramics. The peasant cuisine (we know little of that current among the elite class) was largely confined to such simple foods and to stews compounded from meat and vegetables, to which were added squash seeds and peppers.

131

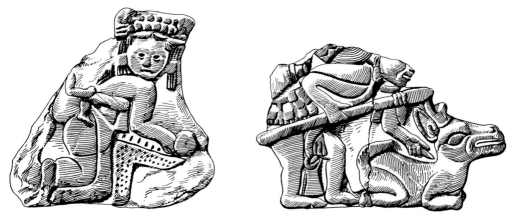

131, 132 (*Left*) Woman grinding maize on a *metate*, from a Late Classic figurine from Lubaantun, Belize. (*Right*) Huntsman slaying deer, on a Late Classic figurine from Lubaantun, Belize.

"Cash crops" were of prime importance to Yucatan. Cotton was widely grown, for the province was famed for its textiles, which were exported over a very large area. Along river drainages in southern Campeche, Tabasco, and Belize and on the Pacific slope of Guatemala groves of cacao trees were planted, but in the north these were restricted to the bottoms of filled-in *cenotes* and other natural depressions. The cacao bean from this tree provided chocolate, the preferred drink of the Mesoamerican ruling classes, but well into Colonial times the beans served as a form of money in regional markets; so precious were they that the Maya traders encountered off the coast of Honduras by Columbus were said to have snatched up any that had dropped as though it was their own eyes that had fallen to the canoe bottom.

Every Maya household had its own kitchen garden in which vegetables and fruit trees were raised, and fruit groves were scattered near settlements as well. Papaya, avocado, custard apple, sapodilla, and the breadnut tree were all cultivated, but many kinds of wild fruits were also eaten, especially in times of famine.

There were several breeds of dog current among the Maya, each with its own name. One such strain was barkless; males were castrated and fattened on corn, and either eaten or sacrificed. Another was used in the hunt. Both wild and domestic turkeys were known, but only the former used as sacrificial victims in ceremonies. As he still does today, the Maya farmer raised the native stingless bees, which are kept in small, hollow logs closed with mud plaster at either end and stacked up in A-frames, but wild honey was also much appreciated.

The larger mammals, such as deer and peccary, were hunted with the bow-and-arrow in drives (though in Classic times the *atlatl*-and-dart must have been the principal weapon), aided by packs of dogs. Birds like the wild turkey, partridge, wild pigeon, quail, and wild duck were taken with pellets shot from blowguns. A variety of snares and deadfalls are shown in the Madrid Codex, especially a trap for armadillo.

132

In Yucatan, fishing was generally of the offshore kind, by means of sweep and drag nets and hook-and-line, but fish were also shot with bow-and-arrow in lagoons. Inland, especially in the highland streams, stupefying drugs were pounded in the water, and the fish taken by hand once they had floated into artificial dams; one of the beautifully incised bones from Late Classic Tik'al shows that this was also the practice in the Peten. Along the coasts the catch was salted and dried or roasted over a fire for use in commerce.

Among wild products of the lowland forests of great cultural importance to the Maya was *pom,* the resin of the copal tree, which (along with rubber and chewing gum!) was used as incense – so holy was this that one native source describes it as the "odor of the center of heaven." Another tree produced a bark for flavoring *balche',* a "strong and stinking" mead imbibed in vast amounts during festivals.

Industry and commerce

Yucatan was the greatest producer of salt in Mesoamerica. The beds extended along the coast from Campeche, along the lagoons on the north side of the peninsula, and over to Isla Mujeres on the east. The salt, which Landa praised as the "best . . . which I have ever seen in my life," was collected at the end of the dry season by the coastal peoples who held a virtual monopoly over the industry, although at one time it was entirely in the hands of the overlord of Mayapan. A few localities inland also had salt wells, such as the Chixoy valley of Guatemala, but it was sea salt that was in most demand and this was carried widely all over the Maya area. Other valuable Yucatecan exports were honey, cotton mantles, and slaves, and one suspects that it was such industrial specialization which supported the economy, not maize agriculture.

Further regional products involved in native trade were cacao, which could only be raised in a few well-watered places (especially the perpetually-damp bottoms of waterless *cenotes*), quetzal feathers from the Alta Verapaz, flint and chert from deposits in the Central Area, obsidian from the highlands northeast of Guatemala City, and colored shells (particularly the thorny oyster) from both coasts. Jade and a host of lesser stones of green color were also traded, most originating in the beds of the Motagua River, but some which appeared on the market could well have been looted from ancient graves.

The great majority of goods traveled by sea since roads were but poor trails and cargoes heavy. This kind of commerce was cornered by the Chontal Maya, or Putun, such good seafarers that Thompson called them "the Phoenicians of Middle America." Their route skirted the coast from the Aztec port of trade in Campeche, Xicallanco, around the peninsula and down to Nito near Lake Izabal, where their great canoes put in to exchange goods with the inland Maya. However, a special group of traders traveled the perilous overland trails, under the protection of their own deity, Ek' Chuwah, the Black God. Markets (*k'iwik*) are rarely mentioned where the lowland Maya are concerned, in contrast with Mexico where they were so large that the Spaniards were astonished, and it is probable that they were unimportant since there was little cause for heavy subsistence goods to change hands in this very uniform land. But we are told by one source that highland Guatemalan markets were "great and celebrated and very rich," and these have persisted to this very day.

It was this trade that linked Mexico and the Maya, for they had much to exchange – especially cacao and the feathers of tropical birds for copper tools and ornaments – and it was probably the smooth business operations conducted by the Chontal that spared the Maya from the Aztec onslaught that had overwhelmed less cooperative peoples in Mesoamerica.

The life cycle

Immediately after birth, Yucatecan mothers washed their infants and then fastened them to a cradle, their little heads compressed between two boards in such a way that after two days a permanent fore-and-aft flattening had taken place which the Maya considered a mark of beauty. As soon as possible, the anxious parents went to consult with a priest so as to learn the destiny of their offspring, and the name which he or she was to bear until baptism.

The Spanish Fathers were quite astounded that the Maya had a baptismal rite, which took place at an auspicious time when there were a number of boys and girls between the ages of three and twelve in the settlement. The ceremony took place in the house of a town elder, in the presence of their parents who had observed various abstinences in honor of the occasion. The children and their fathers remained inside a cord held by four old and venerable men representing the Chaks or Rain Gods, while the priest performed various acts of purification and blessed the candidates with incense, tobacco, and holy water. From that time on the elder girls, at least, were marriageable.

In both highlands and lowlands, boys and young men stayed apart from their families in special communal houses where they presumably learned the arts of war, and other things as well, for Landa says that the prostitutes were frequent visitors. Other youthful diversions were gambling and the ball game. The double standard was present among the Maya, for girls were strictly brought up by their mothers and suffered grievous punishments for lapses of chastity. Marriage was arranged by go-betweens and, as among all peoples with exogamous clans or lineages, there were strict rules about those with whom alliances could or could not be made – particularly taboo was marriage with those of the same paternal name. Monogamy was the general custom, but important men who could afford it took more wives. Adultery was punished by death, as among the Mexicans.

Ideas of personal comeliness were quite different from ours, although the friars were much impressed with the beauty of the Maya women. Both sexes had their frontal teeth filed in various patterns, and we have many ancient Maya skulls in which the incisors have been inlaid with small plaques of jade. Until marriage, young men painted themselves black (and so did warriors at all times); tattooing and decorative scarification began after wedlock, both men and women being richly elaborated from the waist up by these means. Slightly crossed eyes were held in great esteem, and parents attempted to induce the condition by hanging small beads over the noses of their children.

Death was greatly dreaded by all, the more so since the deceased did not automatically go to any paradise. Ordinary folk were buried beneath the floors of their houses, their mouths filled with food and a jade bead, accompanied by idols and the things that they had used while alive. Into the graves of priests they are said to have placed books. Great nobles, however, were cremated, a practice probably of Mexican origin, and funerary temples were placed above their urns; in earlier days, of course, inhumation in sepulchers beneath such mausoleums was the rule. To the Kokom dynasty of Mayapan was reserved the practice of mummifying the heads of their defunct lords, these being kept in the family oratories and fed at regular intervals – a practice which, if even more ancient, may explain why some early royal burials at Tik'al are missing their heads.

Society and politics

The ancient Maya realm was no theocracy or primitive democracy, but a class society with strong political power in the hands of an hereditary elite. To understand the basis of the state in sixteenth-century Yucatan, we have to go right to the heart of the matter, to the people themselves.

In Yucatan, every adult Maya had two names. The first came to him or her from the mother, but could only be transmitted from women to their offspring, that is, in the female line. The second derived from the father, and similarly was exclusively passed on in the male line. There is now abundant evidence that these two kinds of name represented two different kinds of cross-cutting and coexistent descent groups: the matrilineage and the patrilineage. There were approximately 250 patrilineages in Yucatan at the time of the Conquest, and we know from Landa how important they were. For instance, they were strictly exogamous (one had to marry out of the lineage), all inheritance of property was patrilineal, and they were self-protection societies, all members of which had the obligation to help each other. Titles deriving from early Colonial times show that they had their own lands as well, which is probably what Landa meant when he said that all fields were held "in common." As for the matrilineage, it probably acted principally within the marriage regulation system, in which matrimony with the father's sister's or mother's brother's daughter was encouraged, but certain other kinds forbidden.

Now, while among many more primitive people such kin groups are theoretically equal, among the Maya this was not so, and both kinds of lineage were strictly ranked; to be able to trace one's genealogy in both lines to an ancient ancestry was an important matter, for there were strongly marked classes. At the top were the nobles (almehen, meaning "he whose descent is known on both sides"), who had private lands and held the more important political offices, as well as filling the roles of high-ranking warriors, wealthy farmers and merchants, and clergy. The commoners were the free workers of the population, probably, like their Aztec cousins, holding in usufruct from their patrilineage a stretch of forest in which to make their milpas; but in all

133

likelihood even these persons were graded into rich and poor. There is some indication of serfs, who worked the private lands of the nobles. And at the bottom were the slaves who were mostly plebeians taken in war, prisoners of higher rank being subject to the knife. Slavery was hereditary, but these menials could be redeemed by payments made by fellow members of one's patrilineage.

134

By the time the Spaniards arrived, political power over much of the inhabited Maya area was in the hands of ruling castes of Mexican or Mexican-influenced origin. Yucatecan politics was controlled by such a group, which of course claimed to have come from Tula and Zuywa, a legendary home in the west. In fact, any candidate for high office had to pass an occult catechism known as the "Language of Zuywa." At the head of each statelet in Yucatan was the *halach winik* ("real man"), the territorial ruler who had inherited his post in the male line, although in an earlier epoch and among the highland Maya there were real kings *(ahawob)* who held sway over wider areas. The *halach winik* resided in a capital town and was supported by the products of his own lands, such as cacao groves worked by slaves, and by tribute.

The minor provincial towns were headed by the *batabob*, appointed by the *halach winik* from a noble patrilineage related to his own. These ruled through local town councils made up of rich, old men, led by an important commoner chosen anew each year among the four quarters which made up the settlement. Besides his administrative and magisterial duties, the *batab* was a war leader, but his command was shared by a *nakom*, a highly tabooed individual who held office for three years.

The Maya were obsessed with war. The Annals of the Kaqchikels and the Popol Vuh speak of little but intertribal conflict among the highlanders, while the sixteen states of Yucatan were constantly battling with each other over boundaries and lineage honor. To this sanguinary record we must add the testimony of the Classic monuments and their inscriptions. From these and from the eye-witness descriptions of the *conquistadores* we can see how Maya warfare was waged. The *holkanob* or "braves" were the footsoldiers; they wore cuirasses of quilted cotton or of tapir hide and carried thrusting spears with flint points, darts-with-spearthrower, and in late Post-Classic times, the bow-and-arrow. Hostilities typically began with an unannounced guerrilla raid into the enemy camp to take captives, but more formal battle opened with the dreadful din of drums, whistles, shell trumpets, and war cries. On either side of the war leaders and the idols carried into the combat under the care of the priests were the two flanks of infantry, from which rained darts, arrows, and stones flung from slings. Once the enemy had penetrated into home territory however, irregular warfare was substituted, with ambuscades and all kinds of traps. Lesser captives ended up as slaves, but the nobles and war leaders either had their hearts torn out on the sacrificial stone, or else were beheaded, a form of sacrifice favored by the Classic Maya.

133 134 (*Right, above*) Person of high rank in a palanquin, from a graffito incised on a wall at Tik'al. Rulers were carried onto the battlefield in very elaborate palanquins. (*Right, below*) Standing captive from Kalak'mul, incised on a bone from the Temple I tomb, Tik'al (Late Classic period).

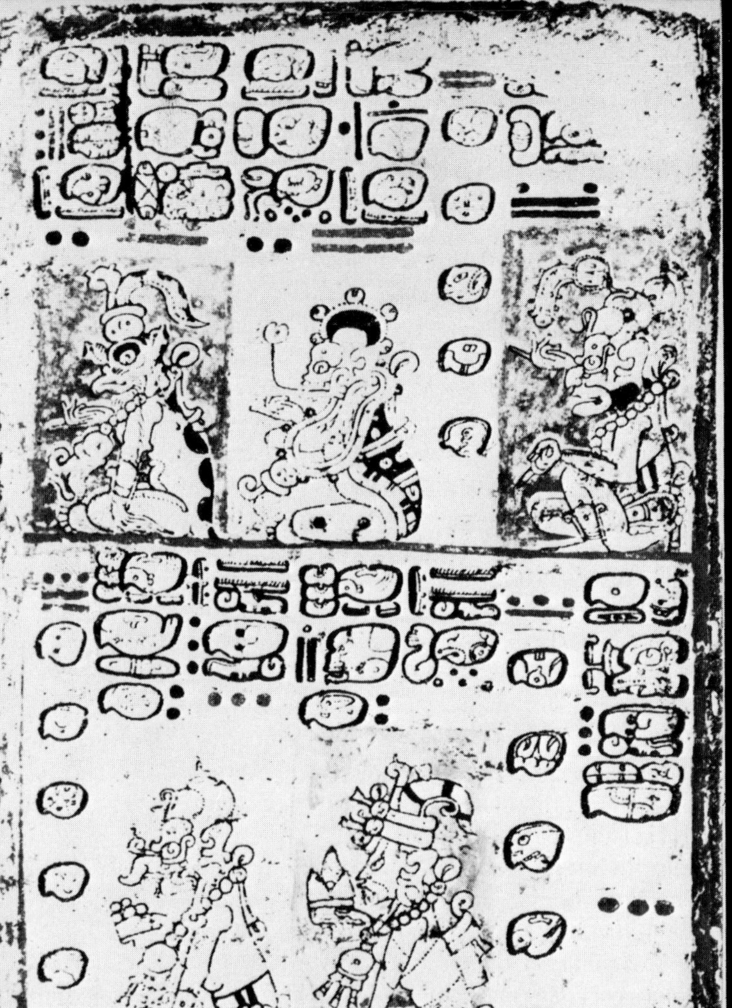

9·Maya Thought and Culture

Like all the indigenous populations of the New World, the Maya are deeply spiritual people; all students of the Maya, and anyone who has been among them for any length of time, can testify to this. Throughout the millennia, their thoughts and actions have been channeled by cosmological concepts of time and space, of the creation of sentient humans, as well as notions of the relation between the agricultural cycle (above all, that of maize, the staff of life) and the supernatural world. This is as true today as it was fifteen centuries ago. The Maya definitely do not "live by bread alone." It should be remembered that to the Mesoamericans (as well as to the civilizations of South and Southeast Asia), time is not linear, but cyclical; while we talk of the irreversible "arrow of time," this is not the case among the Maya and the Aztecs, who have always thought in terms of cycles of creation and destruction. To them, our world is only one in a succession of universes, and while it is doomed to annihilation like its predecessors, Creation will happen again and again.

In the world at large, the ancient Maya are famed for their ability to predict eclipses and for their independent invention of the zero concept in mathematics. Although in almost all the early civilizations of which we have record, it is extremely difficult to separate primitive scientific knowledge from its ritual context, this should not lead one to suppose that a people like the Maya or the Sumerians had not evolved a considerable body of empirically-derived information about the natural world. As we shall see, arithmetic and astronomy had reached a level comparable to that achieved by the ancient Babylonians and surpassing in some respects that of the Egyptians; but one should not exaggerate. Science in the modern sense was not present. In its place we find, as with the Mesopotamian civilizations, a combination of fairly accurate astronomical data with what can only be called numerology, developed by Maya intellectuals for religious purposes.

Nonetheless, our knowledge of ancient Maya thought must represent only a tiny fraction of the whole picture, for of the thousands of books in which the full extent of their learning and ritual was recorded, only four have survived to modern times (as though all that posterity knew of ourselves

135 (*Left*) The Dresden Codex is the most beautiful of the surviving folding-screen books of the Maya. Written on a long strip of bark paper, each page coated with fine stucco, much of it is concerned with 260-day ritual counts divided up in various ways, the divisions being associated with specific gods. The texts immediately above each deity contain their names and epithets. Ht 8 in. (20.3 cm).

136 Rabbit God writing in a folding-screen codex with jaguar-skin covers. Detail from a Late Classic cylindrical vase in codex style, northern Peten or southern Campeche. Eighth century AD.

were to be based upon three prayer books and *Pilgrim's Progress*). These are written on long strips of bark paper, folded like screens and covered with gesso. Pictorial representations on Classic Maya funerary pottery show that in Classic times the codices had jaguar-skin covers, and were painted by scribes using brush or quill pens dipped in black or red paint contained in cut conch-shell inkpots.

According to the early sources, the Maya books contained histories, prophecies, songs, "sciences," and genealogies, but our four examples are completely ritual, or ritual-astronomical, works compiled in the Northern Area during the Post-Classic. The Dresden Codex is the finest, and measures 8 inches high and 11¾ ft long (20.3 by 358.2 cm); while some of its content was certainly copied from Late Classic sources, some of the iconography of the Dresden has been shown by Karl Taube to be Aztec-influenced, so that it must date in its present form to just before the Conquest. The Madrid and the very fragmentary Paris codices are much poorer in execution than the Dresden but probably similar in date. Thompson even suggested that a Spanish priest might have obtained the Madrid Codex at Tayasal – not impossible, since two of its pages apparently incorporate paper fragments with Spanish writing.

In 1971 there was exhibited at the Grolier Club in New York a fourth Maya book which has since been labeled the "Grolier Codex"; it once belonged to a private collector in Mexico and on circumstantial evidence seemed to have been found in a wooden box in a cave near Tortuguero, Chiapas, within the previous three decades. Unfortunately in very bad condition, it comprises about one half of a twenty-page table concerned with the Venus cycle. Although its authenticity was vigorously disputed by Thompson, the radiocarbon date of AD 1230 from its paper is fully consistent with the Toltec-Maya style in which the glyphs and associated deities are drawn. It is now considered genuine by knowledgeable epigraphers, thus making the Grolier the earliest of the four pre-Conquest Maya manuscripts.

To these must be added the Classic Maya inscriptions. And then we have a great deal of very valuable information on Maya ritual in the early post-

137 Pages from the Grolier Codex, a Toltec-Maya book dealing with the planet Venus.

Conquest accounts, and in various esoteric texts like the Books of Chilam Balam and the Popol Vuh, written in Maya but transcribed into Spanish letters. From all these documents it can readily be seen that Maya life was deeply imbued with religious feeling, and that ritual behavior gave meaning and a sense of security to all strata of Maya society.

The universe and the gods

As has been said, the idea of cyclical creations and destructions is a typical feature of Mesoamerican religions. The Aztecs, for instance, thought that the universe had passed through four such ages, and that we were now in the fifth, to be destroyed by earthquakes. The Maya thought along the same lines, in terms of eras of great length, like the Hindu *kalpas*. There is a suggestion that each of these measured 13 bak'tuns, or something less than 5,200 years, and that Armageddon would overtake the degenerate peoples of the world and all creation on the final day of the thirteenth; the Great Cycle would then begin again. Thus, following the Thompson correlation, our own universe would have been created on 4 Ahaw 8 Kumk'u 13.0.0.0.0 (13 August 3114 BC), to be annihilated on 23 December AD 2012, when the present cycle of the Long Count reaches completion.

According to our post-Conquest Maya sources, the last Creation prior to our own ended with a great flood, a belief that is also found among the Aztecs, at the end of which the sky fell on the earth, and there was no light. A kind of interregnum now ensued, a time of magic and heroic doings celebrated in the early chapters of the Popol Vuh – before a new and more perfect world could be formed, the imperfections of the old one had to be expunged. For this task, a pair of twin heroes were necessary. The story begins with the birth of a first set of twins, sons of the old Creator Couple; when they had become young men, this pair are summoned to Xibalba – the Underworld – to be punished for having played a noisy game of ball on the earth's surface. After suffering various grim trials, they are sacrificed by the lords of Xibalba, and the head of one of them (who is none other than the Maize God) is hung in a tree, and magically impregnates Lady Blood, the daughter of an Underworld lord.

In disgrace, Lady Blood is exiled to the earth's surface, and in the house of the old woman gives birth to the Hero Twins, Hunahpu and Xbalanque (their K'iche', not their Classic names). These grow up to be tricksters and monster-killers, a familiar role for twin deities throughout much of the indigenous New World. One of their early triumphs is to transform their jealous half-brothers into monkey-men, and these – called One Howler and One Monkey in the Popol Vuh – become the patron deities of artists, scribes, musicians, and dancers. A more formidable task is to rid the universe of a monstrous, arrogant bird that falsely claims to be the Sun of this penultimate Creation, and this is none other than Wuqub' Kaqix, "Seven Macaw," whom we have already seen in the gigantic stucco masks of the Late Preclassic, and in the huge carved jade head from Altun Ha. The Hero Twins defeat Wuqub' Kaqix by shooting out his teeth with a blowgun pellet, then replacing them with soft maize; the great bird sickens, then dies.

52

At last the Twins achieve their final triumph, the defeat of the Lords of Xibalba. Summoned like their slain father and uncle into the Underworld, they are placed in various torture chambers that they manage to survive through trickery. They also defeat the dread lords in a ballgame, but are eventually killed themselves. The upper world gods do not wish them to die, however, and they are revived, and come into the court of Xibalba disguised as dancers and mountebanks. Through a clever stratagem, the wily youths manage to slay their terrible enemies in a true Harrowing of Hell. In victory,

141

they resurrect their father the Maize God, and rise to heaven as the Sun and the Moon. As Karl Taube has shown, the parallel with the agricultural cycle is patent in this myth. When the farmer plants his *milpa*, he sends the maize into the Underworld down the hole he has made with his digging stick; then, with the coming of the rains, the maize is "resurrected" as a young sprout. As for the Twins themselves, they become the role models for great Maya princes and rulers, certainly as early as Late Preclassic times when Popol Vuh iconography first appears in the archaeological record.

In their ground-breaking *Maya Cosmos*, Linda Schele, David Freidel, and Joy Parker have demonstrated that the next steps in Creation are recorded on several monuments, including Stela C at Quiriguá, and on Late Classic painted or carved vases. In darkness (because the sky is still lying on the earth), on 4 Ahaw 8 Kumk'u, the resurrected Maize God – called Hun Nal Yeh ("One Maize Revealed") in the Classic texts – has been brought by a canoe propelled by two aged Paddler Gods to a special place in the night sky. There he set up three hearthstones, to be seen as three bright stars in our constellation Orion. One of these is the Jaguar Throne, another is the Snake Throne, and a third the Water-lily Throne. At the same time, in the northern sky, within the Milky Way, he made a house of eight partitions (perhaps representing the cardinal and intercardinal points) and raised the Wakah Chan, a great World Tree; and there he started the stars in movement so that they would perpetually revolve counterclockwise around the North Celestial Pole. And atop the World Tree perched the Bird known as "Itzam Yeh," the Classic counterpart of Wuqub' Kaqix, now apparently revived to play a more positive role in our present universe.

Among the Maya, the Milky Way is the road of dead souls into the Under-world. It is thus no surprise to find sculpted on the sarcophagus lid of Hanab Pakal (the great seventh-century ruler of Palenque) a representation of the dead king descending down the Wakah Chan into the gigantic jaws of Xibalba; within his sarcophagus, however, he has been fitted with the green jade mask of the Maize God, so presumably Hanab Pakal is also to be resurrected and will rise to heaven through that same World Tree. 80

Each Maya capital city may have had its own variation on the basic Creation myth, so as to glorify the putative ancestors of reigning monarchs. This is certainly the case with Palenque, and the tablet which Hanab Pakal's son, Kan Balam, had placed in the Temple of the Cross. The opening clauses of the inscription take us back eight years before the 4 Ahaw 8 Kumk'u Creation event, to the birth of First Father (Hun Nal Yeh, the Maize God) and, 540 days later, to the birth of First Mother. From the latter are born K'awil, a snake-footed deity with smoking tube or axe fixed in the forehead, who acted as patron of the royal line throughout the Maya realm, and two enigmatic beings known in the literature only as GI and GIII.

The earth and the gods

Maya notions about our own world are by no means simple to reconstruct from our very uneven data, but apparently they conceived of the earth as flat and four-cornered, each angle at a cardinal point which had a color value: red for east, white for north, black for west, and yellow for south, with blue-green at the center. It was supported by four aged Pawahtuns, the quadripartite form of the old deity who ruled over the days at the end of the year. The sky, in turn, was held up at the corners (according to Landa) by four Bakabs, Atlantean gods with the appropriate color associations. Alternatively, the sky was supported by four trees of different colors and species, with the blue-green ceiba or silk-cotton tree at the center. Classic art and the Post-Classic codices suggest that the flat earth was also thought of as the back of a monstrous crocodile resting in a pool filled with water-lilies. Its counterpart in the sky was a double-headed serpent, a concept probably stemming from 138

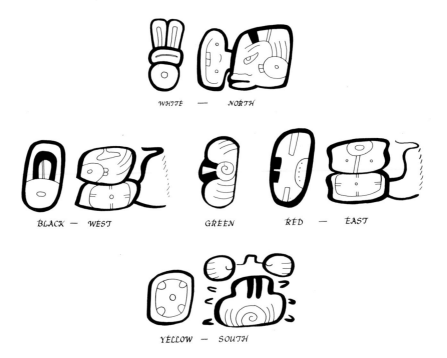

WHITE — NORTH

BLACK — WEST   GREEN   RED — EAST

YELLOW — SOUTH

138 Glyphs for the world directions and associated colors.

the fact that the word for sky, *kaan* or *chan*, is a homonym of the word for snake. Schele and her colleagues are surely right in thinking that this was the ecliptic – the apparent path of the sun, moon, Venus, and other celestial bodies – for their signs are marked on the serpent's body.

Exceedingly little is known about the Maya pantheon. That their Olympus was peopled with a bewildering number of gods can be seen in the eighteenth-century manuscript, "Ritual of the Bakabs," in which 166 deities are mentioned by name, or in the pre-Conquest codices where more than thirty can be distinguished. This theogonic multiplicity results in part from the gods having many aspects. First, in the case of certain gods, each was not only one but four individuals, separately assigned to the color-directions. Secondly, a number seem to have had a counterpart of the opposite sex as consort, a reflection of the Mesoamerican principle of dualism, the unity of opposite principles. Thirdly, some seem to have had young and old aspects, or (especially in Classic times) fleshed and fleshless guises. Fourthly, there was no clear dividing line between humans and animals, or even between species of animals, so that many supernaturals combine these elements in fantastic ways. And lastly, every astronomical god had an Underworld avatar, as he died and passed beneath the earth to reappear once more in the eastern sky.

While some Maya sources speak of a one-and-only god (Hunab K'u) who was incorporeal and omnipotent, this may be a concept introduced by the missionaries. The supreme deity was surely Itzamna ("Lizard House"),

139

pictured as an aged man with Roman nose in the codices, the inventor of writing and patron of learning and the sciences. His wife was Ix Chel, "Lady Rainbow," the old goddess of weaving, medicine, and childbirth; she was also the old Moon Goddess, and the snakes in her hair and the claws with which her feet and hands are tipped prove her the equivalent of Coatlicue, the Aztec mother of gods and men. All the other gods, including the Bakabs, were apparently the progeny of this pair. It is these two who are the old progenitor couple described in the Popol Vuh.

The Sun God, K'inich Ahaw, is very similar to Itzamna in the codices, and may have been one of his aspects. On his night journey beneath the earth, he becomes the Jaguar God of the Underworld of fearsome aspect, often pictured on Classic monuments. It is believed that a young, half-naked lady prominent in the Dresden Codex represents the young Moon Goddess, a youthful variant of Ix Chel known as Ix Ch'up ("The Woman"), who has romantic dalliances with various gods.

At the corners of the world were the benevolent and quadripartite Chak, the Rain God, whose worship, as Karl Taube has demonstrated, goes far back into Olmec times. Chak was deeply venerated by the pre-Conquest Maya who saw him as manifested in thunder and lightning bolts, and is one of the very few deities whose cult has survived among the living Maya. There were also the quadruple Bakabs, each of whom presided over one quarter of the 260-day period in turn.

139 Some gods of the Maya pantheon with their name glyphs, from the Dresden Codex. *a*, Death God; *b*, Chak, the Rain God; *c*, *k'u*, "god" (an image that can be substituted for others); *d*, Itzamna; *e*, Maize God; *f*, Ahaw K'in, the Sun God; *g*, Young Moon Goddess; *h*, K'awil, god of royal descent; *I*, Ek' Chuah, the Merchant God; *j*, Chak Chel, Old Moon Goddess and Goddess of Medicine.

Further, there were patrons of the classes and professions. Heading this list is K'uk'ulkan, a god who succeeded K'awil as presiding deity of the ruling caste; introduced after the Classic collapse, his cult reached a peak in Toltec times. Several war gods were venerated by the soldiers, some of them clearly deified heroes famed for their conquests. For the merchants and cacao growers there was Ek' Chuwah, with black face and Pinocchio nose. He also is of central Mexican origin, succeeding in the role of patron of the merchants the great Classic deity known to us only as "God L"; but the latter was also a war god, and appears in this guise on the world-destruction page of the Dresden Codex. There were also patron deities of hunters, fishers, beekeepers, tattoo artists, comedians, lovers, and even suicides. Assigned to the arts, such as music, dance, and writing and painting, were the Monkey-man Gods whose origin story is so vividly recorded in the Popol Vuh.

The Classic Maya Underworld

The Underworld (Xibalba, "Place of Fright," to the K'iche'; Metnal to the Yucatec) may have been multi-layered with nine corresponding "Lords of the Night"; the several torture houses through which the Hero Twins and their progenitor had to pass suggest that this was the case. This cold, unhappy place was the final destination of most Maya after death, and through it passed the heavenly bodies such as the sun and moon after they had disappeared below the horizon.

140 Rollout of a Late Classic cylindrical vase, probably from Naranjo, Guatemala. This scene takes place in darkness in the palace of God L (right), at the creation of our present era on 4 Ahaw 8 Kumk'u. Facing him are six major deities, including the Jaguar God of the Underworld and the yet-enigmatic GI.

141 Plate in codex style, from northern Guatemala or southern Campeche. Eighth century AD. In the center, the Maize God (Hun Hunahpu) emerges from the split surface of the earth, depicted as a turtle carapace, as he is resurrected by his Hero Twin sons, Hunahpu (left) and Xbalanque (right). The latter pours water from a jar to ensure the sprouting of the corn.

We now know that one important function of Classic Maya pictorial ceramics, whether painted or carved, was funerary, which is logical given that their final destination was as containers for food and drink (especially chocolate) in the tombs and graves of the honored dead. It is thus no surprise to find incredibly explicit pictorial references to the Underworld epic on Classic Maya pottery. The entire epic, of which the Popol Vuh preserves only a fragment, must have been written in codices that would have been the equivalent of the Egyptian Book of the Dead. On vases and on plates appear many of the *dramatis personae* familiar to us from the Popol Vuh: the Maize God, Wuqub' Kaqix, the Monkey-man Gods, and above all, Hunahpu and Xbalanque – the former recognizable from the black spots on his face and body, the latter from patches of jaguar skin. Both of these Hero Twins continued to play the roles of Underworld gods well into the Colonial period in the Maya highlands. Several Late Classic Maya vessels portray them in the act of resurrecting their father at the dawn of Creation, and more than a few celebrate them as the quintessential ballplayers who beat the lords of Xibalba at their own game.

140

pl. XVII

142 Section of paintings and hieroglyphic texts from the walls of Naj Tunich cave, Guatemala. The figure at top left is an *ah k'uhun*, a royal librarian and chief scribe, with his conch-shell inkpot. At bottom left is a ballplayer, complete with protective belt and knee-pad; this is Hunahpu, one of the Hero Twins in the Popol Vuh story. Late Classic, eighth century AD.

Funerary ceramics tell of a strange obsession of the Classic elite. This was the taking of ceremonial enemas by means of a leather or rubber syringe-bag fitted with a bone tube. The aged Pawahtun himself was often the recipient of this treatment, administered at the hands of a beautiful young consort. The exact substance injected remains in doubt, but the vases show the liquid was kept in wide-mouthed jars and had froth on top. This suggests the intoxicating *balche'* mead, and we do know from Aztec accounts of the Huaxtec, linguistic relatives of the Maya, that those people habitually intoxicated themselves by means of "wine" enemas. On the other hand, Peter Furst has pointed to the widespread custom in lowland South America of administering powerful hallucinogens in enemas, and has documented the custom among the contemporary Huichol of western Mexico (who use the potent peyote or spineless cactus buttons for the infusion). Incidentally, the otherwise unexplained bone tubes found in Classic Maya tombs and graves probably represented the surviving remains of the enema apparatus.

142   Deep caverns have always been conceptual entrances to Xibalba for past and present Maya. One such cave, now named Naj Tunich, was discovered in 1979 by local residents in karst terrain near Poptun, in the southeastern Peten. The cave is huge, measuring 2,790 ft (850 m) deep along its longest passage. It has ancient walls, Late Classic burials, and terminal Late

Preclassic pottery, but it was apparently thoroughly looted before archaeologists could get to it. The importance of Naj Tunich lies in its extensive hieroglyphic texts (altogether comprising about 400 glyphs) and scenes, all executed in carbon black on the cave walls. The latter include depictions of the ball game, amorous activities that are probably of a homosexual nature, and Maya deities, which not unexpectedly include the Hero Twins, Hunahpu and Xbalanque. The style of the writing and painting is closely related to Late Classic vases in "codex style," and must have been carried out by one or more artists or scribes skilled in the production of Maya books. According to the inscriptions, Naj Tunich was a pilgrimage site not only for the scribes who wrote these texts, but also for the rulers in whose courts they served.

But beyond their role as points of communication with the Underworld, James Brady of George Washington University has told us that in the Maya mind caves were intimately associated with mountains, and that it is in such caves that it was and still is believed that fertilizing rain is created before being sent into the sky; even today ceremonies are held inside them at the onset of the rainy season. Much of the Maya lowlands consists of limestone karst terrain, and is honeycombed with caves. There is little doubt that the Preclassic and Classic Maya often took care to place their ritual structures over caves so that temple-pyramids and palaces could be validated and energized by them. During a four-year project at Dos Pilas, in the Petexbatun region, Brady located 22 caves; one of them ran directly under El Duende, the largest pyramid in the city, and contained among its offerings Preclassic pottery. At the site of Oxk'intok' in Yucatan, another survey discovered no fewer than 37 caves. In effect, they must exist wherever the underlying geology is karstic, but have eluded discovery because their entrances are often little more than small holes or depressions in the ground. *Cenotes* can also be considered caves, albeit with partly collapsed roofs, and many are known to be considered holy places by the Maya – Brady even suggests that Chich'en Itza itself appears to be laid out around its two main cave features, the Xtolok Cenote, and the Sacred Cenote.

Rites and ritual practitioners

In contrast to that of the Aztecs, the late Post-Classic Maya clergy was not celibate. Sons succeeded their fathers to the office, although some were second sons of lords. Their title, Ah K'in ("He of the Sun") suggests a close connection with the calendar and astronomy, and the list of duties outlined by Landa makes it clear that Maya learning as well as ritual was in their hands. Among them were "computation of the years, months, and days, the festivals and ceremonies, the administration of the sacraments, the fateful days and seasons, their methods of divination and their prophecies, events and the cures for diseases, and their antiquities and how to read and write with the letters and characters," but they also kept the all-important genealogies. During the prosperity of Mayapan, an hereditary Chief Priest resided in that city whose main function seems to have been the overseeing of an academy for the training of candidates for the priesthood, but in no source do we find his authority or that of the priests superseding civil power.

The priest was assisted in human sacrifices by four old men, called Chaks in honor of the Rain God (recalling the sacrificial role of the Classic rain deity Chak), who held the arms and legs of the victim, while the breast was opened up by another individual who bore the title of Nakom (like the war leader). Another religious functionary was the Chilam, a kind of visionary shaman who received messages from the gods while in a state of trance, his prophecies being interpreted by the assembled priests.

Every single Maya ritual act was dictated by the calendar, above all by the 260-day count. These sacred performances were imbued with symbolic meaning. For instance, the numbers 4, 9, and 13 and the color-directions appear repeatedly. Before and during rituals food taboos and sexual abstinence were rigidly observed, and self-mutilation was carried out by jabbing needles and sting-ray spines through ears, cheeks, lips, tongue, and the penis, the blood being spattered on paper or used to anoint the idols. On the eve of the Conquest such idols were censed with copal and rubber as well as ritually fed. Human sacrifice was perpetrated on prisoners, slaves, and above all on children (bastards or orphans bought for the occasion). Nevertheless, before the Toltec era, animals rather than people may have been the more common victims, and we know that such creatures as wild turkeys, dogs, squirrels, quail, and iguanas were considered fit offerings for the Maya gods.

Our understanding of the Yucatecan ritual round is crippled by Landa's sporadic inability to distinguish between what he called "movable feasts," i.e. rites determined by the 260-day count, and those geared to the nineteen months of the 365-day Vague Year. But apparently the greatest ceremonies had to do with the inauguration of the New Year. These took place in every community within the Wayeb, the five unnamed and unlucky days at the close of the previous year, and involved the construction of a special road (perhaps like the Classic "causeways") to idols placed at a certain cardinal point just outside the town limits; a new direction was chosen each year in a four-year counterclockwise circuit. There were all sorts of omens, good or bad, for every year, but an inauspicious augury could be offset by expiatory rites, such as the well-known fire-walking ceremony in which priests ran barefoot over a bed of red-hot coals.

143

Throughout the year, there were agricultural rites and ceremonies for such important economic groups as hunters, beekeepers, fishermen, and artisans, probably geared to the 260-day count if we may rely on the testimony of the Madrid Codex, which seems mainly devoted to such matters. Increase of game, abundance of honey, and wax, and so forth were the purpose of these activities, which so often take the form of the "sympathetic magic" defined by Sir James Frazer, for instance compelling the rain to fall by having the Chaks empty water from pots onto a fire.

Despite past claims that Classic Maya societies were organized as theocracies, that is, as states ruled by priests, there is not the slightest evidence for the existence of priests in Classic times! It is entirely plausible that the office of priest was introduced to the Maya area in the Early Post-Classic by the

143 New Year ceremonies in the Dresden Codex. Below, the Death God sacrifices before the New Year image; middle, the idol of Itzamna in the temple; above, the Opossum God carries out the image of the Maize God to a shrine at the entrance of the town.

Toltecs. Thanks to recent decipherments of ceramic texts by David Stuart, Nikolai Grube, and others, we now know a great deal about Classic scribes, painters, and sculptors, and their supernatural patrons One Howler and One Monkey. They seem to have occupied the highest rank of ancient Maya society, for a highly talented artist/scribe of one vase ascribed to Naranjo is named as the son of the king of that city; and on another unprovenanced vase from the Peten, the king (*ahaw*) himself seems to be named as the scribe! Thanks to the practice of artists – both painters with brush pens and sculptors with carving tools – signing some of their works, we have several titles for such individuals; the most common are *ah tz'ib* ("scribe, painter"), *yuxul* ("his sculpting," a phrase found on both stone reliefs and on carved pottery), and *itz'at* ("wise, learned").

At the top of the scribal hierarchy in the royal palace, and perhaps playing a role equal to that of the grand vizier in Old World courts, was the individual with the title *ah k'uhun*, literally "he of the holy books," that is, the royal librarian. Identifiable by his sarong, unkempt hair wrapped in a headcloth, and bundle of what seem to be quill pens tied to the forehead, the *ah k'uhun* probably oversaw all ritual activities in the kingdom, kept the calendar, made astronomical calculations, taught calligraphy in scribal schools, negotiated royal marriages and diplomatic treaties, and tallied tribute and other offerings. In short, in the hands of this official was all of the learning and sciences of the Classic Maya.

The Classic elite were obsessed with blood, both their own and that spilled by high-ranking captives. Hieroglyphic and iconographic studies, particularly by David Joralemon and David Stuart, have shown the supreme significance of ritually shed blood by the Classic Maya rulers and their families. This was drawn at calendrically important intervals by men from the penis, and from the tongue by their wives. The penis-perforator was usually a stingray spine or bone "awl" end seems to have been ritually adorned and deified. Scenes on stelae once thought to have been concerned with water or maize kernels cascading from the lowered hands of rulers are now known to portray blood dripping from their mutilated members. Thus, "blood" signified noble lineage and descent, as it traditionally did in Europe.

Numbers and the calendar

Otto Neugebauer, the historian of science, considered positional, or place value, numeration as "one of the most fertile inventions of humanity," comparable in a way with the invention of the alphabet. Instead of the clumsy, additive numbers used by the Roman and so many other cultures of the world, a few peoples have adopted "a system whereby the position of a number symbol determines its value and consequently a limited number of symbols suffices to express numbers, however large, without the need for repetitions or creation of higher new symbols."

144 The Maya usually operated with only three such symbols: the dot for one, the bar for five and a stylized shell for nought. Unlike our system adopted from the Hindus, which is decimal and increasing in value from right to left, the Maya was vigesimal and increased from bottom to top in vertical columns. Thus, the first and lowest place has a value of one; the next above it the value of twenty; then 400; and so on. It is immediately apparent that "twenty" would be written with a nought in the lowest place and a dot in the second.

And what kind of calculations were made, and for what purposes? Landa says that the purely vigesimal notation was used by merchants, especially those dealing in cacao, and he mentions that computations were performed "on the ground or on a flat surface" by means of counters, presumably cacao beans, maize grains and the like. But the major use to which Maya arithmetic was put was calendrical, for which a modification was introduced: when days were counted, the values of the places were those of the Long Count, so that

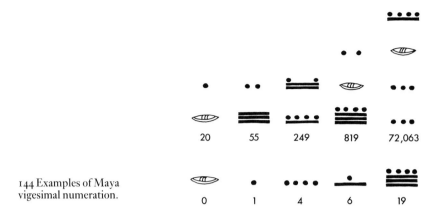

144 Examples of Maya vigesimal numeration.

while the first two places had values of one and twenty respectively, the third was thought of as a tun of 360 days (18 × 20), and so on up the line. For operating within their incredibly involved calendar, which among other things included the permutation of the Long Count with the 52-year Calendar Round, the Maya scribes found it necessary to construct tables of multiples; in the Dresden Codex, such tables include multiples of 13, 52, 65, 78, and 91 (the nearest whole number approximating one quarter of a year). Fractions find no place in their system – they were always trying to reach equations of cycles in which all numbers are integers, e.g. 73 × 260 days equals 52 × 365 days.

145 Glyphs for the cycles of the Long Count. *a*, Introducing Glyph; *b*, bak'tun; *c*, k'atun; *d*, tun; *e*, winal; *f*, k'in.

There are several kinds of dates expressed on the Classic Maya monuments and in the Dresden manuscript. Leading off a typical Classic inscription is the Initial Series, a Long Count date preceded by an Introductory Glyph with one of the nineteen month-gods infixed. This is immediately followed by the day reached in the 260-day count, and, after an interval filled by several other glyphs, the day of the month (365-day count). The intervening glyphs indicated which of the nine gods of the Underworld is ruling over that day (in a cycle of nine days), and lunar calculations which will be considered later.

However, this is not the whole story, for there are usually a number of other dates on the same monument. These are reached by Distance

145

Numbers, which tell one to count forwards or backwards by so many days from the base date, and while the intervals are usually of modest length, in a few examples these span millions of years. And then there are Period Ending dates in the inscriptions, which commemorate the completion of a k'atun, half-k'atun ("lahuntun," that is, ten tuns), quarter-k'atun ("hotun"), or tun. As an example one might cite the k'atun ending 9.18.0.0.0, which was celebrated all over the Central Area. "Anniversaries" also dot the Classic inscriptions; these are Calendar Round dates falling at intervals of so many k'atuns or tuns from some date other than the above-mentioned Period Ending Dates.

Why this apparent obsession with dating and the calendar? What do all the dates on the Classic monuments mean? They were formerly explained as the work of priests working out the positions of calendrical and celestial cycles in a religion which was essentially the worship of time itself. As we shall see, an utterly different explanation is not only possible, but certain.

The sun and the moon

To the Maya the round of 365 days (18 months of 20 days plus the 5 extra days of the Wayeb) was as close to the solar year as they cared to get. This "Vague Year" began among the Yucatec of Landa's time on 16 July (Julian calendar – the Gregorian was not to appear until 1582). Yet the earth actually takes about $365\frac{1}{4}$ days to complete its journey about the sun, so that the Vague Year must have continually advanced on the solar year, gradually putting the months out of phase with the seasons. We know that none of the Maya intercalated days on Leap Years or the like, as we do, and it has been shown that more sophisticated corrections thought to have been made by them are a figment of the imagination. Yet their lunar inscriptions show that they must have had an unusually accurate idea of the real length of the Tropical Year.

Curiously, the Maya went to far greater trouble with the erratic moon. In the inscriptions, Initial Series dates are followed by the so-called Lunar Series, which contains up to eight glyphs dealing with the cycles of that body. One of these records whether the current lunar month was of 29 or 30 days, and another tells the age of the moon on that particular Long Count date. Naturally, the Maya, like all civilized peoples, were faced with the problem of coordinating their lunar calendar with the solar, but there is no indication that they used the 19-year Metonic cycle (on which the "Golden Number" in the Book of Common Prayer is based). Instead, from the mid-fourth century AD each center made its own correction to correlate the two. However, in AD 682 the scribes of Copan began calculating with the formula 149 moons = 4,400 days, a system which was eventually adopted by almost all the Maya centers. In our terms, they figured a lunation to average 29.53020 days, remarkably close to the actual value 29.53059!

Of great interest to Mayanists and astronomers alike have been the eclipse tables recorded on seven pages of the Dresden Codex. These cover a cycle of 405 lunations or 11,960 days, which conveniently enough equals 46 × 260

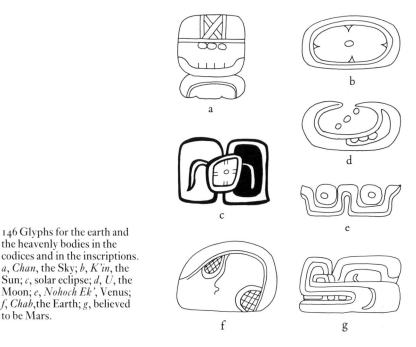

146 Glyphs for the earth and the heavenly bodies in the codices and in the inscriptions. *a, Chan,* the Sky; *b, K'in,* the Sun; *c,* solar eclipse; *d, U,* the Moon; *e, Nohoch Ek',* Venus; *f, Chab,* the Earth; *g,* believed to be Mars.

days – a kind of formula with which the Maya were deeply concerned, for such equations enabled them to coordinate the movements of the heavenly bodies with their most sacred ritual period. The ancients had found out, at least by the mid-eighth century AD but possibly much earlier, that lunar and solar eclipses could only occur within plus or minus 18 days of the node (when the moon's path crosses the apparent path of the sun); and this is what the tables are, a statement of when such events were likely. They also seem to have been aware of the recession of the node (or at least of its effect over long periods of time), and Eric Thompson suggested that the tables were constructed anew every half-century or so.

The celestial wanderers and the stars

Venus is the only one of the planets for which we can be absolutely sure the Maya made extensive calculations. Unlike the Greeks of the Homeric age, they knew that with the Evening and Morning Stars they were dealing with the same object. For the apparent, or synodical, Venus year they used the figure of 584 days (the actual value is 583.92, but they were close enough!), divided into four periods of varying length – Venus as Morning Star, disappearance at superior conjunction, appearance as Evening Star, and disappearance at inferior conjunction. After five Venus "years" its cycle met with the solar round, for $5 \times 584 = 8 \times 365 = 2,920$ days. Such an eight-year table can be found in the Dresden Codex and in the Grolier Codex.

Some have questioned whether the movements of planets other than Venus were observed by the Maya, but it is hard to believe that one of the

Dresden tables, listing multiples of 78, can be anything other than a table for Mars, which has a synodic year of 780 days; or that the Maya intellectuals could have overlooked the fact that 117, the product of the magic numbers 9 and 13, approximates the length of the Mercury "year" (116 days). The Maya savants were, of course, astrologers not astronomers, and all these bodies which were seen to wander against the background of the stars must have influenced the destiny of prince and pauper among the Maya.

With the correlation between the Christian calendar and the Maya Long Count now fixed, it should be possible, by consulting modern astronomical tables, to test the hypothesis, long held by David Kelley, that the Classic Maya inscriptions contain references to the heavenly bodies, above and beyond the lunar data which customarily follow initial Long Count dates on Maya stelae. Floyd Lounsbury of Yale has found confirmation of this hypothesis at the famous site of Bonampak', renowned for its murals. The Long Count position of the date associated with the great battle scene corresponds to 6 August AD 792 (Gregorian); the tables tell us that this date was marked by the inferior conjunction of Venus, by a zenith passage of the sun (as it passes directly overhead on its way to its winter "home"), and by the conjunction of Venus with the star Regulus.

That Venus played a sanguinary role among the Maya similar to that of Mars in the western Old World can be seen in the glyph for war: a Venus sign over another element, sometimes the Emblem Glyph of the site attacked. The date selected by the Bonampak' astronomers for this martial action was, in the words of Professor Lounsbury, "apparently seen as a propitious date for the undertaking, the outcome of which was such as to confirm the opinion." Likewise, the first visibility of Venus as Evening Star on 3 December AD 735, set off an attack on the southern Peten site of Seibal by Dos Pilas, leading to the capture of its ruler the next day. This unfortunate was kept alive for another twelve years, finally being sacrificed at a ritual ballgame timed for an inferior conjunction of Venus. "Star Wars" indeed!

Jupiter was also taken into account by the Classic Maya: the accession, at age forty-nine, and apotheosis twenty-one years later of the great Palenque ruler Kan Balam was set by the planet's second station (the end of its retrograde or east-to-west movement against the background of the stars). And most recently, the art historian Susan Milbrath has suggested a connection between this planet and the supernatural patron of royal lines, K'awil.

The astronomer Anthony Aveni and the architect Horst Hartung have determined that the ancient Maya used buildings and doorways and windows within them for astronomical sightings, especially of Venus. At Uxmal, for instance, all buildings are aligned in the same direction, except the House of the Governor. A perpendicular taken from the central doorway of this structure reaches a solitary mound about 3½ miles (5.6 km) away; Venus would have risen precisely above the mound when the planet reached its southerly extreme in AD 750. In collaboration with Sharon Gibbs, they have shown that in the case of the Caracol at Chich'en Itza, the whole building is aligned to the northerly extremes of Venus at about AD 1000, as is a diagonal sightline in one of the windows of the tower top; another diagonal sightline matched the planet's setting position when it attained its maximum southerly declination.

The Babylonian and Egyptian astrologers divided up the sky in various ways, each sector corresponding to a supposed figure of stars, so as to check the march of the sun as it retrogrades from sector to sector through the year, and to provide a star clock for the night hours. The zodiac of Mesopotamia is the best known of such systems. Did the Maya have anything like it? On this subject there was previously little agreement, but Linda Schele, David Kelley, and their colleagues are now convinced of its existence. The subject is indeed complex. As we have seen, the Maya conceived of the Milky Way as both a great World Tree with its crocodile-headed base in the south, and as the mystic road along which souls walk into the Underworld. Crossing the Milky Way at the constellation Scorpio (seen as a scorpion by both the Maya and ourselves) is the ecliptic, the apparent path of the sun, moon, and planets as they move against the background of stars.

In Maya iconography, the ecliptic appears as a two-headed sky-serpent, its body marked with astronomical signs; a stylized form of the creature can be seen in the "ceremonial bars" carried by Classic rulers. It has been recognized for years that two much-damaged pages of the Paris Codex show a scorpion, a peccary, and other beings pendant from the sky-serpent, and a similar series appears sculpted on the Nunnery at Chich'en Itza. From Bishop Landa's account, we know that the Yucatec Maya called the zodiacal constellation Gemini *ak*, "peccary," just one of a number of clues that the zodiac was present among these people.

The nature of Maya writing

Notable advances have been made in epigraphy, and in the decipherment of the Maya writing system, but if by "decipherment" we mean the matching of a sign or sign group to a specific sound or word in the ancient language, then probably only about half of the script has actually been "broken." Nonetheless, at this point in time we certainly understand the meaning of many more glyphs with some precision, even if we do not always know how they were pronounced in Maya. This means that the ancient Maya are now the only truly historical civilization in the New World, with records going back to the third century after Christ.

A half century ago, however, it could truly be said that few studies had made such little advancement with so much effort as the decipherment of the Maya script. This is not to say that a great deal was not understood, but there is a difference between unraveling a meaning for a sign, and matching it with a word in a Mayan tongue. Progress was most rapid on those glyphs that were of mainly calendrical or astronomical significance. For instance, by the mid-nineteenth century the Abbé Brasseur de Bourbourg had discovered Landa's *Relación*, from which he was able to recognize day glyphs and interpret the bar-and-dot numeration in the codices. It was quickly discovered that Maya writing was to be read in double columns from left to right, and top to bottom. At the turn of the century all of the following had been correctly deciphered by scholars in Europe and America: the zero and "twenty" signs,

147

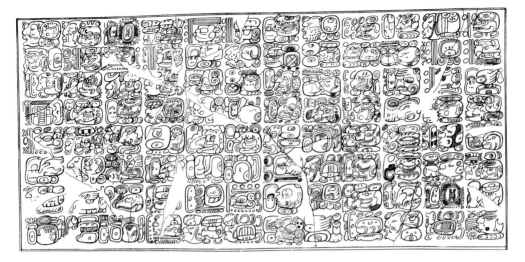

147 Tablet of the 96 Hieroglyphs, from Palenque. A very long text of the Late Classic period, marking the first k'atun anniversary of the accession to the throne by K'inich K'uk' Balam II ("Great Sun Quetzal Jaguar") in AD 764. The text is completely historical, containing the king's descent from Hanab Pakal.

the world directions and the colors, Venus, the months (also in Landa), and the Long Count. In a remarkable collaboration between astronomers and epigraphers, the mysteries of the Lunar Series had been unveiled by the early 1930s. But after these intellectual triumphs, fewer and fewer successes were scored, leading a few pessimists such as Sylvanus Morley and Eric Thompson to the quite unfounded claim that there was little else in these texts but calendrical and astronomical mumbo-jumbo.

It is generally accepted among linguists that all true writing systems express the utterances of a particular language. Earlier generations of scholars once held that some early scripts, such as Chinese and Egyptian, were "ideographic" in that they expressed thoughts directly without the intervention of language, but this has proved to be a delusion. All, we now realize, have a strong phonetic component (they denote sounds), no matter how pictorial some of the signs may look. Yet, even in heavily phonetic scripts including our own alphabetic one, there are some signs (for instance, our mathematical notation) which are purely semantic and can be "read" in any tongue on earth.

True writing emerged simultaneously with the evolution of complex societies in various parts of the Old World. All these early scripts are simultaneously logographic and phonetic: that is, they have a large number of logograms, signs standing for parts of words or (less commonly) whole words, along with phonetic and semantic ("meaning") signs to help in their reading. In logophonetic writing, semantic and phonetic elements are usually complexly intertwined, sometimes in a single hieroglyph or "character," and the logograms themselves require a certain degree of memorization, so such scripts were always more easy to read than to write. In Chinese (and in ancient Sumerian) the auxiliary semantic signs accompany logograms or phonetic signs to indicate the class of things the referred item belongs to (such as "wood," "water," and so on). These are not used in some scripts, but phonetic signs are universally employed to indicate the pronunciation of a logogram. For example, in writing the Maya word *witz*, "mountain," the scribe often prefixed to the logogram for the word the syllabic sign *wi*.

wi

witz

Behind the phonetic signs in all logophonetic systems is the principle of the rebus. While many logograms may have originated as pictures of actual objects, as in Egypt and China, most of the nouns and verbs in a language are more abstract and thus not so easily visualized. But here the scribe could take a pictorial logogram and exploit it for its sound value alone, as the sign for "fire" could be utilized in English as a sign meaning to "fire" or sack a subordinate. As children we have all run across such examples of rebus or puzzle writing as "I saw Aunt Rose," expressed by pictures of an eye, a saw, an ant, and a rose flower. The Mixtecs and Aztecs used such writing to record personal and place names, and it was apparently the only kind of script they knew.

In many ancient logophonetic scripts, the phonetic component takes the form of a syllabary, in which each sign represents a complete syllable (usually a consonant followed by a vowel), although each of the "pure" vowels will have its own sign. This is the case with the *kana* syllabary of Japanese, which gives the grammatical endings for Chinese-derived logograms expressing word roots. Some peoples have eschewed logograms altogether or relegated them to minor importance, and have constructed totally syllabic systems; the two most famous examples are the Linear B syllabary of Bronze Age Greece, and the Cherokee syllabary invented in the nineteenth century by Sequoyah.

The ultimate reduction to an almost (but never completely) phonetic script is the alphabet, perfected by the Greeks from a script handed to them by their Phoenician trading partners in the eastern Mediterranean. In the alphabet, most of the phonemes of the language – the smallest distinctive units of speech – become separately indicated, instead of appearing together as syllables.

With these preliminary remarks, what kind of a system do we then find in the Maya script? Bishop Landa has given to us his famous "alphabet" in 148 which some twenty-nine signs are presented. Several extremely distinguished Maya scholars have stumbled badly in trying to read the codices and the inscriptions with Landa's treacherous "ABC," while some have gone so far as to declare it a complete fraud. A more careful examination suggests that this is really not an alphabet in the usual sense. For instance, there are three

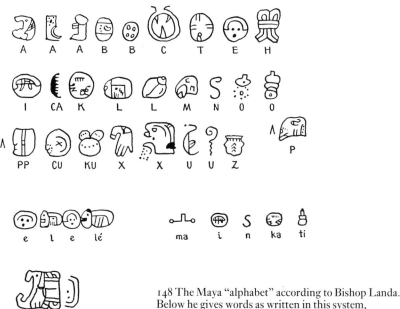

148 The Maya "alphabet" according to Bishop Landa.
Below he gives words as written in this system,
which we now know is syllabic rather than alphabetic.

signs for "A," two for "B," and two for "L." Secondly, several signs are quite clearly glossed as syllables of the consonant-vowel sort, i.e. *ma*, *ca*, and *cu*. We shall consider this important point later.

After the almost complete failure of decipherments along the strictly phonetic lines suggested by the Landa "alphabet," a diametrically opposite line was taken by many authorities, namely that the script was purely "ideographic," with perhaps a few rebus signs imbedded in the texts from time to time. That is to say, any one sign could have as many referents or associations as the priests could think up, and that only they could read the holy signs, which in general character were more ritualistic than linguistic. There is a striking resemblance between this position and that of the would-be decipherers of the Egyptian script before the great discoveries of Champollion.

This resemblance was not lost upon the Russian epigrapher Yuri Knorosov, a student of Egyptian hieroglyphic writing. In 1952, he began publishing a series of studies which re-opened the question of the Landa "alphabet" and the possibility of phoneticism in the Maya script. About 287 signs, not including variants, appear in the codices. If the system were completely alphabetic, then the language of the texts would have contained this many phonemes; if purely syllabic, then there would have been about half this number of phonemes. Both are linguistic impossibilities. On the other hand, if all signs were semantic – representing units of meaning only – then the script represented an incredibly small number of ideas, certainly not enough for civilized communication. With this in mind, Knorosov presented

149

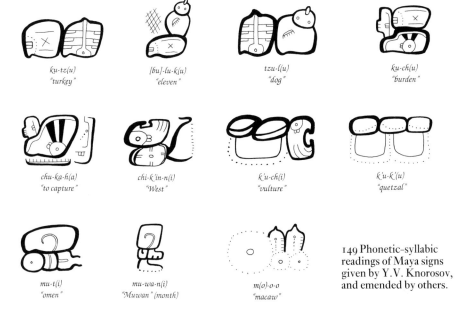

| ku-tz(u) | [bu]-lu-k(u) | tzu-l(u) | ku-ch(u) |
| "turkey" | "eleven" | "dog" | "burden" |

| chu-ka-h(a) | chi-k'in-n(i) | k'u-ch(i) | k'u-k'(u) |
| "to capture" | "West" | "vulture" | "quetzal" |

| mu-t(i) | mu-wa-n(i) | m(o)-o-o |
| "omen" | "Muwan" (month) | "macaw" |

149 Phonetic-syllabic readings of Maya signs given by Y.V. Knorosov, and emended by others.

convincing evidence that the Maya were writing in a mixed, logophonetic system in which phonetic and semantic elements were combined as in Sumerian or Chinese, but that they also had a fairly complete syllabary.

Knorosov's starting point was Landa's "ABC." Thompson had already demonstrated that the bishop's native informant had mistaken his instructions, that is, he gave the Maya sign not for the letter itself, but for the names of the letters; see, for instance, the first "B," which shows a footprint on a road – "road" is *be* in Yucatec, and this is exactly what the Spaniards call that letter. But the point is that this is really a partial and much flawed syllabary, not an alphabet, and Knorosov was able to show that words of the very frequent consonant-vowel-consonant (CVC) sort were written with two syllabic signs standing for CV-CV, the final vowel (usually but not always the same as the first) not being pronounced. The proof of phonetic-syllabic writing is, of course, in the reading, and a number of Knorosov's readings have long been confirmed by the contexts in which the signs appear in the codices, especially by the pictures which accompany various passages of text.

If this were all that needed to be done, it would be a simple job to read the Maya hieroglyphs, but the semantic dimension is very much there. Phonetic complements were often attached to logograms to help in their reading, either prefixed as a representation of the initial sound of the sign, or postfixed as the final consonant; the recognition of these has notably advanced the process of decipherment. Phonetic redundancy of this sort was already being practiced in the Classic; for example, David Kelley was the first to notice that the second part of the name of the great Palenque ruler Hanab

150   Pakal could be written either as a picture of a hand-shield (*pakal*, in Maya), or phonetically as *pa-kal-l(a)*, or both. Epigraphers actively search for such substitutions, for that is the basic way that we learn how the logograms were actually pronounced.

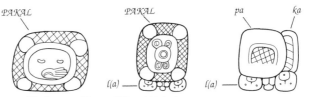

150 Variant spellings of Hanab Pakal's second name. Logograms in upper case, phonetic signs in lower case.

Although ridiculed by Thompson and his followers, Knorosov's phonetic approach is now universally utilized by Maya epigraphers. Since the initial work of Knorosov and Kelley, the recognition of phonetic construction in the script has proceeded at such a pace that epigraphers are now in general agreement on over 140 signs that have phonetic value (some of them, of course, variations on one and the same syllabic sign). It is also now recognized that in Maya, as in many ancient scripts, a number of signs are polyvalent, that is, a particular sign may have more than one phonetic reading, and it may also be read for its logographic value. For example, in English the compound sign *ch* has totally different values in the words *chart*, *chorus* and *chivalry*.

As each new phonetic decipherment has been made, we have been brought closer to identifying the language of the inscriptions and of the surviving books. As has been said in Chapter 1, this has turned out to be Cholti, a now-extinct member of the Cholan branch of Mayan. Even the inscriptions of Chich'en Itza seem to be written in Cholti. But what about Yucatec Maya? To the ancient scribes, this apparently lacked the literary prestige of Cholti, although some Yucatec spellings are found in the Dresden and Madrid codices; even further, the name of Hanab Pakal's son is written as "Kan Balam" rather than in Cholan ("Chan Bahlum," a wrong spelling found in earlier editions of this book).

All four codices deal exclusively with religious and astronomical matters, as is quite obvious from the pictures of gods associated with the texts, from the tables, and from the high frequency of passages geared to the 260-day count. Thus, we have in these texts little more than short phrases of esoteric significance, which often seem to match passages in the Books of Chilam Balam.

History graven in stone

What, then, of the subject matter of the inscriptions? Until quite recently, the prevailing opinion was that this was in no way different from that of the books; and further, that all those dates recorded on the monuments were

151 Some Emblem Glyphs from the Classic monuments. *a*, *b*, Palenque; *c*, *d*, Yaxchilan; *e*, Copan; *f*, Naranjo; *g*, Machakila; *h*, Piedras Negras; *i*, Seibal; *j*, Tik'al. The affixes attached to the left and top of the main signs spell *k'ul ahaw*, "holy king [of]."

witnesses to some sort of cult in which the time periods themselves were deified. The great John Lloyd Stephens was of a different mind, writing about Copan:

> One thing I believe, that its history is graven on its monuments. No Champollion has yet brought to them the energies of his enquiring mind. Who shall read them?

The discovery within the last few decades of the historical nature of the monumental inscriptions has been one of the most exciting chapters in the story of New World archaeology.

It began in 1958, when Heinrich Berlin published evidence that there was a special kind of sign, the so-called "Emblem Glyph," associated with specific archaeological sites, and recognizable from the same kind of glyphic elements which appear affixed to each. Thus far, the Emblem Glyphs for over thirty Classic centers – including Tik'al, Piedras Negras, Copan, Quirigua, Seibal, Naranjo, Palenque, and Yaxchilan – have been surely identified. Berlin suggested that these were either the names of the cities themselves or of the dynasties that ruled over them, and proposed that on the stelae and other monuments of these sites their histories might be recorded. Thanks to the research of epigraphers Peter Mathews, John Justeson, and William Ringle, we now know what Emblem Glyphs really are: they are titles

151

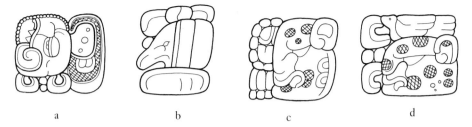

152 Historical glyphs in the monumental texts. *a*, birth ("upended frog"); *b*, accession ("toothache"); *c*, "Shield Jaguar"; *d*, "Bird Jaguar."

of Maya kings describing each as the *ch'ul ahaw* or "divine lord" of a kingdom whose name appears as the main sign of the glyph.

The next breakthrough was by Tatiana Proskouriakoff of the Carnegie Institution, who analyzed thirty-five dated monuments from Piedras Negras. The arrangement of stelae before structures she found was not random; rather, they fell into seven groups. Within a single such group, the time span covered by all the dates on the stelae is never longer than an average lifetime, which immediately raised the possibility that each group was the record of a single reign. This has now proved to be so. The first monument in a series shows a figure, usually a young man, seated in a niche above a platform or plinth; on this stela two important dates are inscribed. One is associated with a

152*b* glyph like an animal's head with a toothache, and has been shown to record the accession to power of the young man; the other appears with the "upended frog" glyph and is that same person's date of birth. Later monuments in a particular group celebrate marriages and the birth of offspring, and Proskouriakoff was able to identify the signs for personal names and titles, particularly of women who are quite prominent in Classic Maya sculpture. Military victories were also marked with great frequency, especially if an important enemy happened to have been taken captive by the ruler.

Thus, virtually all the figures that appear in Classic reliefs are not gods and priests but dynastic autocrats and their spouses, children, and subordinates. As the records for one reign come to an end, the next begin with the usual accession motif. Among the more complete documents which we have for the temporal dynasties which ran the ancient Maya centers are the inscriptions carved on the many stone lintels of Yaxchilan; from these Proskouriakoff reconstructed the history of the extremely militant "Jaguar" dynasty, which ruled the site in the eighth century AD. The record begins with the exploits of a lord whom she called "Shield Jaguar"; he was succeeded in AD 752 by his son "Bird Jaguar." As an example of how much of the writing that accompanies the reliefs celebrating the victories of this ruler can now be read or at

153 least interpreted, we have Lintel 8 of Yaxchilan, which begins with a Calendar Round date falling in AD 755. Below this is Knorosov's *chukah* or "capture" glyph, then a glyph resembling a jeweled skull, which is obviously the name of the prisoner on the right. Above right, the second glyph is that of Bird Jaguar himself (the figure with spear), beneath which is the Emblem Glyph of Yaxchilan.

7 Imix

14 Sek

Chukah
(he
captured)

"Jeweled
Skull"

2nd
captive

2nd captive   "Jeweled Skull"

u bak
(his
captive)

Bird-
Jaguar

Yaxchilan
Emblem
Glyph

153 Lintel 8, Yaxchilan. A record of the capture of "Jeweled Skull" and one other enemy by "Bird Jaguar" and a companion.

Of special interest are those inscriptions that indicate the interference of some centers with the destinies of others. For instance the Yaxchilan Emblem Glyph appears with one of the most prominent women in the Bonampak' murals, and, thanks to a royal marriage, the glyph for Dos Pilas appears on monuments at Naranjo. Piedras Negras is not far downstream from Yaxchilan, and the famous Lintel 3 from that site is now believed to show a royal visitor from Yaxchilan in attendance at a council called in the late eighth century to choose a successor to the Piedras Negras throne. As we shall see below, this interference took on major dimensions in the affairs of a number of cities in the southern lowlands.

In 1973, Linda Schele and Peter Mathews were able to announce at a conference in Palenque that they had worked out the dynastic record of all the Palenque rulers going back to AD 465; this record has since been extended as far back as AD 431, the accession date of Palenque's first ruler, by them and Floyd Lounsbury. Thanks to their research, we can now place such important figures as Hanab Pakal and Kan Balam in relation to the stupendous art and architecture that was created for them. Palenque, like Yaxchilan had entered into the realm of history.

Important glyphs now known to relate to dynastic affairs include the signs for events such as battles (the "star-shell" glyph), inauguration or "seating" in office, ritual blood-letting, and death and burial, in addition to the birth and accession glyphs. As one would expect with ruling families obsessed with noble lineage and marriage affiliation, there are a number of relationship glyphs which have now been recognized, such as "child of father," "child of mother," "child of parent," and "wife" (*atan* in Maya), as well as a sign expressing the relationship (unpleasant in the extreme) between a local dynast and an important captive whom he had taken.

Maya superstates

As the decipherment has evolved, ideas about how the nature of the Classic Maya political system in the Central Area have also been modified. Sylvanus Morley had thought that there had been a great political entity which he called the "Old Empire," but once the full significance of Emblem Glyphs had been recognized, it was clear that there never had been any such thing. In its stead, Mayanists proposed a more Balkanized model, in which each "city-state" was essentially independent of all the others; the political power of even large entities like Tik'al would have been confined to a relatively small area, the distance from the capital to the polity's borders seldom exceeding a day's march. When it became known that warfare between polities was frequent, the main motivation behind these activities was not believed to be control and territorial aggrandizement, but the need for royal captives destined for humiliation and sacrifice.

Based on a better understanding of Classic texts, particularly verbs relating to royal actions, Simon Martin and Nikolai Grube have come up with a model that lies somewhere between an imperial and a Balkan one. Basically, we now know that not all Maya polities were equal: the kings of some lesser states were said to be "possessed" by the rulers of more powerful ones (the phrase *y-ahaw*, "his king," gives away the relationship). Likewise, royal investitures in such vassal states were sometimes witnessed and therefore validated by the foreign "divine ruler" to whom they owed allegiance. Other forms of dominance-dependence relationships included royal visits, gift-giving, joint ritual activity, and marriage.

While city-states such as Palenque, Copan, and Piedras Negras exercised considerable political control over wide areas beyond their borders, the two giant "superstates" were Tik'al and Kalak'mul, the latter being the largest of all Maya cities, and it hardly surprising to find that they were bitter enemies through much of Classic history. As testified by diplomatic activities, Kalak'-mul had extensive influence over Kankuwen, Piedras Negras, Dos Pilas, El Perú, Naranjo, and Caracol, a large and fluctuating alliance directed against Tik'al. K'alakmul's ability to wage war was formidable: in AD 599 and 611 it attacked Palenque, 150 miles (240 km) to the southwest, in 631 it conquered Naranjo, far to the southeast, and in the year 657, Tik'al itself. Tik'al finally had its revenge on 5 August 695, when forces under its great king Hasaw Chan K'awil defeated Kalak'mul and captured its king, Yich'ak K'ak' ("Fiery Claw") – a triumph recorded on the wooden lintel of Temple I, under which Hasaw Chan K'awil is interred.

By the eighth century, the age of superstates was over. No longer could a few powerful polities have hegemony over others. As the system broke down, an intense military rivalry among lesser states sprang up, and the Maya low-

154

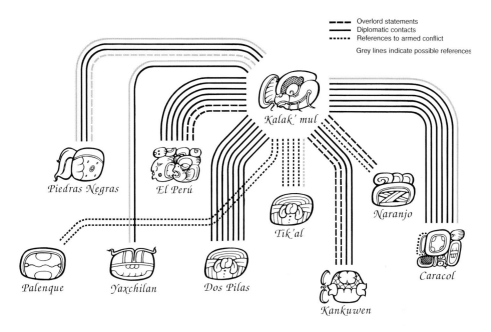

154 Kalak'mul's dominance of the Maya lowlands during the Classic period, as deduced from inscriptions recording forms of diplomatic exchange between the city and nearby kingdoms, With rival Tik'al and Palenque, the relationship was one of armed conflict.

lands became truly Balkanized. Spiralling interregional warfare and its attendant miseries and disruptions (for which the Petexbatun sites give ample testimony) were surely factors in the ultimate breakdown of Classic Maya civilization.

History and the supernatural

If the inscriptions are largely about history, then why the Lunar Series and the calculations far into the past and future? Because the Classic Maya elite believed in astrology, and must have consulted their scribes for lunar and other cosmic auguries at every important civil event, as did the Babylonians, Etruscans, Egyptians, and many other peoples of the Old World. There is a logic to astrology which not only the ancients have found compelling – Kepler and Newton did likewise – so we need not condemn the Maya for their beliefs. Another Maya concern was with royal lineage, and we find figures and dates on some monuments that can only refer to distant ancestors. Thus, Berlin showed that the dates in inscriptions of the Temple of the Cross at Palenque fall into three groups. The first are so ancient that they could only be referring back to deified ancestors of a legendary epoch, immediately before and just after Creation; the next may have to do with distant progenitors of a more intermediate time; and the third are connected with contemporary historical events.

The tablet of the Temple of the Cross celebrates the accession to the

Palenque throne by Kan Balam following the death of his father, Hanab Pakal, in AD 683. Now, Hanab Pakal was born on a day 8 Ahaw in the 260-day count. The very earliest date on the tablet is 3,722 years earlier, and also falls on a day 8 Ahaw, which in itself is suspicious. Floyd Lounsbury has demonstrated that on this initial date, a mythical ancestress was born, but in addition the interval between her birth and that of Hanab Pakal – 1,359,540 days – is an integral multiple of seven different important Maya periods, including the synodic period of Mars! It is inescapable that the initial date was thus contrived to fit the needs of numerology and astrology, thus intertwining religion, genealogy, and history in the characteristic Maya style.

Name-tagging

In recent years, a group of young epigraphers has forged ahead with new readings that throw light on entirely unexpected areas of ancient Maya culture. One of these is what has come to be known as "name-tagging," the labeling of objects with their names and with the names of their owners. The first known case of this concerns a pair of ground obsidian ear spools from a Classic period royal tomb at Altun Ha, Belize. Peter Mathews showed that the texts incised on each read *u tup,* "his ear spool," followed by the ruler's name.

In 1972, I discovered that there is a formulaic, repetitive hieroglyphic text on Classic Maya ceramics, usually placed below the rim, which I christened the Primary Standard Sequence (or PSS). I hypothesized that this was some sort of funerary chant (since these vessels are almost always in burial contexts), but a younger generation of Mayanists has found otherwise: Stephen Houston, David Stuart, and Karl Taube have shown that part of the PSS describes the form of the vessel as well as its contents (such as chocolate or *sak ul,* a white maize gruel). This breakthrough received striking confirmation with an unusual screw-top jar from an Early Classic tomb at Río Azul: the painted text on it said that it contained chocolate (written *ka-ka-w[a],* "cacao'), and subsequent tests carried out by the Hershey Company proved that this had indeed been the case.

On a few Maya vases the Classic artist-scribes went one step further, by signing their own works of art, a custom otherwise unknown in Mesoamerica. And on one vase known to have been painted in Naranjo, the artist gave his pedigree, noting that his mother was a princess of Yaxha, while his father was none other than Naranjo's king. Among the ancient Maya, it seems, artists and scribes belonged to the very highest stratum of a rigidly ranked society. David Stuart, who made this remarkable discovery, has gone on to find the signatures of individual sculptors on carved reliefs from several Usumacinta cities; in some instances, several artists worked on the same relief, which they all signed in their distinctive hands.

Name-tagging was not confined to portable objects only. The Maya who lived in these cities named many other things in the man-made and natural worlds. At Copan, for example, it has been found by Linda Schele, David Stuart, and Nikolai Grube that stelae, altars, buildings, plazas, sections of cities, and even complete cities received proper names. Berlin had posed the question of whether the main signs of Emblem Glyphs are toponyms or the names of ruling lineages. There are now cogent reasons to think that the former is the case. In fact, toponyms have now been found to be widespread in Maya inscriptions of the Classic period, and not just in Emblem Glyphs; there are even toponyms for supernatural places, such as the "Three-Stone-Place" which saw the first moment of Creation, and a mysterious, probably sinister location known as "Black Hole."

Spiritual alter-egos

This new generation of epigraphers has opened a window into the supernatural world of the Maya by another decipherment. The glyph in question appears often in ceramic texts as something possessed by "Holy Lords," that is, rulers of cities. It is read as *way*, a term that remains in use among many Maya groups for an individual's alter-ego spirit or co-essence, conceived as an animal counterpart (which might be anything from a jaguar to a mouse). According to the ceramic texts and accompanying images, each ruler had such a *way*, often a fantastic chimera combining the features of two or three animals, with whom he was in a special kind of relationship.

Way has a further meaning of "sleep" in some Mayan tongues, and it is possible that such mystic contacts were made in dreams; it is certainly suggestive that a few inscriptions point to certain Classic buildings as "sleeping places," where Maya kings may have sought out these spirits, like the vision quest of native North Americans.

The great Maya decipherment is a continuing process, and as it progresses we are taken step by step even further into the mythological and supernatural world that was so important to the ancient Maya. The work of dedicated epigraphers, linguists, and iconographers has put us in touch with realms of Maya thought and behavior that were undreamed of by earlier generations of archaeologists, and has established a bridge to the lives and thoughts of those millions of modern Maya whose culture has survived centuries of oppression.

10· The Enduring Maya

The seven-and-a-half million or so Maya alive in the world today are survivors: they have endured repeated cycles of conquest that continue unabated even today. What have kept the Maya people culturally and even physically viable are their hold on the land (and that land on them), a devotion to their community, and an all-pervading and meaningful belief system. It is small wonder that their oppressors have concentrated on these three areas in incessant attempts to destroy them as a people, and to exploit them as a politically helpless labor force. As the novelist and anthropologist Oliver La Farge put it over a half century ago, "from the Conquest until recently there has been a steady drive, with some reversals, to destroy the Indian ownership of large blocks of land which forms the physical and economic base of tribal solidarity and of freedom from the necessity to work for non-Indians."

La Farge, largely drawing on Guatemalan data, saw five broad stages in the history of the Maya since the initial invasion of their lands by the Spaniards. The first is the *Conquest Period*, from 1524 until the end of the sixteenth century. This was a violent era, shattering Indian cultural structures – although some native polities, particularly in the Peten, were not subdued until the close of the following century. The next stage was *Colonial Indian*, which lasted until 1724, at which time the Spanish Crown abolished the *encomienda* system, an oppressive institution which had given Spanish land barons total right to Indian forced labor in return for the supposed conversion of the natives to the Christian religion. It was a time when Spanish and Christian elements were absorbed wholesale into the fabric of Maya life and somewhat altered to fit the pattern of native culture; many Maya traits were destroyed or mutilated, while others were greatly changed.

During the *Transition Period*, lasting until the colonies broke away from Spain about 1820, life became more tolerable for the Maya, as Spanish control slowly relaxed, and suppressed Maya cultural traits re-emerged. It was during this time that traditional Maya patterns took on the form that they retain today.

Recent Indian I was ushered in by the independence of Mexico and Guatemala, and persisted until the 1870s or 1880s; while La Farge saw this as an era of smooth integration between Spanish and Maya elements, with relative tranquillity, this is true only for the Guatemalan highlands under the country's pro-Indian Conservative government. A different story could be told in Chiapas, with major Indian revolts, and in Yucatan, with the Caste Wars in which the Maya came close to crushing their white overlords.

From 1880 until today we are in *Recent Indian II*, marked by a new tide of intervention in Indian life, and with concerted efforts by governments to force the Maya to become laborers on cash-crop plantations as part of the world market system. Travelers to Guatemala City may drive along the "Avenida de la Reforma," but they surely will not know what the "reform" was: the abolition by President Rufino Barrios of Indian communal lands, and the imposition of a system to supply forced labor from the Maya highlands to the newly-established coffee *fincas* of the Pacific Piedmont zone. Bitter revolts against this injustice took place, but they were put down by the Liberal government of Barrios with a ferocity that foreshadowed more modern developments. Such imposed seasonal migrations were absent in the Yucatan Peninsula, but on the great sisal *(henequén)* plantations which covered much of the north, rock-bottom wages and debt peonage were the rule.

This last period was marked by the emergence of a new cross to be borne by the Maya: the invasion of their lands, villages, and towns by a class of *ladinos*, Hispanic or hispanicized citizens who occupied all the lucrative and politically powerful positions in largely Maya territories; they were the shopkeepers, the labor majordomos, the schoolteachers, the judiciary, the Catholic priests. They spoke Spanish rather than the Indian "dialects" (as the Maya languages were pejoratively thought of), they dressed in Western clothes, and they generally held themselves to be superior to the native peoples. It is a situation that persists.

The new Spanish order

To understand the processes of conflict, accommodation, and integration that have gone on among the Maya since the Conquest, it is necessary to understand what the Spaniards introduced. First and foremost were epidemic diseases previously unknown in the New World, such as smallpox, influenza, and measles. It is generally agreed among scholars that these produced a holocaust unparalleled in the world's history: within a century, 90 percent of the native population had been killed off, including that of the Maya area. Smallpox, in fact, had reached the Guatemalan highlands even before the arrival of Pedro de Alvarado, and it is a wonder that the weakened Maya put up the defense that they did.

Over the next two centuries, then, the Spaniards were able to impose their own cultural pattern on regions that had been devastated by disease. By order of Church and Crown, the scattered populations were "reduced," that is, concentrated into villages and towns on the Spanish pattern, where they could be better controlled and converted. These new settlements were laid out on the grid plan, with rectilinear streets, a central plaza, and a church, a settlement type still to be seen throughout the Maya area. Along with the church, the seat of religious power, there was usually a building housing the *Ayuntamiento*, the civil government run by, or under the thumb of, Spaniards or *ladinos;* and, later on, a *ladino*-run store.

Catholicism brought its priests, its rituals, and its saints, and was usually the principal agent of acculturation. One of its most successful institutions was the *cofradía* (confraternity or brotherhood), adopted enthusiastically throughout the highlands, each dedicated to the care and honor of a particular saint. There are twelve of these brotherhoods, for instance, among the Ixil of the Nebaj region, and they play a crucial role in the ritual life of these people. The Christian sacrament of baptism introduced another element into native social life, namely that of *compadrazgo* or co-godparenthood, which formalizes bonds of friendship between adult Maya.

There was, of course, a great deal of syncretism between Spanish and Maya religious institutions and beliefs, since in many respects they were so similar. Both burned incense during rituals, both had images which they worshiped, both had priests, and both conducted elaborate pilgrimages set by their respective calendars. Both, as Nikolai Grube reminds us, had a hero god who died and was resurrected – for the Spaniards, this was Jesus Christ, and for the Maya, the Maize God. Thus, when the Tzotzil Maya of Zinacantan make pilgrimages to crosses set up on holy mountains, it is really irrelevant to ask if this is a Maya or Spanish custom: to the Tzotzil, both cross and ancestral mountain are a unity.

But the European invaders brought with them more than their civil and religious order: they imposed an economic order as well. Iron and steel tools replaced chipped or ground stone ones, and the Maya took readily to the Spaniards' axes, machetes, and billhooks, which in the lowlands enabled them to cope with the forest as they never had before. Cattle, pigs, and chickens began to replace game as the main source of meat in the diet, although the Maya never took to the heavy use of lard and oil which was such a prominent feature of the Spanish cuisine. The invaders brought in citrus trees, watermelons, and other welcome crops, but the sugarcane and coffee (the latter largely supplanting the native cacao) introduced as cash crops were a mixed blessing as they led to the plantations that put economic shackles on the Maya.

Perhaps the most destructive of these introduced elements was distilled alcohol. The Maya had always used alcohol in their rituals — *chicha* or maize beer in the highlands, and *balche'* (a flavored mead) in the lowlands, but they were unprepared for the power of the Spaniards' *aguardiente*, and many despondent Maya sought relief or oblivion in strong drink, a habit encouraged by the *ladino* majordomos and store owners.

On the plus side, though, was the Roman alphabet, initially used by the earlier missionaries to write down sermons and the like in the native languages. It was not long before educated Maya were using it to transcribe their own ritual and historical texts, which had previously existed in hieroglyphic form, an activity which was probably conducted in secret. To this we owe the preservation of the great K'iche' epic — the Popol Vuh — and the Yucatec Maya Books of Chilam Balam. In Yucatan, there has always been a strong tradition of native literacy, still kept by men who occupy the office of *ah tz'ib,* 'scribe.' It was probably such specialists who produced the large body of surviving letters in Yucatec exchanged between leaders of the Caste Wars of the 1840s and 50s.

In all of this, the various Maya groups have clearly assimilated and altered many disparate foreign, and even threatening, elements to fit their own cultural patterns inherited from the pre-Conquest era. Take the marimba, a percussion instrument ultimately of African origin, but introduced to Guatemala in Colonial times. Today it appears as a typically "Maya" instrument in native performances, both religious and secular; so assimilated is it that many tourists believe that it must be pre-Columbian.

The highland Maya, yesterday and today

Anthropologists and other social scientists agree that about 60 percent of Guatemala's population of ten million is Maya; most of these live in the central and western highlands of the country, the eastern part having been subject to heavy Spanish migration and consequent 'ladinoization' over the centuries. Another million Maya, mainly Tzotzil and Tzeltal, occupy the adjacent Chiapas highlands. All of these populations are rapidly growing and expanding, in spite of Guatemala's recent history of terror.

The highland Maya economy is both a part of, and separate from, the economies of the modern nation-states of Mexico and Guatemala. Most Maya households engage in corn farming, and many produce crafts for local consumption or for sale in Indian-run markets, but in many areas the men must travel long distances to work in the lowlands for part of the year on coffee *fincas*, cotton plantations, and the like. One of the most striking features of the Maya lands in Guatemala, apart from the magnificent landscape, is the vast network of markets and trade routes linking them, producing – as one anthropologist called it – a kind of 'penny capitalism.' These markets can sometimes be spectacular, like the ones at Solola and Santiago Atitlan, near Lake Atitlan, with their row upon row of colorfully garbed Maya women selling produce of all kinds.

It is typical of the Maya highlands that each village will have its own distinctive style of dress. The skirts of the women are usually machine-made, *ikat* wrap-arounds, but their embroidered cotton blouses or *huipiles* mark them as members of a particular community. Recent studies made by Walter "Chip" Morris have shown that the designs on them are not merely decorative, but rather illustrate a complex iconographic system based on native and sometimes Christian cosmology. The men, in contrast, wear clothing more or less based on Spanish modes of dress, but even this has been transformed into something distinctive to the community: Solola men, for example, wear short black-and-white jackets with frogging, but on the back of each is a great emblematic bat, while the Tzotzil men of Zinacantan are clad with broad-brimmed, beribboned straw hats, ponchos, and high-backed sandals recalling those of the Classic Maya.

The old Maya Calendar Round has survived to an extraordinary degree in the highlands. Among peoples like the Ixil and the K'iche', the 260-day count is an integral part not only of native ritual, but of their everyday life, as it was among their distant ancestors. Wherever it is found, there are shaman-priests or "day-keepers" whose job it is to keep track of the round of days, and to conduct rituals for individuals and the whole community in accord with its dictates. The most dramatic of these is the great Eight Monkey or *Wajxaqib Batz'* ceremony, held in the K'iche' community of Momostenango every 260 days. On the day of that name, tens of thousands of Indians gather at dawn at altars formed of mounds of broken pottery; there, over 200 shamans act as intermediaries between individual petitioners and the supreme deity *Dios Mundo* ('God World'). Prayers are made for forgiveness for past sins, and requests that some boon be granted, while each individual adds a potsherd to the pile.

An important function of all highland shamans is divination. This is sometimes done through the mechanism of the 260-day count, along with the casting of certain red seeds or maize kernels, a practice deeply rooted in the pre-Spanish past.

The Tzotzil Maya of Zinacantan

The resilience of the contemporary highland Maya when left in relative peace to work out their own destinies in a changing world is well exemplified by the Tzotzil of Zinacantan, a community that was intensively studied over a period of years by a Harvard project directed by Evon Vogt.

The approximately 12,000 Zinacantecos live in a landscape of rugged mountains; over a thousand occupy the ceremonial center within a densely occupied valley, while the rest are scattered in outlying hamlets. The Zinacanteco world is conceived of as a large quincunx, with four corners and a "navel of the earth" in the middle – actually a low, rounded mound in the ceremonial center. This all rests on the shoulders of the *Vaxak-Men*, the four-corner gods; when one of these shifts his burden, there is an earthquake. The sky above is the domain of the sun, moon, and stars. While the sun, "Our Holy Father," is associated in Zinacanteco cosmology with God the Father or Jesus Christ, the moon is thought to be one with the Virgin Mary.

155 Mountains and hills located near settlements are the homes of ancestral deities, "fathers and mothers"; these supernaturals are pictured as elderly Zinacantecos, living eternally in their mountain abodes, and are referred to constantly in prayers and rituals conducted in their honor; they are sustained by offerings of black chickens, candles, incense, and liquor. Many Mayanists, incidentally, are convinced that these holy, ancestral mountains are directly analogous to the temple-pyramids of the Classic Maya cities, which celebrated the cult of the dead and presumably deified royal ancestors.

Almost of equal weight in Zinacanteco religious life is the Earth Lord – thought of as a fat, greedy *ladino*! – who dwells in caves, limestone sinks, and waterholes. He owns all the waterholes, and controls and produces lightning and rain.

The most sacred objects in Zinacantan are the wood or plaster images of the saints. These have their own legends and associated beliefs (not always the same as those in official hagiographies), and most are kept in three churches in the center.

The Zinacanteco people, on their lowest level of social organization, live

155 A Tzotzil Maya shaman from Zinacantan prays for the soul of a patient at a mountain shrine; in the background is another sacred mountain resembling an ancient Maya pyramid.

in patrilocal, extended families, which in turn are grouped into local patrilineages or *sna*. Each *sna* maintains a series of cross shrines on nearby mountains, for communicating with the ancestral deities, and in caves, for communicating with the Earth Lord. Two to over a dozen patrilineages form a waterhole group (waterholes are highly sacred), and in turn keep up their own series of cross shrines; a particular hamlet will be made up of several waterhole groups.

It will be remembered that the Spaniards imposed a civil hierarchy on each Maya group, and this persists in the ceremonial center of Zinacantan, with strictly ranked officials who are elected to three-year terms. But the more important hierarchy, as can be seen in native communities throughout the New World, is religious. Some of the people with religious power are shamans or 'seers,' of whom there are over 250, almost all adult males. Of overwhelming significance to the community is the system of ranked religious offices which functions on the *cargo* principle, in which each office is conceptualized as 'bearing a burden' (or *cargo*, in Spanish). Within this hierarchy, which fulfills the function of the confraternities found elsewhere, there are sixty-one positions grouped into four levels of seniority. All *cargo*-holders must reside in the center for the duration of the office, and as they rise through the ranks, their expenses grow increasingly exorbitant. After occupying the most senior rank, a Zinacanteco can expect to retire as a poor but highly honored individual. This is a "burden" indeed!

Zinacanteco rituals require formalized eating and drinking, and often large processions to sacred places. The abiding concern with rank shows up in how individuals are placed in these activities. There are many rituals for the curing and well-being of individuals; these often involve a person's innate soul or *ch'ulel*, as well as his or her animal counterpart (every Zinacanteco has such an alter-ego, all of which live together in corrals within a 9,200-ft-high (2800-m) extinct volcano; the *ch'ulel* is clearly cognate with the *way* of the Classic Maya).

There are waterhole and lineage rituals, as well as frequent ceremonies conducted in the ceremonial center by *cargo*-holders. But the greatest of all are the end-of-the-year/New Year *cargo* rites, which reach their culmination in the latter half of January in celebrations held in honor of St Sebastian. Like the myths which surround this Roman saint – themselves the result of four centuries of syncretism – these dramatic ceremonies show a heady mixture of Christian and Maya-pagan elements. Much of the action is pure theater, with actors ritually impersonating monkeys (animals left over from a previous Creation), jaguars, "Blackmen," and Spanish men and women. The entire religious drama is clearly directed towards renewal of the universe and of the community, and ends with the transfer of the sacred objects of office to a new set of *cargo*-holders.

As Professor Vogt has said of these Zinacantan Maya, "they are a shrewd people, and have not retreated from the encroachment of *ladino* civilization. What is most valued and most vital to the culture has been reinforced, for the ritual life is, if anything, more intensified and elaborated than ever before."

The Yucatec Maya

The Spanish conquest of Yucatan was a protracted and by no means completely successful process, and it ended with Spanish control being confined to the northern third of the peninsula, along with portions of the west and east coasts. The foreign overlords lived in villas with European administrative machinery and the usual grid plan; around and between them were hundreds of Maya communities that were forced to pay *encomienda* tribute and more-or-less forced labor, as well as to give up their "idolatry."

The ethnohistorian Grant Jones has documented that to the south and east lay a huge area inhabited by tens of thousands of Maya who had refused to submit to this oppression; this included most of the Peten and Belize, the east coast of the peninsula, and the region to the south of Campeche. At the heart of these defiant lands was Tah Itza (or Tayasal) which, as we have seen in Chapter 7, only surrendered to Spanish arms in 1697. Various attempts to colonize the region by the Spaniards failed time and time again, one reason being, as Professor Jones has found, that vast numbers of Yucatec Maya were arriving from the north where they had fled the terrible *encomienda* system. As a result, the eastern part of the peninsula – including most of what later became the Mexican Territory of Quintana Roo – remained a bastion of Maya independence until very recent times.

The War of the Castes

As in the highlands, the achievement of independence by the modern nation-states that control the Maya meant not a betterment of conditions for the latter, but worsening. The cruelty and misery of the sisal plantations and cattle ranches of Yucatan were amply documented in the books of John Lloyd Stephens, who saw them at first hand. The storm that became known to rich Yucatecan whites as the "War of the Castes" broke out in 1847, not long after Stephens' visit when almost all the Maya of the peninsula took up arms against the hated whites. Eventually, the government troops held only Mérida, some towns along the coast, and the main road leading from Campeche. The Conquest had been reversed!

The dénouement of this story is well known: when the time came for the Indians to plant corn in their *milpas*, the native army disintegrated. Nonetheless, in 1850 a new element was introduced into the conflict. This took place in Chan Santa Cruz, a native village in central Quintana Roo, where a miraculous "Talking Cross" began to prophesy a holy war against the whites. Bolstered by arms and other military equipment received from the British in Belize, the Maya of the region, now formed into quasi-military companies and inspired by messianic zeal, once more battled the armies of the oppressors. Fighting was not to end until 1901, when Federal forces under General Ignacio Bravo took Chan Santa Cruz. But Mexican government control gradually faded away during the ensuing decades, Talking Crosses proliferated, and the Maya of Quintana Roo went their own way (I saw a Talking Cross inside the Castillo at Tulum as late as 1948). Only the frantic development of tourism over the last twenty-five years has managed to spell the doom of Maya culture in this part of the peninsula.

The Maya of Chan K'om

Located in just about the center of the Yucatan Peninsula, during the 1930s when it was the focus of a study by the anthropologists Robert Redfield and Alfonso Villa Rojas, Chan K'om was the typical Yucatec Maya village. It has been since "modernized" considerably, but settlements like Chan K'om as it then was can yet be found throughout the peninsula. With its houses of white-washed walls and thatched roofs, and its women in spotlessly white *huipiles* edged with colorful embroidery, it offered a picture of rural tranquility belied by the turbulent history of victors and vanquished in the Maya lowlands.

Like their counterparts in Zinacantan, most of the Chan K'om Maya were and are maize farmers, but here they practice lowland slash-and-burn, shifting cultivation rather than the fixed-field systems of the highlands. There is the usual Spanish-style municipal government, but nothing like the religious hierarchy that is so striking among people like the Tzotzil. Two types of religious specialists practice here and in other traditional Yucatec Maya settlements. One is the *Maestro Cantor* ('choirmaster'), a layman who nevertheless knows the Catholic prayers that may be used in Christian rituals like baptism, weddings, and funerals. The other is seemingly imbued with far greater spiritual and perhaps real power: this is the *h-men,* "he who does or understands things" – that is, the shaman. *H-menob* are found all over the peninsula, even in large cities like Mérida, but they are an integral part of the agricultural rituals so vital to rural life. Even though the traditional Maya 260-day calendar has disappeared in Yucatan, these specialists still play an important role in divination and prophecy, using their crystals to scry the future.

The supernatural world is ever-present in Chan K'om and in the outlying fields and forest. At the four entrances to the village are four pairs of crosses and four *balam* ("jaguar") spirits, watching to keep evil away from the householders. The benevolent yet feared *balamob* also act as guardians of the cornfields. There are many *Chaakob,* Rain Gods descended from the Classic and Post-Classic deity Chak, visualized as old men on horseback, led by St Michael Archangel. Other supernaturals invoked in agricultural rites are deities of the forest in which the farmer must clear his plot, gods of the bees, and guardians of deer and cattle. Evil winds loose in the world can attack one and cause sickness; also to be avoided are the *aluxob,* leprechaun-like dwarves with large hats who bring misfortune.

Judging from the intensity of farming rituals in Yucatan, anxiety centered on subsistence must be far higher than in the highlands; as we have seen in Chapter 1, the peninsula has generally thin soils, and rainfall is far more sparse than in the south. Underlying the ceremonies performed in the *milpas* of Chan K'om farmers is the idea that "what man wins from nature, he takes from the gods." The nature gods must be asked for favors, and they must be repaid through prayers and offerings, including sacred foods and the first-fruits of the harvest.

These foods are those not consumed in ordinary life: stacks of bean-smeared tortillas cooked in the *pib* or pit, *balche'* mead, *saka* (sacred maize gruel), broth made from fowls, and sacrificed animals. About every fourth year, an individual farmer will sponsor an *u hanli kol* ("dinner of the *milpa*") rite, conducted by a *h-men* at a rustic altar set with these holy foods and drink.

The largest and most dramatic of the Yucatec Maya agricultural ceremonies is the *Ch'a-chaak;* its purpose is to bring rain during times of drought, and thus involves the entire community. The participants are only men, who withdraw for several days to the place on the village's outskirts where the *Ch'a-chaak* is to be held. The rite begins after the *h-men* has consulted his *zaztun* or crystal. The altar is covered with fowl, venison, and the sacred breadstuffs and drink, all set out in predetermined order; under the altar, and tied to its legs, are four boys, who croak like the *wo* frogs which are harbingers of rain in the Maya lowlands. Off to one side is an older man, chosen to impersonate the *K'unk'u-chaak*, the chief of the rain gods, holding in one hand the calabash from which he unleashes rain on the cornfields, and in the other a wooden knife symbolizing the lightning that accompanies downpours.

The Maya *h-menob* have other duties as well, most importantly to cure sickness, which the people of Chan K'om generally hold to come from evil winds and the evil eye; for this, curing rituals are held which include the usual offerings to the gods. As with their highland counterparts, these shamans also engage in divination, either by using their magic crystals, or by separating out cast maize kernels by groups of four (the outcome depending upon whether the number of piles is odd or even, or the remainder odd or even). Witchcraft is an omnipresent danger; the witch takes the form of animal alter ego or *way* (see Chapter 9), and may be male or female. The witch visits sleeping individuals like the incubus of European folklore, and through illicit sex saps that person's strength.

The Lakandon

Visitors to the site of Palenque may encounter near the entrance two or three Maya men with long hair and wearing long, white robes, selling bows and arrows especially made for the tourist trade. These are Lakandon, members of a stubbornly independent tribal group that some say number about 250, and others place at about 500 (a discrepancy that may arise from the fact that some choose to live as *ladinos* for part of the year).

The Lakandon inhabit three small villages in what was once a vast rain forest in eastern Chiapas. Historically, they almost certainly originated as one of the Yucatec-speaking refugee groups who chose to flee to the jungle fast-nesses at the base of the peninsula rather than submit to Spanish rule. While most Lakandon have been converted to fundamentalist Christianity, some have remained fiercely conservative, preserving many elements of the old Maya religion; these latter still make pilgrimages to the ruined temples of Yaxchilan, invoking the gods with their incense-filled pottery censers. At one time they hunted and farmed in an unbroken, high-canopied forest; this was set aside for them in the 1970s by presidential decree, an edict which was soon abrogated, releasing lumber companies to sack its valuable timber. The lumber trucks were followed by an army of landless peasants, largely impov-erished Tzeltal Maya from the highlands, who cut down what remained of the jungle. The final stage in the death of the Lakandon forest has been the conversion of peasant holdings to great cattle *fincas*, supplying beef to feed Americans' hunger for hamburgers.

Uprising in Chiapas

Most of the land, and all of the political life of the State of Chiapas have been in the hands of *ladino* ranch owners and merchants for centuries. Closely allied with Mexico's ruling political party, the PRI, they have managed to keep the Maya majority in their state disenfranchised and land-poor. The signing of the North American Free Trade Agreement (NAFTA) by Mexico and the United States threatened to further worsen the economic situation of the indigenous people in southeastern Mexico, but the Maya seemed powerless. Then, on 1 January 1994, the Zapatista National Liberation Army (EZLN) – a guerrilla force of Tzotzil and Tzeltal Maya, led by a former university student calling himself "Subcommandante Marcos" – stormed San Cristobal Las Casas, one of the major centers of *ladino* power in the state.

This was an unprecedented event in the history of Mexico, where the indigenous peoples have generally been mute and defenceless bystanders in whatever internal conflicts the country has gone through. In spite of the presence of tens of thousands of army troops brought in to control the situation, the Zapatistas have managed to maintain their armed resistance; and through a sophisticated use of the media (including the Internet), they have won considerable sympathy for their cause from the rest of Mexico and the outside world. Their demands include economic, political, and cultural rights not only for the Maya of Chiapas, but also for all of Mexico's indigenous peoples. Whether the PRI – which has always actively pursued a policy of complete assimilation for its native Indians – will ever accede to these demands remains to be seen.

The great terror

The greatest and bloodiest episode in the "cycles of conquest" that have befallen the Maya since the arrival of the Spaniards began on 29 May 1978 in the K'eq'chi-speaking town of Panzos in the Department of Alta Verapaz, Guatemala. There, a unit of the Guatemalan army opened fire on a group of Indians peacefully protesting the government's refusal to award them land titles. Over 100 men, women, and children were immediately killed.

Worse yet for the highland Maya, a second element had entered the picture: the Guerrilla Army of the Poor (later reorganized as the Guatemalan National Revolutionary Unity, or URNG), which had chosen to base its anti-government operations in the western part of the highlands. Consisting largely of Marxist *ladinos*, the guerrillas looked upon traditional Maya culture as an obstacle to the proletarian revolution which they intended to bring about. Nevertheless, the Indian villagers had little choice but to give them support in the way of food and shelter.

Retribution by the Guatemalan government, its army, and its police came swiftly: under a series of military regimes, the official security forces and governmental death squads unleashed a reign of terror against the Maya that was almost unprecedented in its ferocity. It is estimated by anthropologists like George Lovell of Queen's University in Kingston (Ontario) that over one million Maya were displaced. According to a report by the National Academy of Sciences of the United States, approximately 150,000 people were killed, and an additional 40,000 "disappeared" – almost all of these being Maya. By the end of the terrible decade of the 1980s, 35,000 Indian refugees were living in camps in Mexico, and thousands had fled to the United States.

This was indeed ethnocide, if not genocide, on a grand scale. Uprooted communities were forced into "model villages" (a move recommended by American military advisors), where able-bodied men were required to perform service in civil patrols. For hundreds of thousands of K'iche', Ixil, Mam, and other Maya, the traditional ties with the land had finally been shattered – or so the army leaders thought. As these immense disruptions took place, fundamentalist Christian missionaries from the United States, with government support (two recent presidents have been evangelical Protestants), began to make vast numbers of converts among Guatemala's Maya. With whole villages undergoing mass baptism, the effect on the traditional structure of Maya life (the confraternities and *cargo* system, for instance) may well be imagined.

The Maya future

Will the Maya survive? They have been under attack from every side: from the army and death squads in Guatemala, from mass tourism and the destruction of the tropical forest in Mexico, from *ladino* encroachments on their lands everywhere. These almost intolerable pressures have resulted in vast dislocations and migrations throughout the Maya area. But there are signs of hope for them. In Guatemala, many Maya intellectuals have realized that to survive, various Maya linguistic groups, heretofore separate, must come together to save their language and culture. And many more Maya now know that they can stand up to terror by speaking out: Rigoberta Menchu, a K'iche' Maya woman who lost most of her family to the death squads, did so – for which she was awarded the Nobel Peace Prize for 1992.

A turning point in the fortunes of the Maya may now have been reached in Guatemala. In December 1995, with a new and less anti-Maya government in power, the regime signed a series of peace accords with the main guerrilla group, the URNG. Among the provisions (negotiated under United Nations auspices) were an accountability for all of the human rights violations perpetrated by the armed forces over the years, a resettlement of an estimated one million displaced persons (most of them, of course, Maya), and an affirmation of the cultural identity and rights of the indigenous Maya population.

Incredibly, since the accords Guatemala has become a truly multicultural nation on the South African model. Spearheading a virtual Maya renaissance is the Academia de las Lenguas Mayas, established as long ago as 1984, which realized that given the multiplicity of Mayan tongues spoken in the Republic, there would have to be a standardized Mayan orthography (the one adopted in this book). As a result of their efforts, there is now bilingual instruction in several hundred Guatemalan schools, and active teaching of local languages. A government agency has been set up to deal with the rights of the indigenous majority, particularly regarding education and community land ownership. Inevitably, the united Maya will push for their own political party – something unheard of in the rest of the Americas, where native peoples remain completely marginalized. Of course, these developments have already led to opposition in the *ladino*-controlled Congress, where these accords must be implemented, and in the *ladino*-controlled press (with sarcastic articles suggesting that the country be renamed "Guatemaya"), but the participation of millions of Maya in decisions about their own future seems irreversible.

There is now a pan-Maya movement in eastern Mesoamerica, and a profound sense among these people of their glorious past. It is in a way ironic that Guatemala, with its past record of total suppression, should now be moving in the direction that it is, and that Mexico, superficially loyal to the ideals of the 1911 revolution, and happy to exploit for touristic purposes the wonders of the ruined Maya cities, should be trampling the rights of the people who built them.

The Yucatec Maya of the Talking Cross villages in Quintana Roo prophesy a coming Great War, an Armageddon when (as they told Paul Sullivan) a new king will awaken in Chich'en Itza, along with thousands of petrified beings from a past creation, and a petrified Feathered Serpent will come to life and inflict havoc on the creatures of this creation. Messianic predictions like this will surely crop up again and again as pressures on the Maya intensify. Yet the Maya are actually increasing, not dwindling, in numbers, and a heightened awareness that they are all one people with a glorious past, and an adaptability to future change, may help them survive for centuries into the future.

Visiting the Maya Area

General information

There are literally hundreds of Maya sites, of varying size and importance, distributed among five nation states: Mexico, Guatemala, Belize, Honduras, and El Salvador. It would take decades, perhaps a lifetime, to visit all of them. The interested traveler will have to make a balance between budget and available time before deciding on which ones to explore. Those with only a few weeks at their disposal should probably concentrate on the largest and most accessible sites; and it is these that usually have the best local accommodation. For more adventurous travelers, however, willing to put up with less-than-luxurious lodging – which might consist of a hammock slung in a thatched hut – there is the opportunity to explore jungle-shrouded ruins which few other tourists ever see.

When is the best time to go? Although one can travel at any time of the year in the Maya area, it should be remembered that in eastern Mesoamerica, there are two strongly marked seasons. The dry season begins in late November and lasts until the coming of the rains in late May, and it is during that time that most organized archaeological tours take place. Some travel agencies believe that the optimal time is from November through January into early February, when daytime temperatures are relatively cool. But potential visitors should be aware that during those months, cold *nortes* (northers) may occasionally sweep down from Texas, bringing grey skies and often rain to the Yucatan Peninsula. As the dry season progresses, daytime temperatures increase; for many veteran visitors to the Maya cities, the least attractive months are April and May, when the thermometer reaches a maximum, smoke and haze from burning *milpas* obscure the sun, many trees lose their leaves, and (at least in Yucatan) the countryside is brown and sere.

Actually, the rainy season – in spite of the prevailing high humidity – has its advantages. There are far fewer fellow-tourists, seed-ticks (a plague in off-the-beaten-track Yucatecan sites during the dry months) are almost totally absent, and there is a fresh greenness of vegetation that enhances the beauty of the ancient ruins. Except in the southeastern part of the lowlands, the rain itself usually lasts for only a few hours each day, generally in the afternoon or at night, so the mornings can be bright and sunny. There is a downside here, too: backcountry roads and trails can become impossibly muddy and often impassable, even to four-wheeled vehicles, and biting insects, especially mosquitoes, require constant application of repellent.

Even though these are the tropics, and light clothing is recommended for daytime wear, nights can be chilly at any time of year (above all, in the highlands of Guatemala and Chiapas, where freezing temperatures are not unknown in the winter months), so the traveler should always be armed with a sweater. Superior quality hiking shoes, preferably waterproof, are recommended, and hats and other sun protection should be the rule – the sun's rays can be extremely strong and even dangerous at midday in most ruins. And keep in mind that even in the dry months, it can rain at unexpected moments.

Medical advice can be found in any good travel guide to Mexico and Central America. The most common complaint afflicting not only tyros but also seasoned archaeologists, is the ubiquitous *turista* – travelers' diarrhea, which can make an otherwise enjoyable trip a misery. Prevention is imperative here. Under *no* circumstances should one drink any water other than what comes in sealed bottles or which has been boiled at least twenty minutes; ice is equally treacherous. And one should avoid salads, uncooked vegetables and garnishes, and the skins of unpeeled fruits. The good news is that most cases of *turista* clear themselves up in a few days.

Transportation is remarkably good over most of the Maya area. Mexico in particular has good, all-weather roads, with excellent bus service between major cities. For those visitors with ample pocketbooks, car rental gives a great deal of flexibility and the ability to cover many more sites than would be possible by public transportation. Some parts of the lowlands – in particular the Petexbatun area – lack road access, and the travel may be by more primitive means, such as mules or horses, dugout canoes, or by foot.

Should one hire a guide? One of the advantages of an organized tour is that one's group is almost always accompanied by a professional archaeologist or art historian, well-versed in Maya culture history and (optimally) even in Maya hieroglyphic writing. Locally-hired guides, on the other hand, are usually best avoided; in general, they have little or no training, and may well relay information that has no basis in fact. In all fairness, however, there are some exceptions – the guides at Palenque and Copan, for example, are far better prepared and up-to-date than those at most other sites. The true *aficionado* of Maya culture would do best by reading as much as possible about the ancient Maya beforehand, and by attending one of the Maya hieroglyphic weekends or week-long seminars now given in several American cities (such as the March meetings at the University of Texas in Austin).

Good site maps for the major Maya cities are available in various publications, including final reports. It is always a good idea to have Xerox copies of these in hand when exploring a particular ruin. In the more remote ruins, which may not be kept open by clearing, it may be wise to carry a pocket compass along with the map, as well as a canteen of purified water.

The "must-see" sites

Every professional Mayanist – and every seasoned Maya traveler – has his or her own favorite Maya ruins. Those most favored not only are bigger than most of the others, but also possess outstanding architecture and/or a wealth of well-preserved sculpture. Seven appear on almost everyone's list. These are Palenque, Yaxchilan, Uxmal, and Chich'en Itza in Mexico; Tik'al in Guatemala; and Copan in Honduras. No one who has failed to see all of these can really be said to know the Maya area. A determined traveler could probably visit all within a three-week period, although each requires at least three days to know well.

There are, of course, dozens of "lesser" sites, some of which may be even larger than some of the above giants – Kalak'mul (Calakmul) in Campeche and El Mirador in northern Guatemala come to mind – but often these are so hard to get to or are so lacking in above-the-ground attractions that only the most dedicated "Maya buffs" would find it worth the difficulties which must be overcome to visit them.

The Puuk sites

The jumping off point for Uxmal and other sites in the Puuk is Mérida, one of Mexico's more pleasant provincial capitals, with good hotels and a most interesting archaeological museum. Uxmal, with its magnificent Terminal Classic architecture, lies about an hour south of Mérida, along the main highway to Campeche; buildings like its wonderful Governor's Palace and Nunnery Quadrangle inspired Frank Lloyd Wright and other architects of our own age, and are not to be missed. Those wishing to explore not only Uxmal but K'abah, Sayil, and Labna can visit these sites easily by car, but many more remote Puuk sites require a four-wheeled vehicle. While in the area, no Maya enthusiast should overlook Loltun Cave, which now has electric illumination; in this case, a local guide familiar with the cavern is a good idea.

Chich'en Itza and the eastern peninsula

At least three days are required to do justice to Chich'en Itza, an enormous and complex city which is still poorly understood. Easily reached from Mérida via a virtual superhighway, and equally accessible to tourists from Yucatan's "Miami Beach" – the resort of Cancun – it sometimes seems inundated with tourists, yet its sheer size makes it possible to get away from the crowds. Here is a site which has sculptures and reliefs in enormous profusion, all belonging to the Terminal Classic and Post-Classic periods; its Ball Court is the largest in Mesoamerica, and the austere Castillo pyramid and the Sacred Cenote, rich in history, are very impressive indeed.

There are Late Post-Classic sites all along the east coast, some of them almost minuscule. One of the most visited (perhaps too much so) is little Tulum, spectacularly perched on a cliff above the blue Caribbean. Sadly, it is now being "loved to death" by tour and cruise groups. Less thronged with tourists is the inland city of Koba (Cobá), set among a series of beautiful lakes.

Crossing the base of the Yucatan Peninsula is an all-weather highway which gives access to several impressive Río Bec sites such as Xpuhil, Bekan, and Chikanna (Chicanná) as well as a very early (Late Preclassic or beginning Early Classic) pyramid at Kohunlich, with large stucco masks of Maya gods. These can all be visited in a single day, although if one wishes to venture further afield, such as to Río Bec itself, more time and a degree of stamina are necessary.

Palenque and Tonina

If one could see only one Maya site, many are convinced that Palenque should be it: the lush forest setting, with views out over the coastal plain, the delicate architecture, and the beauty of its bas-reliefs and stuccoes are all enhanced by the detailed historical background that modern scholars have provided for this great city. At least two to four days are required to appreciate it, although one could easily spend a week here. One should not miss the beautiful Cross Group, the Palace, and a visit to Hanab Pakal's tomb. There are a number of good hotels in the vicinity, and there is an adequate museum at the site.

The ruins of Tonina, currently under excavation, are accessible by car over an unpaved road from Ocosingo, a town reached from the highway between Tuxtla Gutiérrez (the capital of Chiapas) and the Guatemalan border. Rich in Late Classic three-dimensional sculpture, Tonina has a recently-discovered stucco relief illustrating episodes in the Maya epic, the Popol Vuh.

Yaxchilan and Bonampak'

The easiest way to visit Yaxchilan and Bonampak' is by renting a light plane in Palenque and Villahermosa, although some visitors now travel overland by a road which is promised to be passable even during the wet season. Yaxchilan is much the largest of the two, a Late Classic city arranged on a group of low hills and ridges above the Usumacinta River; there is much sculpture still left at the site. Bonampak' is famed for the wonderful wall paintings contained in one small building, although inept cleaning and restoration, and deterioration due to the elements, have tragically rendered these to but a shadow of what they once were. Yaxchilan, incidentally, is one of several Usumacinta sites which can be visited through a trip down the river on inflatable rafts, but since the river forms the border between Mexico and Guatemala, much depends on the

political situation in these countries. As of 1998, it was still a dangerous region, especially on the Chiapas side.

Guatemala: the highlands and Pacific Coast

The largest museum in Guatemala City is the Museo Nacional de Arqueología y Etnología, in which many of the treasures excavated at the country's Maya sites are housed. The visitor should not, however, miss the more modern Museo Ixchel, which concentrates on indigenous costume and textiles, and the Museo Popol Vuh, which has splendid and well-exhibited pre-Conquest objects. On the western outskirts of the city, in its own park, is what remains of the once-huge site of Kaminaljuyu, but there is little to see other than mounds. Apart from the breathtaking Lake Atitlan, fringed with Maya towns and villages, the highland traveler should see one or all of the great Late Post-Classic capitals: Iximche, Utatlan, and Mixco Viejo, quite accessible by car.

A day trip down to Escuintla and the compact Cotzumalhuapa area is a highly advised side trip. The more important sites are located on coffee and/or cotton *fincas*, and the headquarters of each *finca* usually has a collection of sculptures. If one visits the Finca El Baúl on Sunday morning, one may see Maya shamans conducting ceremonies before the ancient carvings. While on the Pacific Coast plain, be prepared for torrid daytime temperatures.

The Peten

Tik'al is reached by air from Guatemala City, most visitors staying in or near the Peten capital, Flores (site of the Itza island capital of Tayasal); they are then bussed up to the ruins. During the dry season, one can also drive to Flores from the Belize border. To properly appreciate this great and ancient city, with its towering temple-pyramids, one should budget at least three days. Not the least of its attractions is the surrounding tropical forest, with its wealth of birds and animals. The traveler should also not miss the local Museo Sylvanus G. Morley, which has on display many fine objects excavated at Tik'al over the past decades.

There are around ten other major Classic sites in the northern Peten, such as Waxaktun (Uaxactún), but these are usually difficult to reach and may require travel by jeep, mule, or foot over trails which can be extremely muddy at times. Only the most determined enthusiasts should attempt the journey.

Somewhat more accessible are Maya ruins in the southwestern Peten. The base for their exploration is Sayaxche, a *ladino* frontier town with very basic accommodation. To reach these, one must hire an outboard-powered dugout in Sayaxche; there is a certain amount of overland hiking from wherever the boat puts in to shore. Seibal is a very large ruined city on the Río Pasión, upriver from Sayaxche, which was excavated and partly restored by Harvard University; there are still several important stela there *in situ*. One can gain access to the Petexbatun sites to the south and southwest of Sayaxche by boat, but it is a considerable hike over an often muddy trail to reach Dos Pilas, the largest of these sites. Potential visitors should also be warned that one has to bring in camping gear, and that many hundreds of landless peasants have illegally moved into this supposedly protected park area following the signing of the Guatemalan peace accords in 1995.

Belize

Reached only in the dry season by a very rough dirt road, Caracol – the largest site in Belize – lies on the western edge of the Maya Mountains. It has 20 major plazas surrounded by temples, a few of which have been restored. Most of its carved monuments have been removed to the University Museum in Philadelphia, and to the Archaeology Museum in Belmopan, Belize's capital.

So far as its environment and its historical heritage are concerned, Belize is in some ways the most progressive country in the region, with a farsighted, ongoing archaeological program. The two main sites to see here are Altun Ha, a modest-sized Classic center 35 miles (55 km) north of Belize City, along a paved highway; and Xunantunich, a far larger center on the Guatemalan border, near the modern town of Benque Viejo. Neither has noteworthy stone monuments, but Xunantunich is distinguished by some important, ornate stucco facades decorating a large temple-pyramid.

Recommended reading

COE, ANDREW. *Archaeological Mexico: a traveler's guide to ancient cities and sacred sites.* Chico (California) 1998.
KELLY, JOYCE. *An archaeological guide to Mexico's Yucatan Peninsula.* Norman (Oklahoma) 1993.
—— *An archaeological guide to northern Central America: Belize, Guatemala, Honduras, and El Salvador.* Norman (Oklahoma) 1996.

Dynastic Rulers of Classic Maya Cities

Thanks to epigraphic research which has been going on since the early 1950s, a great deal is known about the kings and queens who ruled the Classic Maya cities in the Central Area. In some cases, we are sure about their actual Maya names, but in cases where we are not, scholars refer to them by modern nicknames (indicated by inverted commas). The purpose of these nicknames is purely mnemonic – they may have little relation to linguistic reality. One may reasonably ask, why is it that *all* of these personal names have not been "cracked"? The answer is that most of the glyphs standing for them are the hardest of all to decipher, for they generally are logograms for which phonetic substitutions or complements have not yet been – and may never be – discovered; fantastic animal heads and parts of animals are particularly common in these nominals.

In several cities, above all in Palenque, a number of kings prefaced their names with the title *K'inich*, meaning "Sun-faced," "Sun-eyed," or "Great Sun," probably because those rulers claimed descent from K'inich Ahaw, the Sun God.

In the following lists, compiled by Simon Martin and Nikolai Grube, the first date represents accession to the throne, while the second date is that of the ruler's death. A single date indicates that the ruler is known to be in power at that time. All dates are AD.

TIK'AL
Yax Moch' Xok	?–?
"Scroll Jaguar"	?–?
Siyah Chan K'awil I	c. 300?
"Feather Skull"	?–359?
"Jaguar Paw I"	359?–378
Nun Yax Ayin I	379–?
Siyah Chan K'awil II	411–457
"K'an Boar"	458–c. 488
"Jaguar Paw II"	488–508
"Bird Claw"	?–?

"Lady of Tik'al"	511–c. 527
Kalomte Balam	c. 527
"Double Bird"	537–562
"Animal Skull"	c. 593
"Shield Skull I"	c. 657–679
Hasaw Chan K'awil I	682–734
"Ruler B"	734–c. 760
"28th Ruler"	c. 766
Nun Yax Ayin II ("Ruler C")	768–c. 790
"Shield Skull II"	c. 800
"Dark Sun"	c. 810
"Jewel K'awil"	c. 849
Hasaw Chan K'awil II	c. 869

KALAK'MUL
Tun K'ab Hix	c. 537–546
"Sky Witness"	c. 561–572
Yax Yoat	573
"Scroll Serpent"	579–c. 611
Yukom Chan	c. 619
Tahom Uk'ab K'ak	622–630
"Yukom Head"	631–636
"Yukom the Great"	636–686
Yich'ak K'ak	686–c. 695
"Split Earth"	695?
Yukom Tok'	c. 702–c. 731
Bolon K'awil I	c. 741
"Ruler 8"	c. 751
Bolon K'awil II	c. 771
Kan Pet	c. 849
Ah Tok'	c. 909

NARANJO
"Double Comb"	546–c. 615
"36th King"	c. 630
"37th King"	c. 680
"Lady Six Sky"	682–741
K'ak' Tiliw Chan Chak ("Smoking Squirrel")	693–?
Yax Mayuy Chan Chak	?–744
K'ak' Yipiy Chan Chak	746–?
K'ak' Kal Chan Chak ("Smoking Batab")	755–784
Itzamna K'awil ("Shield God K")	784–c. 814
Waxaklahun Ubah K'awil	814–?

YAXCHILAN

Yoat Balam I	c. 359
Itzamna Balam I	? – ?
"Bird Jaguar I"	378 – 389
"Yax Deer-antler Skull"	389 – 402?
"Ruler 5"	402 – ?
K'inich Tatab Kim I	? – ?
"Moon Skull"	c. 454 – 467
"Bird Jaguar II"	467 – ?
"Knot-eye Jaguar I"	c. 508
K'inich Tatab Kim II	526 – c. 550
"Knot-eye Jaguar II"	c. 564
"Bird Jaguar III"	629 – c. 680
Itzamna Balam II	681 – 742
("Shield Jaguar the Great")	
Yoat Balam II	c. 749
"Bird Jaguar IV"	752 – 768
("Bird Jaguar the Great")	
Itzamna Balam III	769 – c. 800
K'inich Tatab Kim III	c. 808

PIEDRAS NEGRAS

"Ruler A"	c. 431
"Ruler B"	? – ?
"Ruler D"	c. 510
"Ruler E"	c. 560
"Ruler 1"	603 – 639
"Ruler 2"	639 – 686
"Ruler 3"	687 – 729
"Ruler 4"	729 – 757
"Ruler 5"	758 – 766
"Ruler 6"	767 – 781
(Ha' K'in Xok)	
"Ruler 7"	781 – ?

DOS PILAS

Balah Chan K'awil	c. 648 – 698
("Ruler 1")	
Itzamna K'awil	698 – 726
("Ruler 2")	
"Ruler 3"	727 – 741
K'awil Chan K'inich	741 – 761
("Ruler 4")	

PALENQUE

K'uk' Balam I	431 – 435
"Casper"	435 – 487
Butz'ah Sak Chik	487 – 501
Akul Anab I	501 – 524
K'an Hok' Chitam I	529 – 565
Akul Anab II	565 – 570
Kan Balam I	572 – 583
"Lady Olnal"	583 – 604
Ah Ne Ol Mat	605 – 612

"Lady Sak K'uk'"	612 – 615
K'inich Hanab Pakal	615 – 683
("the Great")	
K'inich Kan Balam II	684 – 702
("Chan Bahlum")	
K'inich K'an Hok' Chitam II	702 – c. 711
K'inich Akul Anab III	721 – c. 750
K'inich K'uk' Balam II	764 – ?
Wak Kimi Hanab Pakal	799 – ?

CARACOL

Te' K'ab Chak	c. 331
Yahaw Te' K'inich I	484 – 531?
K'an I	531 – ?
Yahaw Te' K'inich II	553 – 599
"Knot Ahaw"	599 – 618?
K'an II	618 – 658
"Smoking Skull"	658 – c. 685
"Ruler VII"	c. 702
Tum Yol K'inich	? – ?
K'inich Hok' K'awil	c. 798
K'inich Tobil Yoat	c. 810 – c. 835
K'an III	c. 835 – c. 849
"Ruler XIII"	c. 859

COPAN

K'inich Yax K'uk' Mo'	426 – c. 435
"Ruler 2" ("Mat Head")	c. 437 – ?
"Ruler 3"	c. 455
"Ruler 4"	c. 465
"Ruler 5"	c. 480
"Ruler 6"	c. 490
"Water-lily Jaguar"	c. 504 – c. 544
"Ruler 8"	? – 551
"Ruler 9"	551 – 553
"Moon Jaguar"	553 – 578
Butz' Chan	578 – 628
"Smoke Imix God K"	628 – 695
Waxaklahun Ubah K'awil	695 – 738
K'ak' Hoplah Chan K'awil	738 – 749
("Smoke Monkey")	
"Smoke Shell"	749 – 763
Yax Pasah Chan Yoat	763 – c. 820
Ukit Tok'	822 – ?

QUIRIGUA

Yol Tok	426 – ?
Tutum Yol K'inich	c. 455
K'awil-?	c. 652
K'ak' Tiliw Chan Yoat	724 – 785
("Kawak Sky")	
"Sky Xul"	785 – c. 797
"Jade Sky"	c. 797 – ?

Further Reading

There is no up-to-date, comprehensive bibliography on the ancient, Colonial, and contemporary Maya; it might number over 10,000 entries. Here I have tried to concentrate on those articles and volumes which I have found most useful in the preparation of this book, and which might be of interest to those wishing to follow certain topics further. Two important series specializing in Maya culture should be consulted: *Estudios de Cultura Maya*, published since 1961 by the Seminario de Cultura Maya, Universidad Nacional Autónoma de México, and *Research Reports on Ancient Maya Writing* issued since 1985 by the Center for Maya Research, Washington, D.C.

ABRAMS, ELLIOT M. *How the Maya Built Their World: Energetics and Ancient Architecture*. Austin 1994.

ADAMS, RICHARD E. W. (ed.). *The Origins of Maya Civilization*. Albuquerque 1977. (Fifteen essays, but already outdated by more recent excavations in the Peten and Belize.)

ANDREWS, ANTHONY P. *Maya Salt Production and Trade*. Tucson 1983. (Thorough study of an important Maya industry.)

ANDREWS, E. WYLLYS IV, AND E. WYLLYS ANDREWS V. *Excavations at Dzibilchaltun, Yucatán, Mexico*. Middle American Research Institute, Tulane University, Publication 48. New Orleans 1980.

AVENI, ANTHONY F. *Skywatchers of Ancient Mexico*. Austin 1980. (The clearest introduction to Maya astronomy.)

BARRERA VÁSQUEZ, ALFREDO, AND SYLVANUS G. MORLEY. "The Maya chronicles," *Carnegie Institution of Washington, Contributions to American Anthropology and History*, no. 48. Washington 1949. (Yucatec Maya prophetic history based on the Books of Chilam Balam.)

BAUDEZ, CLAUDE-FRANÇOIS, AND PIERRE BECQUELIN. *Les Mayas*. Paris 1984. (Lavishly illustrated introduction to the Maya by two French specialists.)

BAUDEZ, CLAUDE-FRANÇOIS, and SYDNEY PICASSO. *Lost Cities of the Maya*, London and New York 1992. (Low-priced paperback on history of Maya discovery.)

BENSON, ELIZABETH P. *The Maya World*. Revised edition. New York 1977.

——, (ed.). *City-States of the Maya: Art and Architecture*. Denver 1986. (Five essays on Maya cities including Late Preclassic Etz'na and El Mirador, and Terminal Classic Uxmal.)

BENSON, ELIZABETH P., and GILLETT G. GRIFFIN (eds.). *Maya Iconography*. Princeton 1988. (Pioneering essays on Maya art and epigraphy.)

BERLIN, HEINRICH. "El glifo emblema en las inscripciones mayas," *Journal de la Société des Américanistes*, vol. 47 (1958), 111-19. (Article that presaged the historical approach to the inscriptions.)

BRICKER, VICTORIA R. *Grammar of Mayan Hieroglyphs*. New Orleans 1986. (The application of linguistics to Maya decipherment.)

CARMACK, ROBERT M. *Quichean Civilization*. Berkeley and Los Angeles 1973. (Overview of the Post-Classic K'iche' Maya of Guatemala.)

——, *The Quiché Maya of Utatlán*. Norman 1981.

——, (ed.). *The Maya Indians and the Guatemalan Crisis*. Norman 1985. (Eye-witness accounts and interpretive essays dealing with the official violence directed against the Maya of Guatemala.)

CARR, ROBERT F., and JAMES E. HAZARD. "Map of the Ruins of Tikal, El Petén, Guatemala," *Tikal Reports* no. 11. Philadelphia 1961.

CHAMBERLAIN, ROBERT S. *The conquest and colonization of Yucatán*. Carnegie Institution of Washington, publ. 582. Washington 1948.

CHASE, ARLEN F., and PRUDENCE M. RICE (eds.). *The Lowland Maya Postclassic*. Austin 1985. (19 essays covering all aspects of the subject, up to the fall of Tayasal in 1697.)

CLANCY, FLORA S., and PETER D. HARRISON (eds.). *Vision and Revision in Maya Studies*. Albuquerque 1990. (A potpourri of essays, covering subjects from subsistence to epigraphy.)

CLARK, JOHN E. "The beginnings of Mesoamerica: apologia for the Soconusco Early Formative," in *The Formation of Complex Society in Southeastern Mesoamerica*, ed. W. R. Fowler, Jr., 13-26. Boca Raton 1991. (Summary article on the precocious development of settled life along the Pacific Coast of Chiapas and Guatemala.)

COE, MICHAEL D. *The Maya Scribe and His World*. New York 1973. (Iconographic and epigraphic study of Maya vases, along with a description of the Grolier Codex.)

——, "Early steps in the evolution of Maya writing," in *Origins of Religious Art and Iconography in Preclassic Mesoamerica*, ed. H. B. Nicholson, 107-22. Los Angeles 1976.

——, *Breaking the Maya Code*. London and New York 1992. (The history of the Maya decipherment.)

COE, MICHAEL D., and KENT V. FLANNERY. *Early Cultures and Human Ecology in South Coastal Guatemala*. Washington 1967. (Early Preclassic investigations.)

COE, MICHAEL D., and JUSTIN KERR. *The Art of the Maya Scribe*. London 1997, New York 1998. (A study of Maya calligraphy, and of the scribes and artists who produced it.)

Coe, William *Tikal, a Handbook of the Ancient Maya Ruins*. Philadelphia 1967.

——, *Excavations in the Great Plaza, North Terrace and North Acropolis of Tikal*. 6 vols. Tikal Report No. 14. The University Museum. Philadelphia 1990.

COGGINS, CLEMENCY C., and ORRIN C. SHANK (eds.). *Cenote of Sacrifice: Maya Treasures from the Sacred Well at Chichen Itza*. Austin 1984. (Catalogue of objects recovered from the cenote at the beginning of the 20th century.)

COLBY, BENJAMIN N., and LORE M. COLBY. *The Day-keeper: The Life and Discourse of an Ixil Diviner*. Cambridge, Mass., 1981. (Account of shamanistic practices among the contemporary Ixil of the north-central highlands.)

CULBERT, T. PATRICK. *The Ceramics of Tikal*. The University Museum, University of Pennsylvania. Philadelphia 1993.

——, *Maya Civilization*. Washington, D.C., 1993.

CURTIS, JASON H., DAVID A. HODELL, and MARK BRENNER. "Climate variability on the Yucatan Peninsula (Mexico) during the past 3500 years, and implications for Maya cultural evolution," *Quaternary Research*, 46 (1996), 37–47.

DANIEN, ELIN C., and ROBERT J. SHARER (eds.). *New Theories on the Ancient Maya*. Philadelphia 1992. (20 essays prepared for a centennial symposium at The University Museum.)

FASH, WILLIAM L. *Scribes, Warriors and Kings: The City of Copán and the Ancient Maya*. London and New York 1991. (Authoritative introduction to this important city, combining archaeology, iconography, and dynastic analysis.)

FERGUSON, WILLIAM M., and JOHN Q. ROYCE. *Maya Ruins of Mexico in Color*. Norman, Oklahoma 1977. (Color photographs taken from a light airplane of many important Maya sites.)

——, *Maya Ruins in Central America in Color*. Albuquerque 1984.

FLANNERY, KENT V. (ed.). *Maya Subsistence*. New York 1982. (Essays presented at a conference in memory of the Mayanist Dennis Puleston.)

FOX, JOHN W. *Quiché Conquest: Centralism and Regionalism in Highland Guatemalan State Development*. Albuquerque 1978. (Argues for the Gulf Coast origin of the Post-Classic Highland elites.)

FREIDEL, DAVID, LINDA SCHELE, and JOY PARKER. *Maya Cosmos: Three Thousand Years on the Shaman's Path*. New York 1993. (The Creation Myth and cosmology in the lives of the ancient and modern Maya.)

GRUBE, NIKOLAI. "Die Entwicklung der Mayaschrift." *Acta Mesoamericana*, Band 3. Berlin 1990. (The evolution of Maya script.)

GRUBE, NIKOLAI, and WERNER NAHM. "A census of Xibalbá: a complete inventory of *Way* characters on Maya ceramics." *The Maya Vase Book*, No. 4. New York 1994.

GRUBE, NIKOLAI, and LINDA SCHELE. *The Workbook for the XIXth Maya Hieroglyphic Workshop at Texas*. Austin 1995.

HAMMOND, NORMAN. *Ancient Maya Civilization*. New Brunswick and Cambridge, England 1982.

——, (ed.). *Social Process in Maya Prehistory*. London and New York 1977. (Contains 25 essays, including three on the Maya collapse.)

HANKS, WILLIAM F., and DON S. RICE (eds.). *Word and Image in Maya Culture*. Salt Lake City 1989. (Results of a symposium, with 24 essays on Maya linguistics, writing, and iconography.)

HANSEN, RICHARD D. "The Maya rediscovered: the road to Nakbé." *Natural History*, May 1991, 8- 14. New York. (Investigations at a great, Late Preclassic city.)

——, "El proceso cultural de Nakbé y el área del Petén nord-central: las épocas tempranas," in *V Simposio de Investigaciones en Guatemala*, 81-96. Guatemala City 1992.

HARRIS, JOHN F., and STEPHEN K. STEARNS. *Understanding Maya Inscriptions: A Hieroglyphic Handbook*. Philadelphia 1992. (A very clear and useful guide to the Maya calendar and the inscriptions for the neophyte.)

HARRISON, PETER D. *Tikal, City of Lords*. London and New york 1999. (Up-to-date history of the city for the general reader and student.)

HARRISON, PETER D., and B. L. TURNER H (eds.). *Pre-Hispanic Maya Agriculture*. Albuquerque 1978.

HAY, CLARENCE L., *et al.* (eds.). *The Maya and Their Neighbors*. New York 1940. (A now-classic festschrift dedicated to the great Mayanist Alfred M. Tozzer.)

HELLMUTH, NICHOLAS M. *Tikal, Copán Travel Guide*. St. Louis 1978. (A well-illustrated introduction to Maya ruins in Guatemala and Honduras.)

HOUSTON, STEPHEN D. *Maya Glyphs*. London 1989. (Concise overview of Maya epigraphy, including recent advances.)

——, *Hieroglyphs and History at Dos Pilas: Dynastic Politics of the Classic Maya*. Austin 1993.

JOHNSTON, KEVIN. *The "Invisible" Maya: Late Classic Minimally-platformed Residential Settlement of Itzan, Peten, Guatemala*. Ph.D. dissertation, Yale University 1994. (Discovery of "invisible" house mounds, suggesting that the estimates of Classic Maya population have been far too low.)

JONES, GRANT D. *Maya Resistance to Spanish Rule: Time and History on a Colonial Frontier*. Albuquerque 1989. (Documentary history of the independent Maya of southern Yucatan and the Peten.)

——, "The Canek Manuscript in ethnohistorical perspective." *Ancient Mesoamerica*, vol. 3, no. 2 (1992), 243-68.

JONES, TOM, and CAROLYN JONES. *Maya Hieroglyphic Workshop*. Arcata (California) 1995.

JUSTESON, JOHN S., *et al. The Foreign Impact on Lowland Mayan Language and Script*. New Orleans 1985.

JUSTESON, JOHN S., and LYLE CAMPBELL (eds.). *Phoneticism in Mayan Hieroglyphic Writing*. Albany 1984. (Essays presented at a watershed conference on Maya epigraphy, marking general acceptance of the Knorosov approach.)

KAUFMAN, TERENCE, AND JOHN JUSTESON. "A decipherment of epi-Olmec hieroglyphic writing," *Science*, vol. 259 (1993), 1703-1711.

KELLEY, DAVID H. *Deciphering the Maya Script*. Austin and London 1976. (Updates Thompson's 1950 work, but now, due to the fast pace of the decipherment, somewhat out-of-date itself.)

KERR, JUSTIN. *The Maya Vase Book*. Vols. 1-5. New York 1989-97. (A continuing series, presenting roll-outs of Maya vases, accompanied by important essays on ceramic iconography and epigraphy.)

KIDDER, ALFRED V., JESSE L. JENNINGS, and EDWIN M. SHOOK. *Excavations at Kaminaljuyu, Guatemala.* Carnegie Institution of Washington, publ. 561. Washington 1946. (Excavation of Early Classic Esperanza tombs.)

KNOROSOV, YURI V. "The problem of the study of the Maya hieroglyphic writing," *American Antiquity,* vol. 23, no. 3 (1958), 284-9l. (First American publication of Knorosov's revolutionary approach to the glyphs.)

KOWALSKI, JEFF K. "Lords of the Northern Maya: dynastic history in the inscriptions." *Expedition,* vol. 27, no. 3 (1985), 50-60. (Historical texts from the Puuk sites.)

——, *The House of the Governor: A Maya Palace at Uxmal, Yucatan, Mexico.* Norman 1987. (Important architectural and iconographic study of a major administrative building of the Puuk.)

LEÓN-PORTILLA, MIGUEL. *Time and Reality in the Thought of the Maya.* Boston 1973. (An interpretive study of Maya religion and philosophy.)

LOTHROP, SAMUEL K. *Tulum, an archaeological study of the east coast of Yucatan.* Carnegie Institution of Washington, publ. 335. Washington 1924.

LOUNSBURY, FLOYD G. "Maya numeration, computation, and calendrical astronomy," in *Dictionary of Scientific Biography,* vol. 15, supplement I (1978) 759-818. (Full account of these subjects, written for the advanced student.)

——, "Astronomical knowledge and its uses at Bonampak, Mexico," in *Archaeo-astronomy in the New World,* ed. A. F. Aveni, 143-68. Cambridge 1982. (Identification of an astronomically-determined war.)

LOWE, GARETH W., THOMAS E. LEE, and EDUARDO E. MARTÍNEZ. *Izapa: an introduction to the ruins and monuments.* Papers of the New World Archaeological Foundation, no. 31. Provo 1973. (Definitive study of the type site of the Izapan civilization.)

MACNEISH, RICHARD., S. J. K. WILKERSON, and A. NELKEN-TURNER. *First Annual Report of the Belize Archaic Archaeological Reconnaissance.* Andover 1989.

MARCUS, JOYCE. *Emblem and State in the Classic Maya Lowlands.* Washington 1976. (Hypothetical political organization of the Classic Maya, based upon the distribution of Emblem Glyphs.)

MARTIN, SIMON, and NIKOLAI GRUBE. "Maya superstates," *Archaeology,* vol. 48, no. 6, (1995) 41-6. (Highly important paper, presenting evidence that a few giant polities had hegemony over other Classic city-states).

MATHENY, RAY T. (ed.). "El Mirador, Petén, Guatemala: an interim report," *Papers of the New World Archaeological Foundation,* no. 45. Provo 1980. (Investigations at the largest Late Preclassic city.)

MATHENY, RAY, *et al.* 'Investigations at Edzná, Campeche, Mexico," *Papers of the New World Archaeological Foundation,* no. 46. Provo 1980 and 1983.

MAUDSLAY, ALFRED P. *Biologia Centrali-Americana, Archaeology.* Text and 4 vols. of plates. London 1889-1902. (Magnificent photographs and drawings of Maya monuments and cities; a milestone in the history of Maya research.)

MCANANY, PATRICIA. *Living with the Ancestors. Kinship and Kingship in Ancient Maya Society.* Austin 1995.

MCGEE, R. JON. *Life, Ritual and Religion Among the Lacandón Maya.* Belmont 1990.

MENCHÚ, RIGOBERTA. *I, Rigoberta Menchú.* London 1984. (First-hand account of the terror inflicted on the Maya of Guatemala, by the winner of the 1992 Nobel Prize for Peace.)

MILLER, ARTHUR G. *On the Edge of the Sea: Mural Painting at Tancah-Tulum, Quintana Roo.* Washington 1982. (Post-Classic art in the eastern Yucatan Peninsula.)

MILLER, MARY ELLEN. *The Art of Mesoamerica from Olmec to Aztec* (2nd ed.). London and New York 1996. (Excellent introduction to Mesoamerican culture as a whole.)

——, *The Murals of Bonampak.* Princeton 1986.

MILLER, MARY and KARL TAUBE. *The Gods and Symbols of Ancient Mexico and the Maya: An Illustrated Dictionary of Mesoamerican Religion.* London and New York 1993. (Indispensable for understanding the mental world of the ancient Maya.)

MORLEY, SYLVANUS G. *The inscriptions of Petén.* Carnegie Institution of Washington, publ. 437, 5 vols. Washington 1937-8.

MORRIS, EARL H., *et al.* *The Temple of the Warriors at Chichen Itzá, Yucatan.* Carnegie Institution of Washington, publ. 406, 2 vols. Washington 1931.

MORRIS, WALTER F., JR. *Living Maya.* New York 1987. (The text emphasizes the weaver's art, and has photographs of the contemporary Maya of Chiapas.)

PARSONS, LEE A. *Bilbao, Guatemala,* 2 vols. Milwaukee 1967-9. (Description and excavation of a major Cotzumalhuapan site.)

——, *The origins of monumental stone sculpture of Kaminaljuyú, Guatemala, and the southern Pacific coast.* Dumbarton Oaks Studies in Pre-Columbian Art and Archaeology, no. 28. Washington 1986. (Study of a major body of Late Preclassic sculpture.)

PENDERGAST, DAVID M. *Excavations at Altun Ha, Belize, 1964-1970.* Toronto. Vol. 1, 1979. Vol. 2, 1982.

——, "Lamanai, Belize: summary of excavation results 1974-1980," *Journal of Field Archaeology,* vol. 8, no. 1 (1981), 29-53.

POHL, MARY (ed.). *Prehistoric Lowland Maya Environment and Subsistence Economy.* Papers of the Peabody Museum of Archaeology and Ethnology, vol. 77. Cambridge, Mass., 1985. (Agriculture and use of faunal resources among the ancient Maya.)

POLLOCK, H. E. D. *The Puuc: an architectural survey of the hill country of Yucatán and northern Campeche, Mexico.* Memoirs of the Peabody Museum of Archaeology and Ethnology, Harvard University, vol. 19. Cambridge, Mass., 1980.

POLLOCK, H. E. D., *et al. Mayapán, Yucatán, Mexico.* Carnegie Institution of Washington, publ. 619. Washington 1962. (The account of Itza history in Chapter 7 is largely based upon the Roys essay.)

PREM, HANNS J. (ed.) *Hidden among the Hills: Maya Archaeology of the Northwest Yucatan Peninsula.* Acta Mesoamericana 7. Möckmühl (Germany) 1994. (17 essays present the latest thinking about cultural developments in the Northern Area, including Chich'en Itza).

PROSKOURIAKOFF, TATIANA. *An Album of Maya Architecture.* Carnegie Institution of Washington, publ. 558. Washington 1946. (Reconstructions of Maya cities by this great artist-archaeologist.)

——, *A Study of Classic Maya Sculpture.* Carnegie Institution of Washington, publ. 593. Washington 1950. (Stylistic dating of Maya monuments.)

——, "Historical implication of a pattern of dates at Piedras Negras, Guatemala," *American Antiquity*, vol. 25, no. 4 (1960), 454-75. (A now classic paper which established the historical nature of the Maya inscriptions.)

——, "The lords of the Maya realm," *Expedition*, vol. 4, no. 1 (1961), 14-21. (A less technical treatment of the 1960 paper.)

RECINOS, ADRIAN, and DELIA GOETZ. *The Annals of the Cakchiquels. Title of the Lords of Totonicapán.* Norman 1953. (English translation of important documents pertaining to pre-Conquest peoples of the Guatemalan highlands.)

REDFIELD, ROBERT, and ALFONSO VILLA ROJAS. *Chan Kom, a Maya Village.* Chicago 1962. (Classic anthropological study of a Yucatec Maya community.)

REED, NELSON. *The Caste War of Yucatán.* Stanford 1964. (Documentary history of the great 19th-century uprising by the Yucatec Maya.)

REENTS-BUDET, DORIE. *Painting the Maya Universe.* Durham and London 1994. (Beautiful exposition of Maya vase painting.)

ROBERTSON, MERLE GREENE. *The Sculpture of Palenque.* 4 vols. Princeton 1983-91. (The most complete survey of the sculpture of any Maya city, magnificently illustrated.)

——, (gen. ed.). *Palenque Round Table Series (Mesa Redonda de Palenque).* Nos. 1-2, Pebble Beach, Calif, 1974-76. No. 3, Palenque 1979. Nos. 4-5, San Francisco 1985. No. 6, Norman 1991. No. 7, San Francisco 1994. (Much of the recent information on Maya iconography and epigraphy has appeared in this indispensable series.)

ROYS, RALPH L. *The Book of Chilam Balam of Chumayel.* Carnegie Institution of Washington, publ. 438. Washington 1933. (Annotated translation of the most important native Colonial-period text from the Maya lowlands.)

——, *The Indian background of Colonial Yucatán.* Carnegie Institution of Washington, publ. 548. Washington 1943. (Documentary study of Late Post-Classic Yucatán.)

——, *The political geography of the Yucatán Maya.* Carnegie Institution of Washington, publ. 613. Washington 1957. (Should be read in conjunction with the above.)

RUPPERT, KARL, J. ERIC S. THOMPSON, and TATIANA PROSKOURIAKOFF. *Bonampak, Chiapas, Mexico.* Carnegie Institution of Washington, publ. 602. Washington 1955. (Reproduces Antonio Tejeda's copies of the murals.)

RUZ LHUILLIER, ALBERTO. *El Templo de las Inscripciones, Palenque.* Mexico City 1973. (Report on Hanab Pakal's tomb, by its excavator.)

SCHELE, LINDA. *Maya Glyphs: the Verbs.* Austin 1982. (Identification of event glyphs, and how they conformed to Mayan morphology and syntax.)

——, *Notebook for the Maya Hieroglyph Workshop.* Austin 1992. (Broad survey of Maya epigraphy, with emphasis on texts relating to the creation of the universe.)

SCHELE, LINDA, and DAVID FREIDEL. *A Forest of Kings. The Untold Story of the Ancient Maya.* New York 1990. (Major work, presenting Maya history through the ages as told by the Maya inscriptions and iconography.)

SCHELE, LINDA, and PETER MATHEWS. *The Code of Kings: The Language of Seven Sacred Maya Temples and Tombs.* New York 1998. (Applies the history of *A Forest of Kings* and the cosmology of *Maya Cosmos* to the understanding of seven Classic and Post-Classic sites.)

SCHELE, LINDA, and MARY E. MILLER. *The Blood of Kings: Dynasty and Ritual in Maya Art.* Fort Worth 1986, London 1992. (The definitive statement of what is now known about Maya art and culture.)

SHARER, ROBERT J. (ed.). Quirigua Project 1974-1979, *Expedition*, vol. 23, no. 1, 5-lo.

——, (ed.). *Quiriguá Reports* 1, 11. Philadelphia 1979, 1983.

——, *The Ancient Maya* (5th ed.). Stanford 1994. (A new edition of Sylvanus Morley's classic general book on the Maya, with extensive bibliography.)

SHOOK, EDWIN M., and ALFRED V. KIDDER. *Mound E III-3, Kaminaljuyu, Guatemala.* Carnegie Institution of Washington, Contributions to American Anthropology and History, no. 53. Washington 1952. (Excavation of rich Miraflores period tombs.)

SMITH, A. LEDYARD. *Uaxactún, Guatemala: excavations of 1931-7.* Carnegie Institution of Washington, publ. 588. Washington 1950.

SMITH, ROBERT E. *Ceramic sequence at Uaxactún, Guatemala.* Middle American Research Institute, publ. 20, 2 vols. New Orleans 1955. (Established the archaeological chronology of the southern Maya lowlands.)

STEPHENS, JOHN L. *Incidents of Travel in Central America, Chiapas, and Yucatan,* 2 vols. New York 1841. (With the 1843 work, both illustrated by Frederick Catherwood, brought the Maya civilization to the attention of the outside world; still eminently readable.)

——, *Incidents of Travel in Yucatan,* 2 vols. New York 1843.

STONE, ANDREA. *Images from the Underworld: Naj Tunich and the Tradition of Maya Cave Painting.* Austin 1995. (Complete publication of the Naj Tunich paintings and texts, along with a perceptive treatment of the role played by caves in the Maya psyche.)

STUART, DAVID. *Ten Phonetic Syllables.* Research Reports on Ancient Maya Writing, no. 14. Washington 1987. (A major epigraphic advance, building on the methodology pioneered by Knorosov.)

STUART, DAVID, AND STEPHEN HOUSTON. *Classic Maya Place Names.* Washington 1994.

STUART, GEORGE E. "Quest for decipherment: a historical and biographical survey of Maya hieroglyphic investigation," in *New Theories on the Ancient Maya,* ed. E. C. Danien and R. J. Sharer, 1-63. Philadelphia 1992.

——, "The royal crypts of Copán," *National Geographic,* December 1997, 68-93. (Reports the very early and spectacular tombs and structures found deeply buried in Copan's Acropolis.)

STUART, GEORGE E., and GENE S. STUART. *The Mysterious Maya.* Washington 1977. (Popular account of the ancient and modern Maya.)

SULLIVAN, PAUL. *Unfinished Conversations: Mayas and Foreigners Between Two Wars.* New York 1989. (Perceptive account of the extraordinary dialogue in the 1930s between the Maya of Quintana Roo and the Carnegie archaeologists based at Chich'en Itza.)

TATE, CAROLYN E. *Yaxchilan: The Design of a Maya Ceremonial Center.* Austin 1992.

TAUBE, KARL A. *The major gods of ancient Yucatán.* Dumbarton Oaks Studies in Pre-Columbian Art and Archaeology, no. 32. Washington 1992. (Definitive study of Maya religious iconography.)

TEDLOCK, BARBARA. *Time and the Highland Maya.* Albuquerque 1982. (Herself an initiated day-keeper, the author shows how the ancient calendar functions in K'iche' life and society.)

TEDLOCK, DENNIS. *Popol Vuh.* New York 1985. (The definitive edition of the greatest piece of Native American literature, and the key source for the understanding of pre-Conquest Maya iconography and thought.)

TEEPLE, JOHN E. *Maya astronomy.* Carnegie Institution of Washington, Contributions to American Archaeology, no. 2. Washington 1930. (Teeple solved the puzzle of the lunar calculations in the inscriptions.)

THOMPSON, J. ERIC S. *Maya hieroglyphic writing. Introduction.* Carnegie Institution of Washington publ. 589. Washington 1950. (A monumental survey of Maya calendrics, religion, and astronomy, but written before the adoption of the historical and phonetic approaches to the glyphs.)

——, *A Catalog of Maya Hieroglyphs.* Norman 1962. (Covers glyphs of both the monuments and codices. While now in universal use, in bad need of revision.)

——, *Maya History and Religion.* Norman 1970. (Contains first-class studies of Maya ethnohistory. Especially important for its treatment of the Putun Maya.)

TOZZER, ALFRED M. *Chichen Itzá and its Cenote of Sacrifice.* Memoirs of the Peabody Museum of Archaeology and Ethnology, Harvard University, vols. 11, 12. Cambridge, Mass., 1957.

——, (ed.).*Landa's Relacion de las Cosas de Yucatan.* Papers of the Peabody Museum of Archaeology and Ethnology, Harvard University, vol. 18. Cambridge, Mass., 1941. (Thanks to the extensive notes which accompany Landa's text, this is virtually an encyclopedia of Maya life.)

VILLACORTA, J. ANTONIO AND CARLOS A. *Códices mayas.* Guatemala 1930. (Three of the four Maya hieroglyphic books reproduced by line drawings in a useful edition.)

VOGT, EVON Z. *Zinacantan: A Maya Community in the Highlands of Chiapas.* Cambridge, Mass., 1969. (A classic study of the contemporary Tzotzil Maya.)

WILLEY, GORDON R. *The Altar de Sacrificios excavations: general summary and conclusions.* Papers of the Peabody Museum of Archaeology and Ethnology, vol. 74, no. 3. Cambridge, Mass., 1973.

——, "General summary and conclusions," in *Excavations at Seibal.* Memoirs of the Peabody Museum of Archaeology, Harvard University, vol. 17, no. 4. Cambridge, Mass., 1990. (Seibal was a huge Classic city on the Pasión, with important Preclassic and Terminal Classic components.)

——, *et al. Prehistoric Maya settlements in the Belize Valley.* Papers of the Peabody Museum of Archaeology and Ethnology, Harvard University, vol. 54. Cambridge, Mass. (A pioneering work on Maya settlement pattern.)

WILLEY, GORDON R., AND PETER MATHEWS (eds.). *A consideration of the Early Classic period in the Maya lowlands.* Institute for Mesoamerican Studies, publ. 10. Albany 1985. (Combines archaeological and epigraphic evidence.)

ZIMMERMAN, GÜNTER. *Die Hieroglyphen der Maya Handschriften.* Hamburg 1956. (A catalog of the glyphs in the codices, still useful.)

Sources of illustrations

Index